Pobladoras, Indígenas, and the State

POBLADORAS, INDÍGENAS, AND THE STATE

Conflicts Over Women's Rights in Chile

PATRICIA
RICHARDS

RUTGERS UNIVERSITY PRESS
New Brunswick, New Jersey, and London

Library of Congress Cataloging-in-Publication Data

Richards, Patricia, 1971-
Pobladoras, indígenas, and the state : difference, equality, and women's rights in Chile / Patricia Richards.
p. cm.
Includes bibliographical references and index.
ISBN 0–8135–3422–4 (hardcover : alk. paper) — ISBN 0–8135–3423–2 (paperback : alk. paper)
1. Women's rights—Chile. 2. Poor women—Chile—Social conditions. 3. Working class women—Chile—Social conditions. 4. Mapuche women—Chile—Social conditions. 5. Poor women—Chile—Political activity. 6. Working class women—Chile—Political activity. 7. Mapuche women—Chile—Political activity. 8. Mapuche women—Chile—Government relations. I. Title.
HQ1236 .5.C5R53 2004
305.42'0983—dc22

2003018875

British Cataloging-in-Publication data record for this book is available from the British Library.

Manufactured in the United States of America

Contents

List of Abbreviations

ANAMURI   Asociación Nacional de Mujeres Rurales e Indígenas,
National Association of Rural and Indigenous Women

CASEN   Encuesta de Caracterización Socioeconómica Nacional,
National Socioeconomic Characterization Survey

CEDEM   Centro de Desarrollo de la Mujer,
Center for Women's Development

Cedesco   Centro de Estudios de Desarrollo Económico y Social,
Center for Economic and Social Development Studies

CEM   Centro de Estudios de la Mujer,
Women's Studies Center

CEMA   Central Relacionadora de los Centros de Madres,
Central Coordinator of the Mothers' Centers

CONADI   Corporación Nacional de Desarrollo Indígena,
National Corporation for Indigenous Development

CONAMA   Comisión Nacional del Medio Ambiente,
National Environment Commission

CUP   Comando Unitario de Pobladores,
Unitary Pobladores' Command

ENDESA   Empresa Nacional de Electricidad, Sociedad Autónoma,
National Electric Company

FOSIS   Fondo de Solidaridad e Inversión Social,
             Social Solidarity and Investment Fund

IADB   Inter-American Development Bank

MIDEPLAN   Ministerio de Planificación y Cooperación,
             Ministry of Planning and Cooperation

OMEP   Organización de Mujeres Educadoras de Pudahuel,
             Organization of Women Educators of Pudahuel

PEMCI   Programa de Estudios y Capacitación de la Mujer Campesina
             e Indígena,
             Program for the Study and Training of Peasant and Indigenous
             Women

PRODEMU   Programa de Desarrollo de la Mujer,
             Women's Development Program

REMOS   Red de Mujeres de Organizaciones Sociales,
             Network of Women's Social Organizations

SERNAM   Servicio Nacional de la Mujer,
             National Women's Service

Acknowledgments

So many people have contributed to making this book possible. I am deeply grateful to the women who agreed to participate in this study. They honored me with their patience, trust, and honesty. The support, kindness, and expertise of the researchers and staff at the Facultad Latinoamericana de Ciencias Sociales-Chile (FLACSO-Chile, Latin American Faculty of Social Sciences) facilitated my work; I am especially grateful to Teresa Valdés and Mirta Monroy. Teresa also arranged for the formal presentation of my results in Santiago during my return trip in 2001. José Aylwin at the Universidad de la Frontera did the same in Temuco. Magaly Ortiz faithfully transcribed the interviews.

I owe great thanks to my mentors at the University of Texas at Austin. Christine Williams is a constructive critic, and I value her opinions. She has provided thoughtful guidance and encouragement. Bryan Roberts introduced me to the sociology of Latin America and his insights and critiques have made me a better researcher. Charlie Hale, Victoria Rodríguez, Maya Charrad, and Gideon Sjoberg all contributed in important ways to the development of this book. Much of the research for this project was financed through the Andrew W. Mellon Fellowship in Latin American Sociology at the University of Texas at Austin. I am grateful to the Mellon Foundation, Peter Ward, and the rest of the Mellon Committee at the University of Texas for their generosity. The Center for Humanities and Arts at the University of Georgia kindly accepted a proposal to provide subvention funds for the book's cover art, created by Chilean graphic artist Marcia Miranda Manzor. My colleagues and friends at the University of Georgia have provided a supportive environment for the final stages of writing the book. Kristi Long at Rutgers University Press has been helpful and encouraging as an editor. Portions of chapters 1, 5, and 6 appeared in earlier form as an article in *Latin American Perspectives*. The journal has graciously granted its permission to reproduce that material here.

I have been lucky to have the support and company of many wonderful people in my life. Peg, Jim, Greg, Mark, Angela, and Ross Richards, Jerry Ross, Matt Rummele, Scott Beldon, Stacy Drasen, Tam Pellicier, Avri Beard, Stephanie Friedman, Michelle Frisco, Steve Savitski, Franklin Gamble, Catherine Gundersen, Jason Boardman, Merike Blofield, Kelly Goran Fulton, the Finch Family, Rana Emerson, Susan Franceschet, Ben Marcus, Rosamel and Chichi Millaman, Isabel Hernández, Yun-Joo Park, Daniel Ancan, Margrit Blatter, Carmen Melillan, Millaray Painemal, Francisca Llancao, and Sonia Fuentes have variously been bearers of good advice along the way, insightful readers and critics, dear companions, family, and friends.

Pobladoras, Indígenas, and the State

1

WOMEN'S RIGHTS AND REPRESENTING DIFFERENCE

Women's movements throughout the world have argued that citizenship—the relationship between citizens and the state—is gendered. They have worked toward expanding and redefining the content of citizenship in order to achieve the representation of women's rights and interests as part of it. Transitions to democracy in South American countries in the late twentieth century created the opportunity for citizens, including women, to negotiate the content of that democracy. Women's movements took advantage of this opportunity to seek the creation of state agencies, ministries, laws, and policies which would better represent their interests and bring attention to women's rights. In Brazil, women's councils were formed to advise the president, and in Argentina quotas were eventually initiated to increase the number of women representatives in government. In Chile, the Servicio Nacional de la Mujer (National Women's Service), SERNAM, was created to work toward equality between women and men from within the state. While conservative political forces, traditional gender ideology, and competing state priorities have often limited the scope of reforms intended to benefit women, the creation of state women's policy machineries has represented a positive step in the struggle toward equality between women and men.[1]

The idea that women are essentially different from men has been central to women's movements' claims for equal rights throughout Latin America. Many have rooted their activism in notions of domestic and

1

maternal virtues, and have demanded recognition as full citizens on the basis of contributions they have made to the nation through their roles as wives and mothers. Unfortunately, the assertion of difference between men and women has not always translated into recognition of differences and inequalities among women themselves. Poor and working-class women, indigenous women, Afro-Latinas, and others argue that their concerns have been excluded or misrepresented by women's movements dominated by middle-class, educated, lighter-skinned feminists. They draw attention to the ways that race, class, ethnicity, and other factors shape different women's experiences, interests, and priorities. Citizens are not just gendered, they are saying. They also have a race, a class, and an ethnicity.

Indeed, women's movements throughout the world have faced conflicts over the definition of women's rights and interests. Beginning in the late 1960s in the United States, for example, women of color protested the hegemony of white women in the feminist movement (Sandoval 2000). Feminists of color, including bell hooks, Audre Lorde, Gloria Anzaldúa, Cherríe Moraga, Patricia Hill Collins, Maxine Baca Zinn, and Bonnie Thornton Dill, have drawn attention to the ways that white women have contributed to the oppression of women of color by assuming that all women's experiences are the same and by failing to recognize the benefits they derive from their whiteness.

As women's movements have become transnational, conflicts over what constitutes women's interests have taken place internationally as well. Western feminists have tended to both universalize women's experiences and construct third world women as victims of "traditional practices" (Narayan 1997). Moreover, because it is mostly women from the North and educated women from the South who can afford to participate in international women's networks, national level exclusions and inequalities end up being reproduced internationally (Desai 2002). Domitila Barrios de Chungara (1978), for example, poignantly described how class, race, and ethnic differences emerged and transcended national borders at the United Nation's 1975 International Year of the Woman meetings in Mexico.

At the regional level, differences among women have frequently emerged during the Latin American women's meetings known as encuentros (Sternbach et al. 1992). Specifically in Chile, differences in priorities and access to power have complicated relationships between pobladoras (urban poor and working-class women) and middle-class feminists in times of dictatorship as well as democracy (Schild 1994; Valdés and Weinstein 1993). Likewise, feminists have often failed to take Mapuche indigenous women's claims of difference seriously. Latin American women's movements' efforts to deal with inequalities and differences among women have been addressed by authors including Sternbach et al. (1992) and Valdés and Weinstein (1993). Little detailed attention has been given, however, to how well state strategies to represent women have incorporated claims for rights based on difference. In this book, I explore this issue through the cases of Mapuche and pobladora women and their relationship to the women's policy machinery in Chile.

Chile is an excellent case for examining conflicts over citizenship for a number of reasons. First, women's and indigenous movements played important roles in the return to democracy after nearly seventeen years of military rule under Augusto Pinochet (1973–1990). Both movements were successful in getting some of their demands incorporated into the agenda of the Concertación de Partidos por la Democracia (Coalition of Parties for Democracy), the center-left coalition that has launched all three successful presidential candidates since the return to democracy. Indigenous movement actors signed an accord in 1989 with Concertación candidate and future president Patricio Aylwin (1990–1994) that was the blueprint for a 1993 "Indigenous Law" designed to represent a new era in state-indigenous relations. The women's movement persuaded the Concertación to sponsor the creation of SERNAM which would eventually create an Equal Opportunities Plan for Women that stipulated the obligation of all state agencies to establish programs and policies that would lead to greater equality between women and men.

But democracy did not bring about the deep social change for which many had hoped. Under Pinochet's dictatorship, Chile experienced the imposition of what was perhaps the most extreme model of neoliberal socioeconomic reform of all Latin American states. Neoliberal reform is characterized by an export-based economic strategy, opening of the economy to international investment, elimination of trade barriers, privatization of state industries, devaluation of currency, and elimination of much social spending in favor of more restricted targeting of particularly needy sectors of the population. With the return to democratic rule, Concertación leaders left in place many of Pinochet's economic policies. This was true of Christian Democrat Aylwin's government as well as of those of Christian Democrat Eduardo Frei Jr. (1994–2000) and Socialist Ricardo Lagos (2000–2006). This has had particular impacts on women and indigenous peoples. For instance, the de-emphasis on state provision of social services characteristic of neoliberal reform carries with it a corresponding focus on compelling civil society—and in particular women's organizations—to perform what were once state responsibilities. The result is a model of citizenship in which women, particularly in poorer sectors, provide care-oriented services (such as health and child care and domestic violence counseling) for free. Moreover, the now democratic Chilean state continues to ignore indigenous rights when national development is at stake, adding special urgency to Mapuche activism. When paired with an official discourse that emphasizes democracy, decentralization, participation, and equality of opportunity, these situations create a contradictory context within which pobladora and Mapuche women activists negotiate their rights.

Indeed, Mapuche women and pobladora activists have both asserted that they do not recognize themselves in the state's gender discourse. They argue that SERNAM promotes a hegemonic model of the woman citizen that excludes their priorities and concerns. Why do these women feel their priorities are not represented? How do representatives of the state interpret this situation? Is it possible to represent claims for rights based in difference in the state or are conflicts over women's citizenship inevitable? These are the questions I attempt to answer in this book.

CITIZENSHIP, WOMEN'S RIGHTS, AND THE POLITICS OF DIFFERENCE

I locate my work within the debate over social movements and citizenship in Latin America. In the following sections, I discuss citizenship in terms of struggles for the expansion and redefinition of rights from below and as part of state efforts to generate common identity and consent for national goals from above.[2] I then discuss the importance of context to understanding the shifting content of citizenship, and I address how the relationship between citizens and the state plays out in the contemporary neoliberal-democratic context. I present feminist critiques of citizenship and use feminist insights to help explain the disjuncture between the official representation of women's interests and demands for rights based in difference. Next, I discuss the specificities of state-indigenous people relations and the limits of using the concept of citizenship to talk about them. Finally, I summarize Nancy Fraser's distinction between movements based on recognition and those based on redistribution, which I will use throughout the book to help clarify and understand the relationship of Mapuche women and pobladoras to the state.

Citizenship: From Below and Above

In this book, I conceive of the relationship between social actors and the state in terms of citizenship. Citizenship entails more than just a formal status. It refers to the substantive experience of belonging to a given nation, and to the rights and responsibilities associated with that membership. While it has been subject to substantial critique and revision, T. H. Marshall's post–World War II work forms the basis for most contemporary theorizing on citizenship. Marshall viewed citizenship in terms of three distinct but interdependent categories: civil, political, and social citizenship. He considered it to be an evolutionary process in which the consolidation of civil rights in the eighteenth century was followed by political rights in the nineteenth century and finally social rights in the twentieth century.

Rights, as Marshall presents them and as they have been conceived and granted by nation states, are exercised by individuals. Civil rights, in Marshall's view, are those necessary for individual freedom, such as freedom of speech and religion, the right to own property, and the right to equal protection before the law. Political rights are those necessary for individuals to participate in the political process, such as the right to vote or to be elected. Social rights for Marshall (1992, 8) refer to "the whole range from the right to a modicum of economic welfare and security to the right to share to the full in the social heritage and to live the life of a civilised being according to the standards prevailing in the society." Such rights might include public education, income supplements, housing assistance, and health care. For Marshall, social rights were particularly important because the shared basic standard of life and culture they guarantee creates a sense of common identity and mutual responsibility that is essential to people's ability to exercise their civil and political rights to their fullest potential. In the international human rights community, civil and political rights are referred to as "first generation rights" whereas social (and economic) rights are referred to as "second generation."

Marshall viewed citizenship mostly in terms of rights handed down from the state to citizens. In the end, however, citizenship is most usefully understood as the relationship between a state and its citizens. As such, the content of citizenship—civil, political, social, and cultural rights—is shifting and constantly negotiated between citizens and the state.

Much contemporary theorizing of citizenship in Latin America is linked to the analysis of new social movements, which encompass most identity-based movements, such as those dedicated to the rights of women, the gay, lesbian, bisexual, and transgendered (GLBT) community, indigenous peoples, and racial and ethnic minorities. In my view, they have three noteworthy aspects. First, their demands usually focus on achieving inclusion in a given system rather than attaining political control (Jelin 1990). (As shall be seen, this is not necessarily true of indigenous movements.) Second, while my focus is on efforts that are directed at the state, the struggles of these movements are not limited to the political realm or to control over material resources. To the extent that they seek control over meaning—the meaning of their own identities and the meaning of their daily practices in relation to the broader political and socioeconomic context—these movements have a cultural component as well (Escobar 1992; Melucci 1984). They also have a social component, in that they challenge (consciously or not) social roles and relationships, such as patriarchal relationships between women and men (Caldeira 1990). Finally, these struggles—for a stake in the political system, for respect for civil rights, for basic social rights like adequate housing and health care—are impelled from below. That is, they are the struggles of citizens who seek to renegotiate the terms of citizenship and the meanings of rights (Alvarez et al. 1998). Such renegotiation holds particular salience in contemporary Latin America. Under authoritarian states, the citizens of countries including Chile, Brazil, and Argentina had no say in what the content of membership in the nation would look like. As the transition to and consolidation of democracy have taken place, citizens have sought to engage in dialogue with the state, attempting to participate in the creation of the terms of democracy and to expand the content of what it means to be a citizen.

The "citizenship from below" perspective provided by theorists of new social movements provides an important balance to the top-down Marshallian conceptualization. Nevertheless, this bottom-up and participatory notion of citizenship is incomplete as well. To understand the struggles and achievements of movements, I argue that the "citizenship from below" perspective has to be balanced by an understanding of "citizenship from above." By this I do not mean only a Marshallian view of rights being passed down to citizens by the state. Citizenship is also linked to the creation or "imagining" of the nation. "The struggle for citizenship," as Walby (1996, 252–253) puts it, "is a national project and indeed a project by which the 'nation' seeks to obtain legitimacy as a project in the eyes of both that country's inhabitants and the 'international community.'" Approaching citizenship from above thus also entails recognition of the uses of citizenship by the state as well as the restrictions the state places on movements. While it is surely a response to the demands and pressures of social actors, extending or expanding citizenship rights must also be seen as a strategy on the part of the state and elites to control other sectors of the population (Mann 1987).

The "state" refers to the set of institutions established in order to govern or control a given population (Anthias and Yuval-Davis 1989). The state is distinct from government, which refers to "those political officials that occupy the executive and legislative branches of government and are subject to renewal or replacement" (Petras and Leiva 1994, 7). A major contribution of recent feminist research has been to point out that the state is not a unitary actor with intent (Anthias and Yuval-Davis 1989; Pringle and Watson 1998; Waylen 1996b), and it is this understanding that underlies my approach to citizenship. So, for example, an agency like SERNAM and the actors within it can create pro-women policies in an otherwise woman-hostile sociopolitical context. Such a view does not deny that the state represents dominant interests. Franceschet (2001b, 225) explains,

> While it assumes there are certain historically determined instances in which state arenas can be important sites for transforming unequal gender (or other) relations, this view also recognizes that states are, to a great extent, colonized by the interests of the more powerful social groups. What is important is that the hegemony of any particular social group within states is continually being renegotiated as other social groups find ways to contest their subordination.

In fact, the state's legitimacy depends upon its relative autonomy from dominant interests (Alvarez 1990). Underlying this understanding of state-civil society relations is a Gramscian conceptualization of hegemony as not only imposed from above coercively, but as relying on the generation of popular consent through the incorporation of some of the interests of different social actors into state priorities (Hall 1996). In this way, activism on the part of social movements can lead to the deepening or broadening of citizenship, but the granting or expanding of rights by the state simultaneously has the effect of integrating citizens into a hegemonic national identity and generating consent for state goals. Ultimately, the goals of movements that are incorporated into the state are likely to be those that cohere with, or at least do not openly challenge, hegemonic material and cultural objectives.

As shall be seen, different social actors may have varying levels of success in achieving their goals, depending on the ways their goals mesh with hegemonic interests. Understanding the successes and limitations faced by social actors necessitates a perspective that views their struggles within the context of citizenship from above and below. Moreover, viewing citizenship in this way highlights the distinction between citizenship rights and human rights. As opposed to being guaranteed by virtue of membership in a nation, human rights refer to those that are fundamental to the condition of being human, standards that no person should have to live without. I shall argue that though they are problematic in several respects, international human rights agreements are essential to advancing movement claims when states fall short.

Citizenship is Contextual: Neoliberalism and the Limits on Expanding Rights

If we accept that citizenship is a relationship between citizens and the state, and that the content of citizenship is shifting and negotiated, then the sociopolitical context in which this relationship plays out is central to understanding it.

As I see it, "context" is the basis for several critiques of Marshall. Scholars such as Jelin (1996) have noted that throughout the world, citizenship rights have seldom emerged in the evolutionary pattern Marshall laid out. Jelin points out that at many times in Latin American history (particularly under populist regimes) civil and political rights have not accompanied the expansion of social rights. Roberts (1996b, 14) likewise observes that Marshall's view of citizenship as a top-down process assumes "an efficient and disinterested state bureaucracy counterbalanced by a strong civil society based upon a generalized respect for the law" that has seldom existed in Latin America, where the expansion of rights has been more likely to have been impelled from below by the struggles of disenfranchised citizens.

The current scenario in Latin America highlights the importance of context to the practice of citizenship rights, and social rights in particular. While the return of democracy to the region has meant that there is less dispute over civil and political rights, the same cannot be said for social rights. The neoliberal economic restructuring of many developing countries in recent decades has intensified many social needs while simultaneously restricting the ability or will of the state to satisfy them (Roberts 1996a).

One result of these changes is that social policy has been reframed throughout Latin America so as to de-emphasize rights and re-emphasize responsibilities. Specifically, neoliberal economic reforms have been accompanied by a corresponding focus on compelling civil society to perform what were once state responsibilities. Despite rhetoric that emphasizes a desire to "strengthen civil society," the basic question for the state is increasingly how to facilitate civil society's capacity to de-

I note this expression.

liver services and to enhance citizens' ability to "pull themselves up by their own private bootstraps" (Alvarez et al. 1998, 1). Programs and projects sponsored by the state and many international aid organizations reflect this restricted view of citizen-as-economic-actor. This, in turn, has the potential to limit the chances that citizens will be able to make claims for the expansion of social citizenship. Thus, even though democracy exists, the ability of citizens to articulate rights-based claims vis-à-vis the state is restricted by the context of neoliberalism.

A specific look at how neoliberal reforms have played out in Chile is instructive. A central objective of the Pinochet regime was to modernize the country. This was accomplished through a series of structural adjustments to the Chilean economy and the implementation of neoliberal economic and social policies. The military regime liberalized trade, created incentives for foreign investment, privatized state industries, devalued the peso, weakened labor unions, deregulated markets, structured the economy around exports, and drastically decreased social spending. To the extent that macroeconomic indicators improved, these strategies were successful. After the initial application of strict structural adjustment measures in 1975, the country sank into a severe economic crisis with skyrocketing inflation and unemployment on the one hand, and decreasing real wages on the other. By the end of the regime in 1989, however, the economy had rebounded, inflation was low, and Chile had entered a period of sustained growth (Portes 1997). Chile is thus often hailed as a successful example of structural adjustment, and the country gained the status of a South American "Jaguar," an analogy to the "Asian Tigers." Pinochet's economic policies were backed by an ideological discourse through which Chile was defined as modern and nearly developed. Yet the military regime was only able to implement these strategies because it was not answerable to civil society (Portes 1997). The success of the military's strategy came at the expense of human rights, as nearly 3,000 people were either executed or disappeared, and tens of thousands more were detained, tortured, or driven into exile. Moreover, the same strategies that generated unprecedented wealth and growth also led to severe marginalization and inequality.

seems to be a common problem

"nearly developed"

cost. modernity is slavery. historical materialism

The national development goal of the Concertación governments has been to improve Chile's position in the global economy while reducing poverty and inequality. The methods by which the democratic Concertación governments have attempted to accomplish this goal reveal a great deal of continuity with the neoliberal measures put into place by the Pinochet regime. Creating incentives for international

investment, eliminating trade barriers, flexibilizing labor, and maximizing exports—all part of Pinochet's neoliberal reforms—remain important elements in the Concertación's economic development strategy.
National development goals continue to be reinforced by an official national identity discourse that emphasizes modernity, progress, and—particularly important in the Mapuche case—the unitary character of
the Chilean nation state. Generating equality of opportunities and reducing poverty are also part of the state's discourse and policy objectives, but these are to be accomplished primarily through social targeting
and measures oriented around improving individuals' access to the market. Decentralization and participation are at least nominally a part of
this strategy as well, though Chile has remained an exceptionally centralized state throughout this process.

None of this means that struggles for citizenship rights are irrelevant in the current context. Indeed, the focus on participation and
decentralization within the neoliberal paradigm may open up opportunities for making demands for greater citizen involvement in the de-
termination of policy priorities and the design of social programs.
However, as shall be seen, the benefits of these openings are not unequivocal. Two main issues are at stake. First, by "participating" and
engaging with the state, citizens can be unwittingly drawn into the
neoliberal project. Schild (1998) theorizes a dialectical relationship between women's groups and the state in the context of neoliberalism,
through which the state "selectively appropriates" those feminist discourses that fit with an image of citizenship as the "right" and responsibility to be self-reliant economic actors. Through this process (which
takes place with other social actors as well), the terms of citizenship
and belonging are redefined to cohere with neoliberal priorities. This
leads to the second issue, which is that, in the end, to the extent that
citizens' demands conflict with the economic and ideological goals of
the state, they will not be met. Thus, while re-democratization was
largely about the return of citizenship rights, neoliberal reforms have
had a significant impact on how those rights are carried out in practice (Franceschet 2001b).

Citizenship is Gendered

The conceptualization of citizenship presented thus far is based on the
assumption that all citizens are equal members of their society and that
as such they are able to engage in public debate on an equal footing
and exercise rights with the same facility in daily life. These assumptions, however, become problematic when we take account of differ-

ences among citizens on the basis of a variety of factors, including class, gender, age, sexuality, race, and ethnicity.

Feminist scholars have countered the idea of citizenship as universally guaranteed to all members of society. They have shown that, in fact, citizenship has been differentiated on the basis of gender throughout history. In many countries women were systematically excluded from citizenship until relatively recently (Yuval-Davis 1993). Taking the example of post-revolutionary France, McClintock (1997, 91) explains that "a woman's political relation to the nation was thus submerged as a social relation to a man through marriage. For women, citizenship in the nation was mediated by the marriage relation within the family." Nor was the nation imagined as belonging to all men. Despite universalizing pretensions, citizenship effectively entailed a relationship between non-indigenous, non-African male citizens and the state.

Women and men have also been granted different rights and protections and symbolically constructed as different kinds of citizens according to predominant national ideologies. Nation states have historically reinforced and institutionalized traditional roles and stereotypes about women's nature, and women have been constructed as the "breeders of the nation," and the reproducers and guardians of culture (Anthias and Yuval-Davis 1989). This has paradoxically resulted in the extension of social rights under the guise of policies aiming to protect women (particularly in their role as mothers), while simultaneously leaving them to struggle to achieve political rights. In turn, women often need political rights in order to ensure their civil rights, as in the cases of reproductive freedom or the pursuance of justice against abusive husbands (Walby 1994).

Even when women have the same or similar formal rights as men, the way that citizenship plays out in different contexts can have specific disadvantageous effects on women. For instance, as shall be discussed in chapter 2, the impact of the current approach to social rights and policy in Latin America, which emphasizes self-help initiatives and the like, may be particularly harmful for women. In this way, the substantive experience of citizenship under neoliberalism is different for women and men.

Most feminist critiques of citizenship involve a rejection of the distinction between the public and the private. Because women's concerns have traditionally been relegated to the private sphere, they are often excluded from consideration among the rights of citizenship (Franceschet 2001b). Fraser (1997) asserts that the exclusion of private interests from the public sphere and the insistence that there is such a thing as a generalized "common" interest has typically served the advantage of elite males who define the content of "public" and "private." In this way, "women's issues" like domestic violence and child care are defined as private concerns, unconnected to citizenship rights. This restricts women's ability to participate on equal terms in the public sphere and in debates over the content of citizenship.

Many women's rights activists throughout the world have expressed ambivalence about the role of the state, recognizing it as a site for struggle but also an arena where policies and laws can be established to guarantee women's equal and full citizenship. Feminist commentary on citizenship also reflects the debate between "equality" and "difference" feminism. According to Lister (1997), this debate centers on the question of whether women should pursue a "gender-neutral" or a "gender-differentiated" citizenship. The first would guarantee equal citizenship on the basis of women's inherent equality to men, while the second would guarantee recognition of women's specific concerns and values and would revalue their contributions in the private sphere. As shall be seen, both of these debates are important to women's movement struggles in Chile.

While it can be argued that throughout history all women have been excluded from establishing the terms of citizenship, not all women have been constructed as citizens in the same way. Nor do they necessarily share the same interests, or suffer the same consequences of the neoliberal policy environment. Latin American feminists (who tend to be educated members of the middle class) have tended to see their role as encouraging working-class, poor, and racial and ethnic minority women to resist their subordination by men. But many poor and racial/ethnic minority women question whether "equality" with the men in their communities is what they want, since these groups of men are also oppressed. For many women, experiences of exploitation have as much to do with class, race, and ethnicity as they do with gender (Westwood and Radcliffe 1993). In Fraser's terms, then, some women are among the elites that govern interaction in the public sphere. Even when it appears that opportunities exist within the state for social actors to issue their demands (such as SERNAM, for Chilean women), some individuals and groups are likely to be excluded on other bases, such as ethnicity, race, class, or sexuality.

Particular groups (albeit limited by the dominant gender ideology and state context) have greater access than others to influence how certain concepts—such as "woman" or "equality"—are defined. "Multiracial feminism" in the United States, as outlined by Maxine Baca Zinn and Bonnie Thornton Dill (2000), elucidates this point and provides some useful tools for looking at the relationship between different groups of women and state-driven gender discourse. Zinn and Dill describe a women's movement that professes to accept difference, while continuing to centralize the experience of white, middle-class women. The result is the persistent marginalization of women of color through the failure to recognize "the inequalities that cause some characteristics to be seen as 'normal' while others are seen as 'different' and thus, deviant" (ibid., 24). They argue that race is "a basic social division, a structure of power, a focus of political struggle and hence a fundamental force in shaping women's and men's lives" (ibid., 25).

Following Patricia Hill Collins (1991), Zinn and Dill assert that race, class, and gender inequalities are interlocking elements in a "matrix of domination." This means that women experience "being a woman" differently based on their race, class, etc. White, middle-class women have greater access than African American women, Latinas, and others, to determine the content of citizenship. In this interlocking matrix, moreover, "women and men throughout the social order experience different forms of privilege and subordination depending on their race, class, gender, and sexuality" (2000, 26). Women who benefit from particular positions in this social order have power over others and in this sense "women's differences are *connected* in systematic ways" (ibid., 26). Zinn and Dill also point out that while constrained by these various forms of oppression, women continue to exercise agency and "create viable lives for themselves, their families, and their communities" (ibid., 27). While it is clear that United States concepts should not be applied uncritically to other contexts, Zinn and Dill's analysis will prove useful in understanding the conflicts among women in the state, Mapuche women, and pobladoras in Chile.

Indigenous Peoples, Citizenship, and Human Rights

While it is not irrelevant, citizenship does not totally capture the relationship between indigenous peoples and nation states. This is because the historical relationship of indigenous peoples to the state is distinct. For indigenous peoples, the state is the contemporary representative of the entity that usurped their territory, killed many of their ancestors, and had altogether devastating effects on their way of life. Citizenship discourses, rooted in the concept of *mestizaje*, have had an important role in this destruction.

Many Latin American nationalists employed the concept of mestizaje in their struggles for independence from Spain (see Bengoa

[1985] for the Chilean case). This entailed combining aspects of *criollo* identity with images of the "noble savage" or the fierce Indian warrior in an effort to create a new identity which would distinguish Latin Americans from Spaniards and generate loyalty and patriotism among the citizens of Latin American countries.[3] Indeed, the central goals of citizenship discourses, from the perspective of the state, are to create a common sense of national identity and membership and to generate consent among the people within a set territory for a given nation-building project. Although the aims of these projects have been to unify people in the name of the nation, they have historically resulted in the suppression of other forms of identity, and thus have had negative effects on indigenous peoples. Indigenous identities have been appropriated and stereotyped by the "makers" of the nation, and through their symbolic inclusion, the indigenous peoples' right to *not* belong to the new nation has been denied. In addition, mestizaje discourses often have been matched by practices that exploit and do violence to indigenous people. Mestizaje has a gendered content as well, for it is frequently through the feminization of indigenous men that the alternative *mestizo* individual is constructed as ideal, and through dominance over (and, often, the rape of) indigenous women that he comes into existence.

The liberal discourse of individual rights has frequently contributed to the demise of indigenous communities and ways of life. Gould (1998) shows how this happened in Nicaragua beginning in the 1880s. By deeming indigenous people "citizens" within a democratic/equal rights paradigm, national and local elites were able to silence any indigenous claims to collective rights, such as land rights or political autonomy. In a sense, collective rights were (and are) unthinkable within the limits imposed by the liberal democratic discourse. In this way, elites were also able to delegitimate the authenticity of indigenous peoples. If you were a citizen, you were Nicaraguan (mestizo identity). In this context, any claims to additional rights (based on collective, indigenous identity) could be construed as unfair to other citizens. Thus, being made citizens (regardless of whether they were actually granted the substantive rights associated with equal membership) contributed to the loss of indigenous rights and identity.

The implications of citizenship for indigenous peoples are clearly not benign. On the other hand, indigenous peoples today do make claims on the state, seeking to expand what it means to be a citizen to include cultural and collective rights. Cultural rights simply refer to the right of members of a given cultural group/people to preserve and develop their culture (Das 1995). Such rights are often practiced by collectivities, as noted in Gould's example, and in international human rights parlance, are part of the "third generation" of rights. Kymlicka (1995) delineates two major arguments used to justify claims for cultural (or what he calls "group-differentiated") rights.[4] The first argument is made on the basis of equality. To a large extent, claims made on this basis are demands for inclusion, an end to unfair disadvantage, and ultimately, for the representation of difference within citizenship. Such demands might include things like intercultural health care, intercultural and bilingual education, and collective representation. In Chile, these are often referred to as integrationist demands.

On the other hand, many indigenous claims are categorically distinct from those of other social actors and challenge the very notion of citizenship as an obligatory status. Unlike movements organized around the rights of women, racial/ethnic minority groups, or gays and lesbians, many indigenous claims are rooted in their historical status as peoples with their own territory, culture, forms of governance, and so on. Kymlicka's second argument for justifying group-differentiated rights encompasses such claims, which are justified on the basis of history—prior sovereignty or historical treaties, for example. Demands for rights related to these claims are not just for inclusion on different terms, but for the recognition of indigenous peoples' right to be distinct, self-determining, and autonomous peoples. In this sense they are similar to the demands of nationalist movements. In Chile, these are often called autonomy demands. As shall be discussed in chapter 5, the two types of demands do not represent mutually exclusive categories, but rather, exist in dialectical tension.

These two categories of claims for cultural rights imply what Wade (1997) refers to as the centrality of "place" to indigenous or ethnic identity.[5] Indigenous and ethnic identities contain elements of race in the sense of social meaning being assigned to phenotypic differences. But in addition, Wade contends, despite their glorification in mestizo national identities, in Latin America indigenous peoples are ideologically located outside of dominant society. Indigenous people are constructed as separate from "modern" society, and thus, when they leave their communities and migrate to the city, they are often constructed as no longer indigenous. Demands for rights based in difference contest this idea of separateness and the spatial construction of difference, as well as the forced loss of indigenous identity upon entering dominant society. At the same time, Wade points out that indigenous peoples may construct themselves as outside dominant society. This is evident in the second category of rights to such things as autonomous territory and self-determination. Sometimes, claims on these rights involve the elision of within-group differences in order to present a coherent historical identity to the outside world.

The second justification for cultural rights represents a significant challenge to the notion of citizenship as an obligatory status. In fact, along with the desire to distinguish the new nation from the colonial one, the potential threat that indigenous peoples represented to the idea of the nation is a significant reason for their incorporation into national mestizo identities in Latin America. Nevertheless, the equality-based justification (for "integration" rights) also represents a significant challenge to citizenship regimes based on individual rights. This is because, as with collective land ownership, language and religion, and ancestral forms of political representation, these, too, are rights exercised by collectivities. Such rights do not easily cohere with the concept of citizenship as a common set of rights and responsibilities practiced by individuals.

Because they often do not fit within citizenship regimes, indigenous peoples' rights are sometimes better conceptualized in terms of human rights. While these, too, were initially conceived of as rights possessed exclusively by individuals, the international community has given increasing—though qualified—support for indigenous rights. The United Nations declared 1995–2004 the "International Decade of the World's Indigenous Peoples," and a number of accords recognize the rights of indigenous peoples. The most notable of these is the International Labor Organization's Convention 169: Indigenous and Tribal Peoples (1989) which recognizes indigenous peoples' status as peoples and their rights to self-governance, territory, land, and maintenance and development of identities, languages, and religions. It does not, however, recognize indigenous peoples' status as peoples in the sense in which this term has been used by the United Nations to describe the rights of colonized populations in Africa and Asia to national independence. Similarly, though several United Nations agencies now incorporate indigenous rights into their mandates, official documents have often avoided the word "peoples" altogether. Furthermore, despite the progress that has been made, Jelin and Hershberg (1996) caution that the international commitment to human rights does not guarantee that Latin American democracies will respect and extend the rights of all members of society. This is especially apparent with claims to territory or autonomy, which are often seen by states as threats to national development and identity.

In the cases of women and indigenous peoples alike, the universalist language of individual rights occludes the existence of social inequalities and fundamental differences in how citizenship is experienced. Any discussion of rights that does not take into account these substantive differences will reinforce existing inequalities. Moreover, assuring equality of membership on a substantive level may necessarily entail providing specific guarantees in the form of laws and policies designed to mitigate formal and informal discrimination (thereby disputing a universalist notion of citizenship). It also implies that negotiation of substantive citizenship takes place within civil society, as well as vis-à-vis the state, since it is often the actions of citizens themselves that restrict other citizens' access to equal membership.

Making Sense of Social Movement Claims: Recognition and Redistribution

Throughout this book, I classify the demands of the poor and working-class *pobladores* and of the Mapuche—and more specifically, of pobladoras and Mapuche women—according to Nancy Fraser's (1997) distinction between movements whose claims are based on recognition and those whose claims are based on redistribution. Recognition claims, according to Fraser, are based on a cultural understanding of injustice, forms of which might include cultural domination, non-recognition, or disrespect. The goals of recognition-based movements are to end injustice while maintaining and valorizing their "difference." Ultimately, these are the movements we associate with identity politics. In contrast, redistribution claims focus on socioeconomic injustice, which, according to Fraser, may take the form of exploitation, economic marginalization, or deprivation. Movements that base their demands in redistribution are seeking their difference—socioeconomic inequality—to disappear. Typically, these are class-based movements or movements that operate with a class-based logic.

Of course, these are ideal types, and in the real world, movements mix the two kinds of demands (Fraser 1997). Claims based on recognition as well as redistribution are present in the demands of both pobladores and the Mapuche. But ideal types are useful precisely for the clarity they can provide in the analysis of complicated social realities. In the Mapuche case, I argue, demands that are ultimately rooted in recognition of their status as a people predominate (though they are certainly not unconnected from development-oriented or material goals), while poor urbanites' demands, which typically include access to jobs, education, housing, and health care, tend to emphasize redistribution above recognition.

While I find Fraser's conceptual distinction between redistribution and recognition-based claims useful, I am not applying her general argument to the cases examined in this book. In one essay, Fraser uses the redistribution/recognition typology to critique Iris Marion Young's (1990) delineation of five faces of oppression. She maintains that Young's categories, which include exploitation, marginalization, powerlessness, cultural imperialism, and violence, eventually come down to redistribution and recognition, and that, to the extent that it reifies group differentiations and tends to lend itself to multiculturalism as a policy response, the emphasis on recognition has worked to the detriment of many contemporary social movements. Fraser goes on to argue that there are different types of differences which should alternatively be eliminated, universalized, or enjoyed, depending on the extent to which they cohere with redistributive goals. Elsewhere, she supports a movement strategy that focuses on deconstructing and destabilizing group differentiation while simultaneously focusing on socialist remedies for structural inequalities.

In a 1997 reply to Fraser, Young firmly argues that "her dichotomy between political economy and culture leads her to misrepresent feminist, anti-racist, and gay liberation movements as calling for recognition as an end in itself, when they are better understood as conceiving cultural recognition as a means to economic and political justice" (1997, 148). Young also accuses Fraser of retreating from "New Left theorizing which has insisted that the material effects of political economy are inextricably bound to culture" (ibid., 148). She points out that culture, identity, and recognition have material sources and consequences, but are not reducible to economic exploitation. One struggle cannot be reduced to the other—indeed, as shall be seen in chapter 5, this is what the Chilean state often does in responding to Mapuche claims. Although I think Young's criticisms distort Fraser's intent in establishing the typology—Fraser does not deny that some groups are victims of both cultural and socioeconomic injustice and, indeed, argues that justice today requires both recognition and redistribution (1997, 12)— they are important reminders that ideal types are only tools for understanding complex realities, and are not in themselves strategies for action.

Moreover, while Fraser's solution is attractive, it is not entirely appropriate when applied to the case of indigenous movements, whose struggles focus not just on rectifying cultural and socioeconomic injustices within a given system, but, sometimes, on gaining autonomy from that system. Young assesses the case of indigenous peoples thus:

Movements of indigenous peoples, to take another example, certainly consider recognition of their cultural distinctness an end in itself. They also see it as a crucial means to economic development. They assert claims to land for the sake of building an economic base for collective development and for achieving the effective redistribution of the fruits of white colonial exploitation. Many also believe that the recovery of traditional indigenous cultural values provides vision for forms of economic interaction and the protection of nature whose wider institutionalization would confront capitalism with transformative possibilities. (1997, 158)

Fraser herself recognizes that an "affirmative recognition strategy of cultural nationalism" can, in some cases, be a successful approach to "decentering Eurocentric norms" (1997, 30). For my own purposes, I am less interested in Fraser's own conclusions about what kind of strategies are most likely to lead to transformative social change as I am in using the distinction between redistribution and recognition to understand conflicts among women in Chile. I suggest that conceptualizing demands of different groups of women in terms of redistribution and recognition can help us to understand why, when, and how social movements are successful in achieving their demands. I suggest that how the state responds to demands depends on not only what those demands are, but on who makes them and in what context.

METHODOLOGY

In order to understand how demands based in difference are represented in the state women's policy machinery, I used a three-pronged research design. My principal method was semi-structured, open-ended interviews. These were conducted with Mapuche women leaders in Chile's capital city of Santiago and Region IX (in ancestral Mapuche territory), pobladora leaders in Santiago, non-governmental organization workers, and government employees (most of them femocrats, or women who promote gender equality from within the state) from diverse national, regional, and municipal governmental offices with which pobladoras and Mapuche women interact. Respondents were selectively sampled based on their representativeness and willingness to participate. The selection of sites for the Mapuche interviews merits some explanation. According to the 2000 Encuesta de Caracterización Socioeconómica Nacional (CASEN, National Socioeconomic Characterization Survey), a little over 20 percent of the Mapuche now reside in Santiago, though the 1992 Census put this figure at around 50 percent (MIDEPLAN 2002). Region IX, also known as the Araucanía, is the part of ancestral Mapuche territory in the south of Chile with the highest concentration of Mapuche residents (over 25 percent of the total population).

Almost all of the pobladoras in the sample were part of the women's movement during the dictatorship. They were activists, and as such may or may not represent the views of the majority of poor urban women, who do not participate in organizations. In addition, since these pobladoras were part of the women's movement, their views were more likely to be associated with the political left. The Mapuche women interviewed were all current or past leaders of Mapuche organizations, and as such may or may not represent the views of Mapuche women at the community level. Their politics also tended to lean toward the political center or left, which is certainly not true of all Mapuche, though several eschewed party politics altogether. All of the Mapuche women interviewed had at least a minimal degree of engagement with women's issues and/or interaction with SERNAM, and thus did not necessarily represent the views of all Mapuche women leaders, some of whom choose not to interact with SERNAM at all. They also did not necessarily represent the views of women leaders in Regions VIII and X, which also have significant Mapuche populations. Most of the women in both groups ranged in years of formal education from three to twelve; a couple of the Mapuche women had technical or university degrees.

I chose in-depth interviews as my main method because I was interested in how the women described and explained their own actions and interactions with others, the motivations behind their own actions, and their interpretations of the actions of others. In other words (and guided by Symbolic Interactionism) I was interested in ascertaining why the women I interviewed do what they do in their points of view and why they think others do what *they* do. By understanding and contrasting individuals' motivations and explanations for their behavior, I could begin to understand why there appeared to be so little overlap among women about what "women's interests" were and how well they were represented in the state.

I also conducted participant observations in both regions. This entailed attending meetings, cultural celebrations, and events held by Mapuche associations and pobladora organizations in Santiago and the Araucanía, participating in seminars and workshops conducted by nongovernmental organizations or by Mapuche and pobladora grassroots organizations, observing formal interactions between organizations and representatives of state agencies, and visiting rural Mapuche communities. These observations were an essential part of this project because they allowed me to get to know many of the women I interviewed, witness what they expressed (and did not express) in the interviews, develop a greater understanding of their goals and motivations, and talk informally with leaders, organization participants, and non-governmental organization and government workers whom I did not interview. Finally, I also collected documents from the organizations and SERNAM, as well as written state and media representations of Mapuche and pobladora women. More detailed information on the sample and methodology can be found in the appendix.

ETHICS AND POWER IN FIELD RESEARCH

Conducting field research brings with it a series of dilemmas, most of which have to do with the issue of power. I went into this project knowing that I would need to confront power imbalances on several levels: United States researcher/Chilean "third world" subject; formally educated sociologist/community leader without much formal education; representative of the most powerful nation on Earth/poor indigenous woman or urban squatter; white blue-eyed blonde/Mapuche in a country that values blue-eyed blondness and disparages *rasgos indígenas*. Power issues were also likely to emerge in my relationships with middle-class femocrats, some of whom might resent my presence as a United States researcher and my interpretations of their interactions with pobladoras and Mapuche women. These issues bring up some difficult questions: What place did I, as a white *gringa* sociologist, have studying conflicts among women in Chile? To what extent was my research facilitated by my own country's place in the global system (that is, to what extent was it facilitated by United States imperialism)? Would my research be good for the women I was studying? What *were* my motivations? What was my responsibility to the pobladoras and Mapuche women? To middle-class Chilean feminists and femocrats? What truth would I be telling? Whose reality would it reflect? I do not pretend to have resolved all of these issues. It is nonetheless important to consider their impact on the analysis presented in the chapters to come.

Power, of course, is diffuse and dynamic within any relationship. While I had the power to make myself present, design the research, and ask the questions, respondents had the power to determine the extent to which they would respond and the content of what they would reveal. Developing trust with respondents and openness in their responses was difficult in some cases. Especially in the case of Mapuche women in Santiago, I spent a good deal of time getting to know the women at events or in initial meetings before conducting each interview. Some Mapuche respondents expressed suspicions about why I wanted to study them, reflecting a reluctance to have their cause separated in any sense from that of the Mapuche people as a whole. For example, before we began our interview, Ana Llao, a former president of the Mapuche organization Ad Mapu (in Mapudungun, Ad Mapu refers to the body of laws and religious traditions inherited from the ancestors), expressed misgivings about consenting to interviews in general. She said that she had had negative experiences in the past, though not so much with interviews as with photographs; she had discovered photos of herself in traditional Mapuche dress, used without her permission, in calendars or on posters. She added that she is not fond of interviews, either, because she never knows exactly where the information is going and because words and intent can be distorted so easily. She concluded by consenting to the interview, but noted that there were certain things that she would not talk about because she considered them her intellectual property. I said that all of this seemed reasonable to me, and that she would have access to my results. The interview was one of the most informative I conducted, perhaps because Llao's misgivings were on the table from the start.

As leaders of organizations and public figures, many of my respondents were accustomed to being interviewed. They were also accustomed to seeing little come of the process. Some expressed their expectations as to what would happen with the results. For instance, María Hueichaqueo, who led a small Mapuche organization in Santiago, reflected,

> I think that the work that you (social scientists and students) are doing, in wanting to work in indigenous issues, is very important. I think that maybe you don't know it, but you are doing, you are supporting us in our work, you know? . . . For me personally, it is very important, because probably it will become a little piece of paper, but that little piece of paper will probably be read by another person, and another, and another. So there we go creating a chain, about what is happening with our people here in the urban sector.[6]

Juana Huenufil, another Mapuche leader from Santiago, reinforced this perspective, though with some ambivalence: "Well, the only thing I could tell you is that for us it is nice to collaborate, as long as the answers that we give serve to spread a little bit the thoughts and way of working that we Mapuche have, even though we are sometimes a little tired of so many interviews. But all the same, it is not lost time, although sometimes (I have to) put things aside (in order to give an interview). But I tell you that it is also the only way of getting people to talk about us." While many of the pobladora leaders were accustomed to being interviewed, some expressed misgivings about the process. For instance, Jessica Vergara from the Organización de Mujeres Educadoras de Pudahuel (OMEP, Organization of Women Educators of Pudahuel) said members of her organization often wondered what happened to the interviewers after they left, and wished they could maintain contact. Relationships develop over the course of fieldwork, and even over the course of a two-hour interview. Respondents and researchers alike can be left with a sense of emptiness, bringing to the forefront the utilitarian character of the relationship between the researcher and the researched.

Hilda Muñoz who led Mikempai (in Diaguita, Women of Peace), a pobladora organization that focuses on preventing domestic violence, commented on the possibility of being "used" by social scientists. When I asked her at the end of our interview if she had anything to add, she said,

> No, the only thing that I . . . is the concern that at this time, there are so many people that are interested in knowing what it is that we, the *dirigentas*, do (and) how the organizations are doing. . . . This is a question that I have right now, because I say, we were utilized for a long time, a long time. But I know that now they are not going to use us, that it is history, our history, which, in some way, could be publicized. And well, right here (in the consent form) it says that it could come out in a book, right? But this is just a concern.

Muñoz's anxieties seemed to resonate with the feelings of many of the women who participated in this study. They wanted their stories told, but how did they know they could trust me to do the telling? To what extent do I perpetuate the "utilization" of these women by telling this story?

Perhaps because of these anxieties, many of the women, particularly Mapuche leaders, expressed a desire to see the results of the research. I returned to Chile in 2001 in order to present respondents with a written copy of my initial analysis. In many cases, I discussed the findings with them in private meetings, and I also invited them to formal presentations of my work. Presentations were held in Santiago and Temuco, and were each attended by approximately fifty people, including Mapuche women, academics, and representatives of SERNAM. These events were occasions for these groups of women to come together and discuss their differences, and equally importantly, for the women to directly comment on and critique my work. In most cases, the work was received positively. The return trip also permitted the women to clarify things they had told me, hopefully reducing the risk that I misrepresented their views. At a smaller meeting, I also presented results to pobladora members of the Red de Mujeres de Organizaciones Sociales (REMOS, Network of Women's Social Organizations).

Respecting respondents' rights was a major ethical concern in all stages of this project. I wanted to ensure that the respondents did not feel they were under any obligation to participate in the study. Respondents were informed about my background and motivations, the subject of the book, and its possible future uses. While many of the respondents had been interviewed before, assuring that they understood their rights often entailed a lengthy discussion: they had the right to be anonymous or not, to refuse to be audiotaped, to answer only the questions they felt comfortable answering, to end the interview at any time, to contact me or my supervisors at a later date, and so on. No respondents refused an interview after discussing their rights. They signed consent forms per Human Subjects Committee specifications. Most chose to allow me to audiotape the interview, and most also chose to be identified with their real names. Some women simply did not care one way or the other if their names appeared; as public figures they were used to revealing their opinions and standing behind them. Others insisted that their comments be attributed to them by name. A number of pobladoras observed that "we are not in dictatorship anymore" and that it was thus no longer necessary to fear that one's life would be threatened as a result of participating in an interview. In this sense, not claiming anonymity was an assertion of freedom of expression for some of the women.

Some had other reasons for appearing by name. Pobladora Hilda Muñoz viewed appearing by name, in print as well as in her activism, as the main "inheritance" she could leave to others: "If I were a rich woman, and giving what I am giving now, I would do it anonymously. . . . But at this moment, no. I am a pobladora, same as anyone, with the same needs as anyone, and maybe I can be an example for others. . . . I at least want to leave my inheritance in knowledge to the organizations. That is my greatest desire, and that is what brings me to dedicate myself very strongly within this *comuna* (municipality)." Many Mapuche women also were emphatic that their words be attributed to them by name. For example, at the end of our interview, social work professor Hilda Llanquinao commented, "The only thing I would ask of you, is that if you have to let these thoughts be known, do not have any doubts in letting them be known, nor do you have to—I think that if you were to shut up, to not say who said it . . . you would be denying me my thoughts, and I don't like that. All this time, I have fought, you know, so that no one denies me my thoughts." Again, I respected each individual woman's desire. Most appear by name. A limited number of women chose to appear anonymously; these cases are noted in the text or in the appendix.

All of the women in this study—pobladoras, Mapuche women, and femocrats alike—were integral to its telling. Though I did not always agree with them or even sympathize with their positions, I have tried to represent their intent truthfully and without distortion. In addition, I have tried to be attentive to the way ambiguity entered into their explanations of themselves and of others, as I believe that ambiguity often has more to tell us about the way people understand their worlds than do seemingly straightforward statements of truth. I have also made an effort to understand how Mapuche women and pobladoras themselves theorize difference and "marginality." As Bacigalupo (2003a) explains, "We need to attend to theories that start from the 'Margin' and see how they analyze and position themselves with regards to the 'Center'—and in turn look at how the presence of the Other creates the 'Center'." I believe this task can contribute, however slightly, to challenging the racism, classism, and ethnocentrism that continues to be present in much feminist theorizing and activism, and to developing new ways of thinking about women's rights, difference, and solidarities across borders both metaphoric and geographic.

Women's social locations are central to the analysis presented in this book. Perhaps the most important thing for me to acknowledge, then, is that my own social location as a white feminist sociologist from the United States, from the working class but no longer of it, is also a central part of this story. My social location impacted how the women I spent time with treated me, and what they would and would not tell me. Equally importantly, the analysis herein is filtered through who I am. I have done my best to reflect the interpretations and understandings of the women I studied, but ultimately, it is I who tells the story (and I who benefits most from telling it). This became clear to me when I returned to Chile to share my interpretations and ideas with the women I studied. Often, they identified with what I was saying, sometimes they did not, and sometimes, they expressed ambivalence, as if I had the right idea, but it just didn't sound right coming out of my mouth. Mapuche leader Elisa Avendaño summarized this issue for me during our interview. She said that she respected feminism because "anyone who struggles (for a cause) has some source of sorrow." She also emphasized, though, the difference between a Mapuche woman telling her own story and a non-Mapuche (feminist) advocate interpreting it: "They can be very studious, they can be very knowledgeable about the culture, but they don't feel it. Because it's one thing to say it and another to feel it. Because we say it with feeling, with pain, with strength, with the feeling that *we* have, you know, with suffering, and other people aren't going to have that." With this in mind and heart, I present the chapters that follow as my own interpretation of contemporary conflicts over women's citizenship in Chile. I stand by it as the most truthful reflection I can offer.

In chapter 2, I set up the context for examining the representation of Mapuche women's and pobladoras' priorities in the contemporary Chilean state. I look at the representation of women by the state and women's activism in Chile under Allende, Pinochet, and the Concertación. I argue that throughout each of these eras, the state promoted and used women's roles and images in different ways, responding more or less favorably to women's demands depending on the national interests of the moment. Simultaneously, on both ends of the political spectrum and across historical periods, women's movements have mobilized around women's supposed essential difference from men to achieve their goals. However, to the extent that it has involved a focus on the return and expansion of citizenship rights, women's activism on the left differs from that on the right. In the contemporary era, two central changes mark gender politics in Chile. First, the state has publicly committed itself to women's equality with men through the creation of SERNAM. At the same time, differences among women have become increasingly salient. Women of distinct groups contest the state's gender discourse, calling into question the very concept of "women's interests." This context is important for the rest of the book, in which I examine how state gender discourse and practices come into conflict with the priorities and identities of Mapuche women and pobladoras.

Historically, pobladoras' claims and activism have centered on class issues. In chapter 3, I discuss how changes in economic and social policy that were put into place during the Pinochet dictatorship and the successive Concertación governments have affected poor and working-class Chileans (pobladores). I explain that pobladores' demands on the state historically have focused overwhelmingly on issues of redistribution. I argue that by de-linking social policy from universal social rights and applying market principles to social service delivery, the state's policy model restricts the possibilities for the achievement of pobladores' demands. I argue that Concertación rhetoric that refers to a "social debt" with the Chilean people and a commitment to reducing inequality represents an effort to combat poverty without modifying macroeconomic goals, and I outline some of the specific effects this has had on poor women. I conclude the chapter by discussing the implications of the changing sociopolitical context for making demands for redistribution.

The background provided in chapters 2 and 3 sets the context for chapter 4, in which I explore the issues and conflicts that have emerged in the relationship between pobladora activists and femocrats (women who work in the state women's policy machinery). I show that both class and gender are manifest in pobladoras' identities and activism, and contrast pobladoras' and femocrats' explanations of the contradictions that are involved in their contemporary interactions, particularly as they involve the concept of participation. The pobladora case demonstrates that women's experience of rights in Chile today is differentiated on the basis of social class. Power differences among women have meant that middle-class women have more access than pobladoras to determine how women's interests and priorities are defined in the state's agenda. And the state context for dealing with poverty and inequality—set up in the previous chapter—effectively structures the steps that femocrats can take to address pobladoras' concerns.

I then move to the case of Mapuche women, whose claims are situated within the wider struggle of the Mapuche people. In chapter 5, I explore the state's discourse and practices around national identity and development as they relate to the Mapuche. I discuss Mapuche movement goals and review the commitments made by the state to the Mapuche at the return to democracy, showing that many of them have been broken in the name of national development. I then discuss Chile's national identity discourse, which is based on a unitary notion of the "Chilean people" and is used to reinforce and justify national development goals. I point out that while it was once possible for the Chilean state to deny the existence of the Mapuche, this is no longer the case. The Mapuche movement's support of the return to democracy and continued activism, as well as international standards regarding the treatment of indigenous peoples, demands a more active state response. I discuss this response in detail, arguing that it continues to reflect the state's mutually reinforcing goals of strengthening Chile's position in the global market and maintaining a unitary Chilean national identity. I conclude the chapter by addressing the implications of state goals for the Mapuche struggle for cultural rights and recognition.

In chapter 6, I examine the issues, contradictions, and conflicts involved in interactions between Mapuche women and the state women's policy machinery. I discuss how indigenous identification and gender are manifest in Mapuche women's identities and activism. Mapuche women's claims—based on a sense of cultural difference or what they call *visión de pueblo*—are distinct from those of pobladoras. Nevertheless, SERNAM's representation of Mapuche women's interests is inadequate for reasons similar to the pobladora case. Power differences among women result in restricted access for indigenous women to decision making about the content of women's citizenship as well as policy and program objectives. In addition, SERNAM's actions are framed by the context of the Chilean state, which, as demonstrated in chapter 5, is slow to recognize cultural rights.

Throughout the book, it will become apparent that Chile's national development goals often conflict with the demands of indigenous peoples and the poor. Moreover, the state's response to those demands is conditioned by its goals and reinforced by national identity discourse. Nevertheless, the response is not uniform in the two cases. Rather, it varies according to the basis for those demands: recognition or redistribution. Linked to redistribution and thus integration into the Chilean system, the demands of the poor do not represent a challenge to national identity. To the extent that they are linked to social inequality, however, their demands cannot be met without substantially changing macroeconomic policy, and thus come into conflict with national development goals. In the Mapuche case, where demands for recognition—and the radical redistribution they entail—represent a potential threat to national development goals and unitary national identity, the state employs its unitary national identity discourse in order to delegitimize Mapuche claims for political autonomy and status as a people, and implements policies that highlight "diversity" as well as more integrative redistribution or development-related demands. In both cases, state policy responses impact women in particular ways.

I compare the two cases in chapter 7 and address their implications for representing women's interests in the state and for our understanding of rights, difference, and national identity in a global context. My findings indicate that, as they assert to be the case, many of the priorities of Mapuche women and pobladoras (particularly those that are linked not just to being women, but to being indigenous or poor) are excluded from the work of the state women's policy machinery. The factors that lead to this exclusion are similar in the two cases. Mapuche and pobladora women do not have access to the limited power made available to women within the Chilean state. Furthermore, insofar as they conflict with hegemonic socioeconomic and ideological goals, many of the claims of pobladora and Mapuche women (and of poor and Mapuche people more generally) remain unaddressed. Thus, what Mapuche women and pobladoras are able to achieve is structured by SERNAM's expectations for how women should perceive their gender interests, and also by the state's expectations for how rights will be conceptualized in the democratic-neoliberal era.

However, class and ethnic differences and inequalities structure women's identities and interests distinctly. Pobladoras seek socioeconomic redistribution. They also seek redistribution of decision-making power in SERNAM, and they do so because they perceive their gender-related goals as at least similar to those of middle-class women. Mapuche women, in contrast, focus more on cultural recognition, and their demands are related to creating space for recognizing difference *and for being Mapuche* within SERNAM, or sometimes, alongside it.

Pobladora and Mapuche women's struggles for rights in Chile are instructive for efforts to advance women's rights worldwide. They indicate that power differences among women on the basis of race, class, ethnicity, etc. must be taken into consideration when women's struggles for rights are defined. They also show that the economic and political context in which these struggles occur places equally important strictures on what different groups of women are able to achieve. Poor and indigenous women's struggles are framed not just in reference to dominant perspectives on women's rights, but in reference to dominant class and ethnic ideologies as well. These two cases—and the ways they contrast with one another—constitute an important case study for examining how we understand differences among women. I therefore end this book by relating my findings to a broader discussion of struggles for women's rights throughout the world, noting the importance of recognizing differences among women, and of understanding the wider national and global context in which assertions of difference are made, if all women's rights are truly to be advanced.

2

WOMEN'S ACTIVISM AND
THE CHILEAN STATE

My objective in this chapter is to provide historical background for the relationship between women and the state in Chile. I examine the representation of women by the state (from above) and women's activism (from below) during the Allende, Pinochet, and Concertación regimes. I contend that two central changes mark gender politics in the contemporary democratic era. First, the state has committed itself to women's equality with men through the creation of SERNAM. For the first time in Chilean history, promoting women's equality is an explicit goal of the state. At the same time, differences among women have become increasingly salient. As women of distinct groups question the state's gender discourse, SERNAM's ability to represent women's interests is contested, and indeed, the very concept of "women's interests" is called into question.

I frame the discussion in terms of citizenship. Throughout the world, women's experiences of citizenship, both substantive and formal, have been different from those of men. Feminist scholars have pointed out that while the concept of "citizenship" proclaims a universalist notion of "citizen" as individual bearer of rights, not all citizens are granted rights at the same time or in the same order (Dietz 1989; Walby 1994). As Walby (1994) asserts, "Access to citizenship is a highly gendered and ethnically structured process." For instance, as noted in chapter 1, women have often been granted some degree of social rights (under the guise of protection), while they are left to struggle to achieve political and civil rights (ibid.). Likewise, ethnic and racial minority groups across the world have not been granted civil and political rights as a matter of benevolence; these rights have been hard-won through the struggles of social movements.

Four themes are interwoven throughout this chapter. First, the struggles of the women's movement that emerged during the dictatorship were struggles for the return and expansion of rights. Some women focused on the civil and political rights that were suspended by the military regime. Poor women struggled for social rights like access to food for their children, decent employment, housing, and health care. Feminists emphasized the ways that the absence of all these rights affected women in particular, and fought for women's equality in the country and in the home. Indigenous women worked against violations of cultural rights. All of these efforts can be conceptualized as struggles for the expansion of citizenship.

Second, as has been the case with women's movements throughout the world, in all three eras discussed in this chapter, differences that problematize the concept of "women's interests" emerged among women. These differences fall into two general categories. The first category includes differences asserted by women who struggle for the expansion of rights, but whose priorities are linked to class, ethnic, sexual, and other issues that lead them to feel that their interests are not represented in women's movements dominated by white, middle-class, non-indigenous women. These differences have been more or less salient over time, taking a back seat to the struggle against the dictatorship, but coming to the forefront after the return to democracy.

The second category involves ideological differences that have led some women to struggle not for the expansion of women's rights but for the preservation of women's traditional roles. Such women, generally associated with the political right, have had a significant activist presence in Chilean history, particularly in the first two eras discussed here. They have made claims on the state for the protection of their status as wives and mothers, without linking this to the expansion of rights or opportunities. In this book, I focus primarily on the first group of women, those who are fighting in some way for the expansion of rights. Yet in order to have a complete picture of women's activism over the latter half of the twentieth century, it is necessary to outline all its forms. Women's activism on the right *and* the left, and all the variations in between, has been key to the way political events in Chile have played out.

Although their end goal often differs (inciting the coup versus ending the dictatorship, for example), the factors that have motivated women to action have often been quite similar on both ends of the political spectrum. The third theme thus involves the importance assigned to women's essential difference from men as a basis for activism. This is clearly the case of those who have struggled for the preservation of women's traditional roles. And to a great extent, it has also been the case of those who have struggled for the expansion of women's rights. As shall be seen, difference feminism has been a much more potent force in Chilean women's struggle for rights than arguments based on women's inherent equality with men. Chilean women have principally fought for the expansion of women's rights on the basis of their inherent difference from men, reflected in superior morality and maternal and cooperative values. They have maintained that their rights should be defended and that they should be granted equality on the basis of the contributions they have made to society as wives and mothers. As should be clear from the above paragraph, however, "difference" as a basis for women's activism does not preclude the existence of differences among women themselves.

The final theme has to do with the state, which has promoted and used women's roles and images in different ways over time, responding more or less favorably to women's demands in different periods, depending on the national interests of the moment. This remains true today. Though women's activism substantially influenced the Concertación's agenda, the state continues to promote women's opportunities and rights in accordance with broader (now "neoliberal") national goals. In addition, sexist and morally conservative sectors continue to exercise influence over the state. In this chapter, I discuss the Allende, Pinochet, and Concertación eras sequentially, addressing the state's representation of women and their interests, as well as women's activism. I conclude the chapter by discussing the implications of these four themes for the expansion of women's citizenship rights, suggesting that the creation of SERNAM and the increasing salience of differences among women combine to make the contemporary era an important case for examining how women's interests are represented in the state.

WOMEN AND THE STATE DURING THE UNIDAD POPULAR ERA

Until recently, Latin American states generally viewed women as noncitizens or as reproducers of the nation's future (male) citizens. When women's interests were addressed, they were linked to the strategic goals of the state or political parties, rather than concern for women themselves (Miller 1991). For example, in several countries, women were granted suffrage in order to generate votes for the ruling party. Whether this was the case or achieving suffrage was the product of women's activism, it was "almost universally portrayed by its advocates as the means to a more moral society, with a platform that emphasized social motherhood issues and peace more than gender equity" (ibid., 97).[1] Social motherhood was emphasized in the suffrage campaigns of many European and North American countries as well. Evans (1989), for instance, documents United States suffragists' claims that women's higher moral standards and maternal instincts would contribute to cleaning up a corrupt political system and establishing better social policies. In addition, they argued that the practice of voting would help women themselves be better able to educate the future sons of America to be good citizens. Motherhood has thus shaped women's citizenship throughout the world.

In the 1960s and early 1970s, women's formal involvement with politics tended to occur through participation in the women's wing of political parties, and their activities involved the extension of women's traditional roles as wife and mother (Miller 1991). The state similarly mobilized women around stereotypical female roles. For example, in Chile, Eduardo Frei Sr.'s Christian Democrat administration (1964–1970) created the Central Relacionadora de los Centros de Madres (CEMA, Central Coordinator of the Mothers' Centers), a governmental organization led by the wives of political leaders that institutionalized and coordinated thousands of Centros de Madres (Mothers' Centers), many of which already existed throughout the country. Before as well as after the creation of CEMA, the centers played an important role in generating support among poor and working-class women for the various regimes.

When his Partido de la Unidad Popular (Popular Unity Party) was elected into government in 1970, many women rallied around President Salvador Allende, imagining a new era and an end to the extreme class inequality that divided the nation. Women were central participants in education and public health campaigns, often working through the Centros de Madres. To a large extent, however, women remained peripheral during the Allende administration (1970–1973). Despite the view, typical of socialist movements, that all people, regardless of sex, would benefit from a move toward class equality, and also despite his own belief that the integration of women at all levels would be essential for the success of the movement, Allende did little to incorporate women, who often ended up in supportive roles (Miller 1991). A traditional view of women was reflected in Allende's discourse: "When I say 'woman,' I always think of the woman-mother. . . . When I talk of this woman, I refer to her in her function in the nuclear family. . . . The child is the prolongation of the woman who in essence is born to be a mother" (in ibid., 183). Today, many women who were active in the Unidad Popular note that they were usually relegated to roles that fit well with traditional expectations for women's activities (Vecchione 1993).

While the Unidad Popular does not appear to have challenged the patriarchal character of Chilean society, the 1973 coup meant that many initiatives undertaken during Allende's government never had the chance to fully develop. Teresa Valdés et al. (1989) observe that unlike other regimes, in which women were viewed entirely as wives and mothers, Allende addressed them as mothers, workers, and citizens. Elsewhere (n.d., 46) Teresa Valdés notes that by presidential decree, Allende created the Secretaría Nacional de la Mujer (National Women's Secretariat), which was intended to create policies that would encourage "the incorporation of women into society." The Secretaría was in charge of issues typically associated with women's concerns, such as price controls and the supply of food and household necessities, women's health and education, and child care. However, it also organized debates about issues like paternity laws and legalizing divorce, and provided women with information about the services and rights to which they were entitled. While these tasks were suspended after the coup, many of the same issues were later taken up under the Concertación with the creation of SERNAM.

Growing political antagonism during Allende's administration brought out women activists on the other end of the political spectrum as well. Women's activism against Allende was organized principally by Poder Femenino (Feminine Power), which was linked to but independent from the right-wing organization Patria y Libertad (Fatherland and Liberty). These women "demanded protection for women's traditional roles against what they perceived as the economic and social threats of Allende's socialist policies" (Valenzuela 1998, 51). Their chosen forms of resistance included the infamous 1971 "March of the Empty Pots and Pans," during which over five thousand women took to the streets to protest food shortages as well as a visit by Fidel Castro to the country. Poder Femenino also encouraged simultaneous banging of empty pots and pans from within women's homes, and harangued members of the military by calling them "chickens" for their policy of non-intervention (Power 2000).

The Unidad Popular—and many scholars since—portrayed women who opposed their government as old and rich and implied that all poorer women supported Allende. In reality, however, women's political views did not follow class lines. Only 30.5 percent of women voted for Allende in 1970, compared to almost 42 percent of men. And women's opposition to the Unidad Popular, while organized by the wives of centrist and rightist elites, involved cross-class mobilization of women around an idealized notion of womanhood (Miller 1991). Power (2000) examines why poor and working-class women would oppose Allende. She explains that when shortages of food and other necessities occurred, many poor and working-class women blamed their inability to carry out their roles as mothers and wives on the Unidad Popular. Power (ibid., 301) acknowledges that some of these problems were related to shortcomings of the Unidad Popular's economic policy, but maintains that the creation of shortages was also a central part of the opposition's strategy to undermine the government.

> The real sources of the shortages were the Chilean landowners who destroyed their own crops, limited agricultural production, or sold their goods on the black market, and the industrialists who cut back on their manufacturing or limited the sale of their goods. In addition, the U.S. government refused to extend the Allende government needed loans or to sell Chileans necessary spare parts for equipment or vehicles. As a final coup de grace the U.S. government financed striking truck drivers in October 1972, an act which effectively halted the transportation of food and other products to and from the urban centers.

Wealthy and middle-class Chileans hoarded goods as well. Power (ibid., 302) argues that poor women were often the most negatively affected by the shortages: "Despite the increases in their husband's salaries, poor and working-class women could not afford the skyrocketing prices charged on the black market. Unlike the upper- and middle-class women, they could not send their maids to stand in lines to wait for food. Nor could they travel to their country estates for needed food, as the wealthy did." Thus, women who opposed Allende's government had diverse motivations. Wealthy women were defending their class interests, while poor and working-class women sought an end to the political and economic disorder that prevented them from fulfilling their roles as wives and mothers. Women's role in undermining the Unidad Popular government cannot be underestimated; their activism gave rightists the moral authority they needed to wage a military coup (Miller 1991; Power 2002). Altogether, women's activism on both ends of the political spectrum during this time indicates that all women do not share uniform interests. Even among those of the same social class, personal interpretations of the crisis at hand led women to react in distinct ways.

WOMEN'S MOVEMENTS AND THE STATE DURING THE DICTATORSHIP

Pinochet and his junta (1973–1989) relied heavily on rhetoric about women's traditional roles as a method of social control. For instance, the junta's *Declaración de principios* (Declaration of Principles) proclaimed that it was women's responsibility to make the family the "spiritual rock of the motherland" (in Cleary 1987, 116). Women's role was to socialize children for future loyalty to the nation; to do otherwise was considered anti-patriotic. Moreover, Pinochet asserted that through their activism against Allende women had shown that they "sought the shelter of a strict authority that would reestablish order and public morality in our country" (in Pratt 1996, 1). In this way, women's "support" was used to legitimate the dictatorship.[2]

Pro-Dictatorship Organizing

The official rhetoric of the Pinochet regime was reinforced by two state women's organizations, the newly named CEMA-Chile and a reorganized Secretaría Nacional de la Mujer. Headed by Lucía Hiriart de Pinochet (the dictator's wife) and staffed mainly by other military wives, CEMA-Chile was charged with "de-politicizing" the Centros de Madres, reflecting the belief that Unidad Popular had brought in "foreign values" that destabilized the family (Cleary 1987). In practice, however, CEMA-Chile was not at all apolitical. Its main task, organizing women to better serve the family by training them in various tasks and providing some health and housing services, was linked to the nationalistic and patriarchal goal of helping women to be the reproducers of a great nation. The Secretaría, directed by the presidency, included among its goals the "conservation, reproduction, and diffusion of the patriarchal order through an organization of women" (ibid., 139). Again, the defense of the family against "foreign values" was directly linked to the defense of the nation against communism, which, it was thought, would inevitably follow from a change in values.

Women who mobilized under the auspices of the dictatorship included two main groups: military wives (also known as the *voluntariado* for the volunteer work they engaged in) and pobladoras. The pobladoras who participated in the Centros de Madres were in many ways distinct from those who participated in the women's movement, who will be discussed in the following sections. In fact, many pobladoras suspended their participation in the Centros precisely because they opposed the dictatorship, and the number of Centros never recovered pre-dictatorship levels (Valdés et al. 1989). According to Valdés et al. (ibid.) and my own interviews with two Centros de Madres, those pobladoras who did participate in them did so for several reasons. Many ideologically identified with the dictatorship. For others, the Centros were one of the only sources of resources for their families, an opportunity to get out of the house, and a place to socialize and develop skills. Finally, a few women whose families were opposed to the dictatorship participated in the Centros to dispel suspicion among their neighbors.

Pobladoras and the voluntariado came together in the newly reorganized Centros de Madres. Members of the voluntariado were assigned to a Centro, where they would coordinate and sometimes implement activities and services in benefit of the group. One of the main activities that occurred in the Centros involved training courses in various manual skills that included sewing, cooking, macramé, baking, embroidery, hair cutting, etc. Pobladoras had to pay for these courses; if they did not pay, they could not attend. CEMA-Chile organized fairs and workshops for the sale of the women's handicrafts. Members also had access to some material assistance and services provided by CEMA-Chile, including health care and medicine at CEMA-Chile clinics, low price generic goods, free food, clothing, school supplies and scholarships for children, and so on. Pobladoras paid a price for these benefits, however. Members were prohibited from talking about politics in the Centros (even innocuous phrases like "the situation is very bad" were censored) and if exposed, communist members were expelled. The women's attendance was monitored; they were punished if they missed meetings, and rewarded with food for their families or access to health care for behaviors like attending pro-Pinochet political events. Women who did not attend these events could be punished or kicked out of their Centro. Centros as a whole also received a "grade" from CEMA-Chile based on their compliance with rules established by CEMA-Chile, and leaders were usually picked by the CEMA-Chile representative, apparently based on their adhesion to the military regime (Valdés and Weinstein 1993). By creating a relationship of dependency between poor women and the military wives, CEMA-Chile functioned as a mechanism of control and surveillance (Cleary 1987).

The Secretaría Nacional de la Mujer and CEMA-Chile reflect a strategy of reliance upon traditional values in order to neutralize women's potential as a progressive political force (ibid.). Yet there is a certain irony here: these wealthy women and military wives saw the "need to break with their 'natural' role as mothers and housewives in order to save the family and nation from 'Marxist chaos'" (ibid., 116). Though Poder Feminino was forced to suspend its activities after the coup (possibly, as Power [2002] suggests, because the skills they displayed in bringing down Allende were too incompatible with the junta's ideas about women's proper place) many of its members went on to channel their abilities through CEMA-Chile or the Secretaría. As Valdés et al. (1989) observe, while CEMA-Chile served to monitor and discipline the poor women who participated, it also provided the military wives involved with the chance to work outside of the home and take leadership positions. It is important not to diminish the fact that many women of all social classes *did* see (and continue to see today) the socialist values of Unidad Popular as a threat to their ability to raise and protect their families. Nevertheless, the incongruity of rhetoric that advocated women's "essential" role as creators of patriotic subjects with the daily experience of material and social deprivation ultimately led many women of all social classes to mobilize against the Pinochet regime.

The Chilean Women's Movement

Frohmann and Valdés (1993) document three main branches of women's activism against the dictatorship: human rights groups, economic survival organizations, and feminist groups. Together, they made up what came to be referred to as the Chilean women's movement. These organizations were not mutually exclusive. For example, one woman might participate in a feminist organization as well as a human rights organization. Moreover, the objectives of many organizations encompassed human rights, economic survival, and feminist concerns. As shall be seen, many human rights organizations and economic survival groups grew in feminist orientation as time went on, though there were sometimes differences of opinion as to what the most important issues were. Nevertheless, while some focused more intently on feminist issues, others on the human rights atrocities committed by the dictatorship and alliances with political parties, and others on the social and economic needs exacerbated by structural adjustment, the dictatorship gave the women who participated a common enemy, leading to a fairly united women's movement as well as to links with other types of organizations and parties that opposed Pinochet.

Human Rights Organizations. Women were the first to take to the streets to denounce the detention and disappearance of their loved ones under the dictatorship. Organizations like the Families of Political Prisoners and the Families of the Detained and Disappeared became famous for marching with poster-sized photographs of their loved ones that read, *¿Dónde Están?* (Where are they?). Women's ability to mobilize in defense of human rights in the midst of political oppression is attributed by some scholars to the social protection that results from stereotypes of women as non-political and worthy of protection and honor. The hypothesis is that regimes willing to commit extreme violence against male activists may risk losing legitimacy if they publicly treat women in the same inhumane manner (Chuchryk 1994). This factor may partially explain why it was women who predominated in human rights groups that demanded the return of the disappeared and an end to state-sponsored violence.

However, this argument only goes so far. It may have been *safer* for women to mobilize than it was for men, but it certainly was not *safe*. Women have suffered sex-specific forms of torture, rape, and murder at the hands of authoritarian governments across the globe, including in Chile. Demanding the return of the disappeared was, moreover, directly linked to women's traditional role of protecting their children and preserving their families. For many women, violence against their families made their private roles public issues, inspiring them to mobilize across classes around human rights (Chuchryk 1994). Their mobilization in defense of their families and human rights entailed substantial sacrifice, risk, and bravery.

Pobladoras' Economic Survival Organizations. Economic survival groups emerged in response to the severe economic reforms initiated by Pinochet. These reforms, which are discussed at greater length in chapter 3, caused high levels of inflation, unemployment, and poverty. Like participants in human rights groups, women residents of the *poblaciones* (shantytowns) often organized to defend their roles as wives and mothers. Pobladoras who saw their ability to fulfill their mother roles threatened mobilized to start communal soup kitchens, collective work groups, and neighborhood daycare centers. The Catholic Church and external aid agencies often played an essential role in financing and providing organizational space as well as legal and social aid for these groups (Schild 1995).

Although, as noted earlier, some pobladoras who participated in the Centros de Madres did so to provide resources for their families, those women's activism was largely isolated from that of the women discussed in this section. It was relatively uncommon for women to participate simultaneously in the two types of organizations, because CEMA-Chile was run by Pinochet's wife, and the survival organizations and their supporters were usually critical of the dictatorship. Moreover, they were often staffed by leftists. Lucía Hiriart de Pinochet solidified this separation in 1976 when she mandated that all Centros de Madres choose to ally themselves with either CEMA-Chile or Cáritas-Chile, a charitable organization reliant on the Catholic Church, which provided similar types of support (Valdés et al. 1989).

While the pobladora organizations on the left usually did not begin with an explicitly feminist agenda, and most of the pobladoras active in the groups today do not self-identify as feminists, participating in them and meeting other women who experienced similar difficulties often led women to develop greater gender consciousness. The very act of participating in these organizations was a challenge to the patriarchal nature of these women's home lives and the association of women with the private sphere (Caldeira 1990; Schild 1990). The development of gender consciousness is also linked to the fact that Church-sponsored groups were often led by feminists and leftist women who integrated socioeconomic and human rights concerns with feminist and Freirean consciousness-raising and educational activities. When in the mid-1980s the Catholic Church veered back to the right, many of the feminists and leftists were fired or chose to leave and form independent non-governmental organizations (Schild 1995). However, many of them maintained contact with pobladora organizations, providing them with technical and financial support.

This is not to say that tensions did not exist between pobladoras and middle-class feminists. Rather, feminist discourses of rights and equality provided pobladoras with the tools not only to reconsider their place in the world, but also to challenge the inequality and paternalism inherent in their relationships with the feminists who guided the groups (Schild 1994). These new "meaning-making resources," as well as their oppositional ideological perspective, are what distinguish these groups from the Centros de Madres of the same era (Schild 1990). Thus, women's economic survival groups frequently ended up being much more, as they linked their class-based activities to their oppression as women in general and within the context of the dictatorship in particular. Importantly, though, many of the class tensions between pobladoras and middle-class feminists became increasingly salient as Chile transitioned to democracy. These tensions, as well as the class aspects of pobladora activism and identities, will be dealt with at greater length in chapter 4.

Middle-Class Feminists and Political Activists. Middle-class women on the left focused their activism on feminist concerns and on ending the dictatorship. They combined the two issues to varying degrees.

The precursors for the Chilean feminist movement can be found among working-class women who organized to put women's issues on union agendas in the early 1900s (Frohmann and Valdés 1993). Chilean women went on to mobilize for suffrage in the 1930s and 1940s, which they finally achieved in 1949. This was followed by a period of little political and feminist activity. However, feminists re-emerged during the dictatorship with the motto "democracy in the country and in the home," which eventually became the rallying cry for the women's movement as a whole (ibid.). Linking authoritarianism in the country to authoritarianism in the home, and the dictatorship to widespread societal patriarchy, Chilean feminists throughout the 1980s were active in organizing cross-class umbrella groups, working with pobladoras, participating in anti-dictatorship organizations and parties with men, and creating documents and platforms demanding women's rights.

Women came to feminism in different ways. Some had become disillusioned with their experiences in leftist movements, while others were exposed to European and North American feminism while in exile and brought it back to Chile. Many of them returned before the end of the dictatorship and established consciousness-raising groups and women's non-governmental organizations. The international women's movement influenced the development of feminism in Chile in other ways as well. European and North American women supported feminist and grassroots groups through direct financial and social support. Maryknoll nuns and lay workers with feminist orientations, for example, often lived and helped establish women's organizations in the poblaciones. In addition, the United Nations Decade for Women (1975–1985) and the Convention on the Elimination of All Forms of Discrimination against Women (1979) contributed to a global awareness of gender inequality and women's rights.

The first explicitly feminist organization in contemporary Chile was the Círculo de Estudios de la Mujer (Women's Studies Circle), which emerged in 1977. In 1983, the Círculo lost its Church support and split into the Centro de Estudios de la Mujer (Women's Studies Center) and Casa de la Mujer la Morada (La Morada Women's Center), which focused on feminist activism. Also central were Mujeres por la Vida (Women for Life) and the Movimiento Pro-Emancipación de la Mujer Chilena '83 (MEMCh83, '83 Chilean Women's Emancipation Movement, founded in 1983 and named in homage to a women's suffrage organization founded in 1935). Mujeres por la Vida was founded by sixteen political women who wished to "set an example of unity to the rest of the political anti-Pinochet establishment," which was rife with infighting (Frohmann and Valdés 1993, 11), whereas MEMCh83 was established to coordinate all women's organizations that opposed the dictatorship. Both of these organizations became cross-class umbrella organizations, incorporated feminist and non-feminist women, and grew in feminist orientation as time went on. Mujeres por la Vida was responsible for a 1983 "women's meeting" at the Caupolicán Theater in Santiago. The meeting, attended by over ten thousand women and intended to demonstrate women's ability to mobilize in unity, was the largest display of opposition to the dictatorship up to that point (ibid.). Other women's organizations, such as Women for Socialism, focused on women's issues within the dynamics of party politics. Undoubtedly, the work of feminist women was central to the overall mobilization of women—and of the general populace—during the dictatorship.[3]

The Dominance of Difference Feminism and Militant Motherhood. Difference feminism was, and continues to be, influential among Chilean feminists. Early (and to some extent continuing) debates among feminists in North America involved two main camps: "equality feminists" and "difference feminists." For equality feminists, according to Fraser (1997), the goal of feminism was to do away with essentialized categories of difference between women and men, which they argued, were imposed upon them within a sexist system. Exposing and eliminating these differences, they maintained, would result in gender equality. Fraser says that difference feminists, on the other hand, believed that gender differences were real, and that the goals of equality feminists were andocentric and devalued women's activities and perspectives. The solution was to revalue feminine characteristics and values, recognizing women's "difference" as morally superior (as in the case of nurturing versus militaristic attitudes), or at least, as a second and equally valuable "voice."

Whereas in North America "difference" and "equality" feminisms usually have been portrayed as separate camps (whose proponents often come into conflict with one another), Argentine feminist Elizabeth Jelin's (1996) portrayal of the Latin American case suggests two sides of feminism that are connected but always in tension with one another.

The principle of women's difference has been central to women's move-ments throughout Latin America. Jelin points out that feminism has made claims not just for equal rights, but also for "the right to a differ-entiated treatment and to the social recognition of women's unique-ness" (ibid., 178–179). Molyneux (2000, 45) explains that more so than in Europe and the United States, women's movements in Latin America have made gains based on a gender discourse that appropriates aspects of binary gender ideology and focuses on essentialist differences between women and men. They have rooted their activism in notions of do-mestic and maternal virtues, and have demanded recognition as full citizens on the basis of contributions they have made to the nation through their roles as wives and mothers.

All three sectors of the Chilean women's movement—human rights activists, economic survival activists, and feminists—used women's dif-ference as a justification for their activism and for making claims on rights. Human rights activists rooted their claims in their rights to be good mothers and wives, as did economic survival activists. Chuchryk (1994) calls these forms of activism "militant motherhood." Valdés and Weinstein (1993) observe that Mujeres por la Vida and other women's organizations' focus on "life" involved reframing motherhood as a de-parture for activism.[4] Franceschet (2001b) notes that women's differ-ence was used as a justification for many radical demands made by Chilean feminists in the 1980s as well. For example, many of the de-mands presented in 1986 by Mujeres por la Vida to the Asamblea de la Civilidad (an oppositional civilian assembly) and incorporated into its demands for the return to democracy, were linked to women's concerns as wives and mothers, such as respect for human rights, better wages and dignified jobs, and improvements in education, housing, and health care. But their demands also included "feminist issues," such as free con-traception, legal divorce, and promotion of women's political partici-pation. Mujeres por la Vida justified these demands by emphasizing women's essential qualities, noting that their "participation will gen-erate a political renovation, with non-authoritarian styles of debate, or-ganization, and direction" (in Franceschet 2001b, 153–154). Other documents, including one released by MEMCh83, made similar de-mands based on similar justifications. The feminist movement's *Demandas de las mujeres a la democracia* (1988) also focused on civil, reproductive, family, and labor rights, and attempted to link women's agenda to the broader democratic agenda (in Valenzuela 1998). This document also called for the creation of a women's policy machinery to promote women's interests from within the state. In this document, for the first time, the feminist movement qualified the oft-established direct link between maternity and women's rights as citizens. The document reads, "We value our maternal role and we exercise it with great commitment and responsibility, but our realization as persons is not exhausted by it," and asserts that "women's liberty to choose whether to be mothers or not must be respected" (in Franceschet 2001b, 156–157). In Fraser's terms, at this point the Chilean women's movement's demands shifted from a focus on recognition alone to one that encompassed redistribution as well.

The three types of organized women discussed in this section played important roles leading up to the transition to democracy. Women's protests—as diverse as parading with photos of the disappeared, developing feminist demands for democracy, establishing community kitchens, and creating tapestries depicting the economic and political suffering of the Chilean people—were central expressions of discontent within society. Women were also important actors in the plebiscite of 1988, mobilizing the "No" vote against eight more years of dictatorship.[5] After the "No" won, feminists actively sought inclusion of women's demands in the various party platforms, and women's activism during the dictatorship gave them the leverage to have some of their demands addressed. In 1990, an autonomous women's coalition in support of the Concertación de Partidos por la Democracia called the Concertación Nacional de Mujeres por la Democracia (CNMD, National Coalition of Women for Democracy) was successful in getting gender-based demands incorporated into the Concertación's agenda, an incredible accomplishment in a country where conservative forces insisted on women's "natural" place and feminism continued to hold extremely negative connotations.

Mapuche Women's Participation in Relation to the Women's Movement

Indigenous women are seldom mentioned in scholarly work about women's interests and the women's movement in Chile. This omission reflects a deeper-seated denial of ethnic and cultural diversity. Though some changes have occurred since the 1992 Census, which showed that indigenous peoples represented approximately 10 percent of the Chilean population, there is a widespread belief among Chileans that theirs is a racially homogenous society of European origin. Few Chileans self-identify as mestizo, the Spanish term that indicates a mixed Spanish-indigenous heritage, and the only incorporation of indigenous people in collective self-imagery is the glorification of the brave Mapuche who defeated the

Spanish in times gone by (Aylwin 1998). It follows, then, that Mapuche women and their interests would be generally ignored as the women's movement developed and became a subject of academic study.

There is an important exception to this, however. A small group of women dedicated themselves to working with Mapuche women beginning in the early 1980s. Angélica Willson of the Centro de Desarrollo de la Mujer (CEDEM, Center for Women's Development) explains that these women began organizing in 1982 as a group called the Programa de Estudios y Capacitación de la Mujer Campesina e Indígena (PEMCI, Program for the Study and Training of Peasant and Indigenous Women. As the name of the group implies, its work was dedicated to the dual goals of academic investigation and strengthening the "organization and social fabric" of peasant and indigenous women during the dictatorship. In PEMCI's early years, the group published a book of life histories of Mapuche women who had migrated to Santiago. The program's work eventually came to focus on Region IX, where they established the Casa de la Mujer Mapuche (Mapuche Women's Center) in 1985, with the goal of supporting rural Mapuche women in the areas of health, production and marketing of traditional weavings and recuperation of traditional designs, legal aid, and social organization. The Casa de la Mujer Mapuche was eventually handed over to Mapuche women who continue to run it as a non-governmental organization in Temuco, working with associated groups of women throughout the region. The Program for the Study and Training of Peasant and Indigenous Women was eventually subsumed by the non-governmental organization CEDEM, which continues to conduct studies of issues that affect rural and indigenous women as well as supporting initiatives that foster their development and sociopolitical participation. Also thanks largely to the initiative of CEDEM, Mapuche women were later involved in the preparation process for the World Women's Conference in Beijing.

Like the pobladora and middle-class feminist women discussed in the previous section, many Mapuche women actively resisted the dictatorship, and worked toward the expansion of their own rights. Nevertheless, unlike pobladora activists who linked their class struggles to women's issues and much of whose activism took place in the context of the broader women's movement, the bulk of Mapuche women's activism took place in the context of the Mapuche movement. For the most part, this remains true today. Because of this, Mapuche women's activism will be discussed at greater length in chapters 5 and 6.

WOMEN'S MOVEMENTS AND THE STATE IN CONTEMPORARY CHILE

How have Chilean women fared under the Concertación governments? By taking advantage of the political opportunity provided by the transition to democracy, the women's movement was able to assure that some of its demands were incorporated into the Concertación's agenda. As a result, important gains have been made in terms of policies and legislation that favor women's equality with men. Women have also achieved greater access to the state. But these gains are not unequivocal, and measures taken to work toward greater equality between women and men have met with opposition from rightist and religious forces in Chilean society. Moreover, differences among women have become more salient since the end of the dictatorship, again raising the question of whether it is legitimate to talk about "women's" interests and rights at all. In this section, I discuss the gains made by the women's movement since the return to democracy, which center on the creation of SERNAM. I also address the limitations faced by SERNAM and by women's movement activists more generally. I outline the way that differences among women along a number of fronts have led to fissures in what, by many accounts, can no longer be called the Chilean women's movement. Finally, I discuss where SERNAM and the women's movement fit into the state's socioeconomic goals.

The Servicio Nacional de la Mujer

During the Pinochet dictatorship, the Chilean women's movement struggled not just for the return to democracy, but for inclusion in that democracy as full subjects of rights. The relationship between women's movement actors and the state today demonstrates some successes as a result of prior efforts as well as some new limitations. The Concertación Nacional de Mujeres por la Democracia's demand for the establishment of a women's agency in the state was taken on as part of the Concertación's agenda. In a speech during his candidacy Patricio Aylwin adopted women's demand for "democracy in the country and in the home" as his own (Frohmann and Valdés 1993). The creation of SERNAM represents the women's movement's most significant accomplishment since the return to democracy. Nevertheless, the inclusion of women and their interests in the state has been contested, and significant institutional and political barriers have limited what SERNAM has been able to accomplish.

Like the development of feminism in Chile, the creation of SERNAM was influenced by international activism around women's rights. Guzmán (n.d., 14–15) notes that in the conclusions of the 1975 World Women's Conference held in Mexico, it was suggested that "the establishment of an interdisciplinary and multi-sectoral machinery within the government, such as national commissions, women's offices, and other bodies, with adequate staff and resources, could be an effective transitional measure for accelerating the achievement of equal opportunities for women and their total integration in national life." This recommendation was taken quite seriously in Latin America, and today nineteen countries in the region have state agencies for women. In Chile, the establishment of SERNAM, though demanded from below by women's movement activists, was influenced by this international context.[6]

SERNAM's *Creation: Opposition and Compromise.* The women's movement actors who proposed SERNAM modeled their ideal agency after Spain's Women's Institute. They wanted the agency established by law, rather than presidential decree, to make it more difficult to remove the agency should rightists take power. The "imaginers" of SERNAM were also concerned that the agency not become a "women's ghetto" within the state. They thus proposed an agency that would coordinate the efforts of other state ministries and agencies to integrate a gendered perspective and promote women's rights.

The bill proposing the creation of SERNAM was presented in 1990. It met with substantial opposition from rightist and conservative Catholic forces who alleged that feminists would infiltrate SERNAM and use it to subvert the family (Valenzuela 1998). Baldez (1999) suggests that conservative political actors curtailed the power of SERNAM from the start. Even before SERNAM was created, the Concertación Nacional de Mujeres por la Democracia left issues like abortion and divorce off their agenda in an attempt to make their demands more palatable to conservatives. Rightist politicians nevertheless vehemently opposed the principles of equality, non-discrimination, and state intervention to guarantee women's rights, all of which were behind the creation of SERNAM.

As Franceschet (2001b) notes, Aylwin and at least some segments of the Concertación wanted to promote women's interests, but they also wanted to assure a peaceful transition to democracy. Fear of another coup was palpable throughout the early years of democracy, a fear that was intensified because the military still enjoyed (and enjoys) significant autonomy from the state and Pinochet was sitting as a senator for life, a provision he had worked into the Constitution. Nor did

Concertación leaders wish to upset moral conservatives among the Christian Democrats—the largest party in the Concertación and the party of the first two democratic presidents—or the Catholic Church, which maintains a moral voice on social issues in Chile today (Franceschet 2001b). As a result, the Concertación compromised on several issues in the creation of SERNAM. Central compromises involved emphasizing the importance of women's role in the family and acknowledging essential differences between men and women. When the law establishing SERNAM was passed in 1991, its phrasing reflected these compromises. The second article, for example, states the purpose of SERNAM in this manner:

> The National Women's Service is the organism charged with collaborating with the executive branch in the study and proposition of general plans and measures that will lead to women enjoying equal rights and opportunities with respect to men in the process of the political, social, economic, and cultural development of the country, respecting the nature and specificity of the woman, which emanates from the natural diversity of the sexes, including adequate concern for family relations.

The law was subject to other compromises, as well. SERNAM was established as part of the Ministry of Planning and Cooperation (MIDEPLAN, Ministerio de Planificación y Cooperación), where programs for the poor, youth, and indigenous peoples are also housed. Baldez (1999) interprets this as an attempt to diminish the political content of women's demands. According to former deputy director of SERNAM Natacha Molina, a provision that would have legally created a "space for listening to the community" (i.e., women's non-governmental and grassroots organizations) was also taken out of the bill. She reflected, "Politically, in some way, they didn't want SERNAM to have a direct relationship with women."

Political limitations have hounded SERNAM since its creation. Morally conservative forces among the Christian Democrats have limited SERNAM's potential as a feminist force within the state. The first two directors were Christian Democrat party activists with no links to the women's movement, much less to pobladoras. And in an effort to avoid confrontation with the Catholic Church, rightist parties, and morally conservative Christian Democrats, the content and objectives of SERNAM have often been deliberately toned down. For example, in many cases, women continue to be represented as a vulnerable social sector and not as adult citizens. Natacha Molina explained that SERNAM often legitimates itself by presenting women as victims:

SERNAM continues to be an island and the way to legitimate oneself as SERNAM or any other organism that worries about equal opportunities for women is through victimization. That is why the law against intra-family violence came out so quickly, because, "Poor little one, the beaten woman." The Women Heads of Households Program has more resources than others because, "the women heads of households, poor little ones, they are alone and have families." So, what legitimates it is a traditional image. To break with this, and talk about equality and a gender perspective—that is seldom achieved.

An example of this victimization was displayed in Frei's 1998 presidential address, in which he discussed the Equal Opportunities for Women Plan in the "Rights of the Weakest" section of his speech. In Lagos's speeches as well, which often (as shall be seen in the following sections) have included fairly progressive stances on women's rights, discussion of women's issues generally has been followed by references to how to best support the family. This represents some consistency with earlier regimes in that women are implicitly denied the right to be complete human beings; either they are able to act only on behalf of their families, or they are too weak to act and must be protected.

Other limitations are budgetary. For instance, SERNAM has little funding of its own, and is expected to generate support and funding among the other ministries for policies and programs that benefit women. Its budget at the time it was founded was U.S.$2 million plus $1.5 million in additional funding from international agencies. In response to pressure, the budget more than sextupled over the following six years (Valenzuela 1998). Still, according to Baldez (1999), the portion of SERNAM's budget that is designated by the state (i.e., not counting international funds) is less than 0.1 percent of the total governmental budget. Valeria Ambrosio, SERNAM's program director, explained that approximately one-third of the budget is pre-assigned to specific programs, such as the Women Heads of Households program described below. Another third goes to salaries, and only one-third is money that SERNAM is free to determine how to spend (fieldnotes, August 16, 2000). In addition, conservatives achieved the creation of an advisory council that has the power to audit all SERNAM programs with international funding (Baldez 1999).

Successes and Limitations in SERNAM's Operations. In practice, SERNAM's principal objectives are to put women's issues on the public agenda and to achieve the incorporation of a gender perspective in all government ministries. It makes formal agreements (*convenios*) with the other ministries at the national and regional levels, and proposes, coordinates, and trains state employees in how to create policies that promote equal opportunities for women. However, although SERNAM's national director is a member of the president's cabinet, SERNAM is not a ministry. This imposes a serious practical limitation: only ministries can implement their own programs. A "service" like SERNAM can only implement pilot programs, which must be turned over to an appropriate ministry after a given period of time. While SERNAM's designation as a service in part reflects the desire to integrate a gender perspective throughout the state, it poses a major limitation when combined with widespread resistance to SERNAM within the state. According to Waylen (1996a) and my discussions with several femocrats, there is no formal mechanism by which SERNAM can oversee and evaluate the work of other ministries or enforce the convenios. As a result, it must depend on the goodwill of the individuals assigned as contact points in the other ministries. Valeria Ambrosio, director of programs at SERNAM, noted that this is problematic, because the person assigned to work with SERNAM in a given ministry may lack decision-making power or may be socially conservative and resistant to feminist values. Moreover, the high turnover of personnel in some ministries makes developing working relationships difficult.

Most of the SERNAM employees I interviewed noted that reliance on people's goodwill is a central difficulty in instituting more than a rhetorical dedication to women's equality in the state. Erika López, director of SERNAM in Region IX from 1994 until 2002, explained that this difficulty is often very intense at the regional level. When her regional government initiated the development of a Regional Indigenous Development Plan, SERNAM was not invited to participate in the process. López personally called to ask why, and was told that it simply had not occurred to regional authorities to include SERNAM. López concluded that institutionalized sexism and SERNAM's lack of legitimacy among other state actors are major limitations for achieving the representation of women's interests.

The pilot programs established by SERNAM have both advantages and disadvantages. Programs established thus far have focused on specific groups of women, including victims of domestic violence, young pregnant women, *temporeras* (women seasonal workers in the agriculture industry), and *jefas de hogar* (single mother heads of households). An additional program established Centros de Información de los Derechos de la Mujer (CIDEMs, Women's Rights Information Centers), to which women have free access, at SERNAM's regional offices throughout the country. By far the most publicized, and in some respects successful, program is the Programa de Habilitación Laboral para Mujeres de Escasos Recursos Preferentemente Jefas de Hogar (Labor Force Training Program for Low Income Women, Preferably Heads of Households), through which SERNAM coordinates the activities and financial support of over ten state agencies in order to provide education, health and child care, and job training to young single mother heads of households. My interviews with women who participated in the jefas de hogar program indicated that they benefited from access to health and dental care for themselves and their children, and felt they had gained in self-esteem. However, few of them were able to acquire jobs in the area in which they were trained. The program can do little to combat labor market discrimination against women, and participants complained that employers are reluctant to hire women if they are older than thirty-five, especially if they are single mothers. Some success stories exist, however, as in the case of a pharmacy chain that hired several program participants from the municipality of Cerro Navia in Santiago who had been trained as stockroom workers. The chain even committed to further training some of them to become pharmacy aides (fieldnotes, September 12, 2000). Pilot programs by SERNAM also appear to have increased knowledge about SERNAM and awareness of women's issues among the general public. However, some criticize these programs, noting that they draw needed staff and resources away from intersectoral coordination, which is SERNAM's intended purpose (Matear 1995). One non-governmental organization worker described to me the case of a woman at SERNAM who was responsible for simultaneously coordinating SERNAM's work with the housing, justice, national assets, and rural sectors.

The National Women's Service, SERNAM, is a decentralized agency with offices in each of Chile's thirteen regions. However, as is the case throughout the Chilean state, decision making and budgeting are still highly centralized. Erika López explained that existing efforts at decentralization of decision making in SERNAM have mainly focused on administrative issues, such as allowing regional directors to establish the daily stipends of subcontracted professionals working with SERNAM. As a result, making programs adequate to regional realities is difficult. López gave three examples. First, the jefas de hogar program requires that municipalities have a minimum population. This excludes the majority of municipalities in Region IX which are predominantly rural despite containing towns of significant size with the presence of women who could benefit from the program. Second, while many women in

Region IX are temporary workers, they mostly work in the forestry, fishing, and tourism industries. SERNAM's temporeras program, however, focuses exclusively on the agricultural exports industry, and thus most temporeras in Region IX are not eligible for the protections and services the program provides. Finally, of all Chile, Region IX has the highest proportion of Mapuche residents. Because program design and decision making is centralized, there is little possibility to make SERNAM's programs in the region adequate to the needs and priorities of Mapuche women (fieldnotes, August 18, 2000).

In order to institutionalize commitment to equal opportunities for women at the local level, SERNAM has encouraged the creation of Municipal Women's Offices. These offices are now fairly widespread (forty-eight of fifty-two municipalities in the Metropolitan region have them, for example). They are financed and staffed entirely by the municipality, and receive no money from SERNAM except for funds designated for the jefas de hogar program. The quality of these offices therefore varies according to the resources available in a given municipality; poorer municipalities are able to designate fewer resources to women's services even though there may be a greater need than in wealthier areas. Equally important is the mayor's personal commitment to women's equality. The poor and working-class municipality of Renca is a case in point. Over six years, Manuel Caballero, the former mayor of Renca, increased the municipal funds designated for the Women's Program by more than six times. It was called a program rather than an office, moreover, to connote the importance the municipality designated to women's services. Caballero frequently noted in public that investing in women was the best way to invest in the community. At a 1999 Municipal Women's Congress co-organized by the Renca Women's Network and the Women's Program, for example, Caballero said, "I am convinced that you, the women of Renca, constitute an important motor for our actions, you are the true protagonists of progress in the municipality" (in Orrego and Martínez 1999, 4).

When I visited Renca's Women's Program in 2000, Jessica Orrego, the social worker who directed the program, had a lawyer and a psychologist available for consultancies, provided workshops on women's rights and domestic violence, coordinated women's access to the jefas de hogar program and other educational services, and had helped establish a network of women's organizations with the capacity to make demands of the municipal government. The Women's Program was located in a former schoolhouse with four separate rooms, in addition to a kitchen and bathroom. Other Women's Offices do not even have a single room of their own, and often the person who runs the office is also in charge of programs for the elderly, children, and other groups. Renca's program changed drastically at the end of 2000, however, when Caballero retired and a new mayor, Viky Barahona, a woman from the Unión Demócrata Independiente (Independent Democratic Union), a rightist party associated with Pinochet supporters and the Opus Dei fundamentalist Catholic movement, won the election. The new mayor drastically reduced women's services and changed the program's staff (fieldnotes, August 2, 2001). Thus, efforts to institutionalize women's rights as a permanent priority at the local level have encountered mixed results.

The greatest success of SERNAM has been in generating legal reforms. Thus far, laws that SERNAM has successfully sponsored have included the criminalization of domestic violence, the establishment of equality among legitimate and illegitimate children in terms of receiving inheritances, the provision of time off from work for either parent to care for sick children, and the prohibition of pregnancy tests as a condition for employment (Franceschet 2001b). However, these reforms have been limited by the political barriers faced by SERNAM. For instance, the violence law refers to "intra-family" violence rather than violence against women, and no funding was allotted to enforce the law. And many women report that employers continue to demand pregnancy tests. A particularly egregious case occurred when female custodial workers employed by a Santiago municipality were tested prior to the renewal of their one-year contracts. A number of the women were pregnant and lost their jobs. When Municipal Women's Office employees protested, they were told that the municipality simply could not afford to pay the maternity benefits that would have been entailed were the women's contracts renewed.

Changes under Lagos. There have been some positive changes in the representation of women and their interests under Socialist president Ricardo Lagos. The first national director Lagos designated was Adriana DelPiano, a member of the Partido por la Democracia (Party for Democracy, PPD) who worked in the Secretaría de la Mujer under Allende and was active in Women for Socialism during the 1980s, though party politics, rather than women's issues, have been the focus of her career. Several women, including DelPiano, had key posts in Lagos's campaign, and his agenda included "Full Integration of Women" as one of ten key objectives.

While it has steadily increased from around 30 percent at the beginning of the 1990s, at 39 percent, Chilean women's labor force participation rate remains one of the lowest in Latin America.[7] Lagos and SERNAM have made increasing this rate a central priority, and consistently denote women's employment as a precondition for their equality with men. The issues addressed in Lagos's campaign agenda focused mainly on labor market participation, deploring the discrimination faced by women, and promoting shared parenting responsibilities as a solution to women's double workload. In the agenda, Lagos also promised to make work more compatible with motherhood, improve child care services and working conditions, and increase the availability of training programs. By referring to such issues, the Lagos administration has given at least rhetorical attention to the ways that the workplace can be a site of oppression for women. However, it is important to note that the Chilean state has a dual interest in increasing women's employment: it might promote women's equality, but it will also help improve Chile's position in the global marketplace (Franceschet 2001b). In Lagos's 2000 presidential address, he declared that women's low labor force participation rate "reflects the inequality and discrimination in our society for the woman, who is not completely integrated." He added that Chile must confront this "form of backwardness," and that "to incorporate women, to improve the labor participation rates, is to better utilize the other half of Chile, which is our women." Clearly, there is more at stake than advancing women's rights.

In non-work related initiatives, Lagos made a commitment in his campaign agenda to improve health coverage and promote women's political participation. He promised to combat discrimination and promote equal opportunities through the new Equal Opportunities Plan. He also appointed five women to ministerial posts, as opposed to none under Aylwin and three under Frei, as well as several women as undersecretaries, intendents, and governors. The language he uses when he addresses the nation is gender inclusive (*amigos y amigas, conciudadanos y conciudadanas*, and so forth). He has also promoted legalizing divorce, and it is likely that divorce law (albeit, a conservative one) will pass the Senate by the end of his tenure as president. However, even under Lagos, the Concertación has continued to bow to conservatives and the Church on the issue of abortion, all forms of which are illegal in Chile. For instance, at the Beijing +5 meetings held in 2000 in New York, SERNAM's then director DelPiano announced, much to the dismay of many Chilean feminists, that Chile was a pro-life nation. The extent to which women's priorities are substantively addressed by Lagos's government is thus complicated by hegemonic political and economic objectives.

SERNAM's Model of Women's Citizenship. The existence of SERNAM as an agency responsible for promoting women's equality represents an important change in the way the Chilean state views women. Despite the institutional and political limitations faced by SERNAM, as a result of the struggles of the women's movement, the official image of the Chilean citizen is no longer exclusively male. Today, the responsibility for promulgating the rights and responsibilities of women citizens falls largely on SERNAM's shoulders. While women's movement struggles were often based on a notion of women's essential difference from men, SERNAM's citizenship discourse focuses principally on the concept of equality, especially as related to opportunities. This is demonstrated in the Equal Opportunities Plan for Women, 1994–1999 and the Plan for Equal Opportunities between Women and Men, 2000–2010, which were adopted as part of Frei and Lagos's campaign agendas, respectively. For instance, in its discussion of "A Culture of Equality" in the second plan (2000–2010, 22), SERNAM states, "Equality is a recent value in history. Modern societies, by affirming universal rights and formal equality before the law, eliminated customs, norms, and beliefs that predetermined people's place in society in accordance with their sex, and social, religious, ethnic and cultural origin." The authors of the Plan maintain that in Chile, equality is not yet generalized and as a result, women have fewer opportunities than men. The Equal Opportunities Plans are not law, but they lay out lines of action governmental agencies need to pursue in support of equal opportunities for women. While, as shall be seen, there is a great deal of debate over what women's interests are and how well the state represents them, the Plans have been of central importance in putting women's rights on the public agenda. Nevertheless, the factors described here have resulted in a Women's Service fettered by political limitations, an unstable relationship between the Service and women's movement actors, and a tendency to center policies on women's roles as mothers and wives rather than basing them on feminist claims for women's rights.

The Increasing Salience of Differences among Women

Scholars of women's movements throughout the Americas note that by restricting the practice of formal politics, authoritarian governments unintentionally provided the necessary space for alternative forms of political expression to grow, including activism around women's rights (Fitzsimmons 2000; Friedman 1998). The consolidation of democracy, however, often seems to have been detrimental to women's movements. Indeed, the return to democracy has in many respects meant the return to "business as usual," where the political scene is dominated by party politics and party politics are dominated by men. In addition, the absence of a central, unifying cause has left room for underlying tensions among women to emerge (more accurately, perhaps, to re-emerge) on several levels. The women's movement has still not managed to encompass the interests of socially and politically conservative women. And among feminists, some advocate an autonomous women's movement while others believe engagement with political parties and the state is essential to advancing women's rights. Some have argued it is necessary to remain outside of the state, while others have become *femócratas*. (After the "femocrats" in the Australian state [see Eisenstein 1991], this refers to bureaucrats who promote women's equality from within SERNAM and other state agencies.) Class differences have become increasingly salient as pobladoras sense that middle-class feminist women who work in non-governmental organizations and the state have abandoned them. Poor, rural, and indigenous women claim that their interests are seldom represented and that they are rarely invited to participate in decision making on issues that impact them. All of these issues have contributed to the fragmentation of what was once a vibrant women's movement in Chile.

Although the women's movement and the Concertación Nacional de Mujeres por la Democracia imagined themselves as representing the demands of women across the political spectrum, in reality it was mostly women who identified with parties of the center and left who made up the movement (Baldez 1999). Women's movements in some other Latin American countries transitioning to democracy have been more successful in establishing cross-party collaboration. Hipsher (2001) documents alliances between the Salvadoran feminist movement and rightist women in the legislature around political rights, domestic violence, and paternal responsibility (she acknowledges, though, that agreement on economic issues or sexual rights is rarer). Metoyer (2000) notes that in Nicaragua women of all parties have likewise posed a fairly united front when it comes to expressing women's demands. However, political differences continue to divide women in Chile today, and conservative women rarely identify themselves with the work of SERNAM or the women's movement.

Key differences also began to emerge *within* the women's movement once it became apparent that the return to democracy was imminent. A central conflict emerged around the issue of feminist autonomy versus "double militancy" (an expression that refers to using the feminist movement as well as political parties to pursue feminist goals). Those who argued for feminist autonomy questioned the effectiveness of addressing their demands through formal politics and state policies while underlying social values remained unchanged. They argued that subordination and cooptation were likely to result from any interactions between the women's movement and the state. Those who advocated double militancy, on the other hand, saw in the transition an opportunity to have women's interests represented in the state, and argued that taking advantage of any such opening was essential if women were to impact the formal political process and policy formation (Valenzuela 1998; see Alvarez 1990 for similarities in the Brazilian case). The autonomy/double militancy debate thus developed in part from concern over the relative invisibility of women in the formal political process under democracy as compared to their central role in the oppositional movements of the 1970s and 1980s.

After the return to democracy, women's non-governmental organizations went on to specialize in a multitude of areas, dispersing the focus of the movement and making articulation difficult among the various groups. Many of the non-governmental organizations that worked directly with pobladoras have disappeared altogether, due to lack of funding (Weinstein 1997). Many feminists joined the state women's machinery as well. As a result of all these factors, gaining and retaining political leverage has become problematic (Frohmann and Valdés 1993).

Most Chilean feminists today acknowledge the need for some degree of interaction with the state. A new quandary has emerged, however, related to whether to pursue feminist goals from within or outside of the state. This debate is partially an extension of the autonomy/double militancy question. Sometimes, this debate is characterized as one between "institutionalized" feminists or femócratas on the one hand and *autónomas* ("autonomous" feminists) on the other. In reality, however, many of the feminists who have remained outside the state are connected to it in some way (receiving state funds to conduct studies, implement programs, and so on), rendering the concept of autonomy extremely problematic. For my purposes, I distinguish between femocrats who work in the state and those whose sources of employment and activism are outside of the state (recognizing though, that most of them are not financially "autonomous" from SERNAM, and do not isolate themselves from interactions with the state).

Feminists who have remained outside of the state (and SERNAM, specifically) sometimes argue that the feminist ideals of those who enter the state bureaucracy are lost or coopted. The femocrats I interviewed at SERNAM had interesting perspectives on this issue. One anonymous femocrat who formerly held a high-level position at SERNAM said that the cooptation asserted by the autónomas did occur to a great degree. Natacha Molina, a socialist feminist who worked in a feminist non-governmental organization, was offered a position as the deputy director of SERNAM under President Frei. She explained that after much deliberation, she took the position because she wanted to be consistent with her view that it was necessary to use the state to pursue the goal of women's equality. She admitted that to a certain extent the criticisms of non-femocrats are correct but maintained that the reasons for this have more to do with state bureaucracy than with cooptation.

> On a personal level, it wasn't easy, you know? It wasn't easy because . . . well, the rate of work was much more intense, and it didn't let you think a lot. The state doesn't think, the state acts, right? So that situation of making decisions very quickly and exposing yourself to error is a very different logic and dynamic from what you find in the social movement institutions and organizations, where you have time to reflect, to evaluate the pros and cons. There (in the state) you do that, but you have to do it at a much faster rhythm and velocity.

Molina, who estimated that almost half of the women who work in SERNAM have come from the women's movement, went on to explain the conflicts she encountered in dealing with women's movement actors once she was in a position of authority within SERNAM:

> At the beginning in the movement, there was a lot of happiness and (a sense of) legitimacy: "How great that for once a woman from the movement, feminist, well-known, gets a position (in SERNAM)." It was applauded by the women. And I always maintained open doors in terms of dialogue with the different groups of women. . . . But at the same time, there were criticisms too, in the sense that one begins to appropriate what you are doing. You get enthusiastic with what you are doing, and when you test those things with the movement, you realize that there is a lot of criticism. One tends to forget to be critical. So, as an anecdote, I remember that one time, I went to Grupo Iniciativa (a network of women who work in feminist NGOs), to tell them about, I don't know, some policy, a new plan. . . . I was very enthusiastic . . . so one of them, when she heard me, she said, "It's

impressive how much you've changed. Now, everything that SERNAM does is good. You've forgotten that years ago we made severe criticisms of SERNAM." I told her, "You're right, it's true, because you get so into this that you lose a critical perspective."

Molina noted that she "still doesn't know" how she feels about the experience of having worked in SERNAM; the personal contradictions she encountered are evidenced by the above passages. Another woman, who worked in SERNAM's Metropolitan Region office, echoed the difficulty of coming from the movement into the state. She said that the role of SERNAM vis-à-vis the movement is still in the process of definition, and this is complicated by the fact that so many women in SERNAM have come from the movement and feel sympathetic to its goals. However, once they are in SERNAM, she said, their work stops being of the movement and becomes public policy, which is restricted by the wider requirements of the state. At the same time, many of them still feel that they owe loyalty to the women's organizations. The themes that SERNAM deals with *are* the themes that emerged from the women's movement, she observed, but many times, the movement does not understand the limits of what can and cannot be dealt with from within SERNAM (fieldnotes, March 27, 2000). Valeria Ambrosio had a somewhat different reaction to the criticisms that come from movement actors:

> My opinion is that there is still so much to be done in this country that all of us, from distinct places, could work for women, and not because some are here and others are there, can one disqualify the other. That is, a women's movement is very important for the state. . . . It interests me that there be a women's movement that is critical, that mobilizes, that moves the system. For me, the more women who are organized, the better, and I think we can work together in favor of women's situation, or for greater freedoms, for more possibilities and opportunities for women and not just that we (SERNAM) do all the work, and not only them, but that all of us work from distinct angles, because we have different roles.

These women's statements are interesting because they reflect the nonunified character of the state and the multiplicity of perspectives held by those it employs. In all likelihood, the state both coopts and promotes women's interests through SERNAM. Nevertheless, even though its existence was a major demand of the women's movement at the return to democracy, and despite the clear commitment to women's rights on the part of many women who work there, SERNAM's ability to represent women's interests is contested.

Class differences are also increasingly salient in post-dictatorship Chile. Few pobladoras directly participated in drafting women's demands for the new democratic government, but many felt hopeful for a democracy in which their participation would be invited in establishing priorities and making policy decisions. Pobladora activism has diminished as well, as many women have "gone back to their homes" in the absence of an urgent cause for activism, and others have found paying jobs. Today, many of the remaining pobladora activists sense they have been abandoned by the middle-class feminists with whom they developed close relationships during the dictatorship. Pobladoras' shared history with many of the women who came to staff SERNAM led them to think that their opinions and participation would be solicited in the process of creating plans and policy objectives. Unfortunately, as will be examined in chapter 4, pobladoras indicate that this has not been the case. The resentment felt by many pobladora activists extends beyond women who work in the state to include those who continue to work in non-governmental organizations. As Schild (1998) notes, middle-class feminists who are willing to take on the role of project implementers are more likely to achieve access to the state today, while pobladoras are excluded.

Indigenous women, of course, were never really integrated into the Chilean women's movement. Like pobladoras, rural and indigenous women from organizations like the Asociación Nacional de Mujeres Rurales e Indígenas, (ANAMURI, National Association of Rural and Indigenous Women) and other organizations are increasingly vocal about the ways they are excluded and how their own interests and priorities differ from those of middle-class, urban, non-indigenous women. These differences will be addressed at greater length in the chapters to come.

All of this fragmentation leads to the question of whether a women's movement exists in Chile today. Many of the women I interviewed say there is no longer a women's movement, or if there is, it is much reduced in scope and influence. Most scholars similarly acknowledge that the women's movement exerts much less influence and is much less coherent as a social actor than it was during the dictatorship. This has resulted, according to Valenzuela (1998, 59), in a situation in which "SERNAM has come to play a de facto leadership role by default, blurring its functions as a government institution and as a representative of the women's movement." The problem with this, of course, is that a state agency (poorly funded and with limited power) cannot substitute for an active women's movement or for effective dialogue between women's groups in civil society and the state.

WOMEN'S ACTIVISM AND "NEOLIBERAL" GOALS

Questions have also arisen regarding how to mount a successful struggle for women's rights in the age of neoliberal economic and social policies. As noted above, contemporary state discourse focuses on improving women's rate of employment, a measure that would clearly favor state goals in the world marketplace. A second policy area vis-à-vis women has been poverty. Provoste (1997) and Matear (1995) note that many programs targeted at poor women tend to reduce women's issues to poverty, failing to perceive the ways that poverty and poverty alleviation programs are themselves gendered. And as shall be seen in chapter 3, even though alleviating poverty is ostensibly a central goal of the Concertación, the tactics used to achieve this often lead to increased social exclusion and marginality. As appears to be the case throughout Latin America, the state utilizes rhetoric that emphasizes "strengthening civil society" and "participation" in order to compel citizens to perform what were once state responsibilities, taking advantage of the neighborhood organizations and solidarity movements that developed during the dictatorship. This places a particular burden on women, since they traditionally have been responsible for community work and household welfare (Benería 1992; Moser 1996). In addition, by framing women's issues in terms of employment and poverty alleviation through individual empowerment, the state often fails to address other issues of central concern to women.

Exclusion of some women's groups and discourses may be an additional strategy on the part of the state to limit women's participation in this context. As noted in chapter 1, Schild (1998) maintains that the state "selectively appropriates" feminist discourses that fit within the overall neoliberal project. Most of the appropriated discourses belong to non-governmental organizations that end up working as project implementers or subcontractors of state policy. By focusing in particular on the economic realm, Schild notes, the state takes an important role in defining women's struggles. In the end, this new model of the state creates a very different context than that faced by women's movements in prior eras. Thus, neoliberal policies exacerbate an already tenuous situation of institutional and political restrictions on the representation of women in the state, and fragmentation among women themselves.

CONCLUSION: TAKING DIFFERENCE TO THE STATE

Women's activism over the past thirty years has played an important role in instigating social and political change in Chile. Women on both ends of the political spectrum have rooted their activism in notions of domestic and maternal virtues. Indeed, in spite of, and often because of, cultural emphasis on women's roles as wives and mothers, women were central participants and leaders in movements against Allende and Pinochet. Both groups of women sought to fulfill their roles as wives and mothers. But unlike the women who struggled against Allende, the women who struggled against Pinochet also linked their activism to human, socioeconomic, political, and civil rights. In this sense, they were working for not just the return of a previous disorder-free era, but for a new era represented by the ideals of democracy, political and economic justice, and participation. For many of the women who joined the Chilean women's movement, restrictions on their ability to play out these roles also led them to link authoritarianism and repression in the country to the authoritarianism and repression they experienced in their daily relationships with fathers, husbands, and sons. They have demanded recognition as full citizens on the basis of contributions they have made to the nation through their roles as wives and mothers, and increasingly, on the basis of the ideal of equality as well.

In each of the eras described in this chapter, the state has responded to some women's demands. This was true of Allende, who made important efforts to "incorporate" women into society, and it was true of Pinochet, who claimed the coup was a response to the pleas of Poder Femenino. It is also the case, however, that women and their interests have tended to be represented in accordance with the broader objectives of the state itself. Not until the transition to democracy had women built a movement with the capacity to significantly influence the agenda of the ruling political coalition. The establishment of SERNAM responded to national and international women's movements' efforts to bring attention to women's rights. While conservative political forces, traditional gender ideology, and competing state priorities have often limited the scope of reforms aimed to benefit women, the establishment of SERNAM has represented a positive step in the struggle of the Chilean women's movement toward equality between women and men.

The ability of SERNAM to represent women's interests is contested, though, and differences among women have become increasingly salient in democratic Chile. Unfortunately, the assertion of difference between men and women has not always translated into recognition of differences or power imbalances among women themselves. As women of distinct groups challenge the state's gender discourse, the very concept of "women's interests" is called into question. However, little detailed attention has been given to examining how well SERNAM has incorporated claims for rights based on difference. In the remainder of this book, I therefore explore the claims of two groups that have challenged SERNAM: Mapuche women and pobladoras.

In the following two chapters, I address the pobladora case. In chapter 3 I document changes in social policies, comparing the years before, during, and after the dictatorship. The socioeconomic policy environment, in combination with the history of the women's movement presented in this chapter, sets the context for pobladoras' claims vis-à-vis the state. In chapter 4, I examine interactions between pobladoras and femocrats, in order to assess how the women's policy machinery, as the promoter of women's rights and opportunities in Chile today, fares in terms of representing claims for rights based in class differences.

3

NATIONAL DEVELOPMENT, SOCIAL POLICY, AND THE POOR

The military coup of 1973 represented a break with Chile's long democratic tradition, the recent socialist regime, economic policy that emphasized import substitution, and a social policy tradition based on universal social rights. Changes in all these areas had profound effects on the lives of Chileans. In this chapter, I focus on how changes in economic and social policy have affected poor and working-class Chileans. I begin by discussing collective identity and action among the popular sectors during the dictatorship and today. I suggest that the pobladora organizations are essentially what remains of the poor people's movement that began to emerge during the years of the dictatorship. I explain that pobladoras' demands on the state focus overwhelmingly on issues of redistribution, though they are also rooted in a conception of popular identity, which Oxhorn (1995) calls *lo popular*. In the following section, I outline how Chile's social policy regime has changed over time. Next, I argue that by de-linking social policy from universal social rights and applying market principles to social service delivery, the state's policy model restricts the possibilities for the achievement of pobladores' demands. I argue that Concertación rhetoric that refers to a "social debt" with the Chilean people and a commitment to reducing inequality represents an effort to combat poverty without modifying macroeconomic goals. I also outline some of the specific effects this change has had on poor women. I conclude the chapter by contrasting the demands for social equality and integration expressed through lo popular with the type of integration offered by the contemporary social policy model, and discuss the implications of the changing social policy arena for making demands around social rights.

LO POPULAR, POBLADOR ACTIVISM, AND DEMANDS FOR REDISTRIBUTION

During the dictatorship, pobladores (the poor and working-class residents of Santiago's shantytowns, or poblaciones), suffered extreme economic hardship as well as political repression. It is estimated that at the worst points of the crises that resulted from structural adjustment, unemployment reached 80 percent in some poblaciones (Chuchryk 1994). A wealth of economic survival organizations sprang up in response to the crisis, including community kitchens, bulk buying initiatives, and informal businesses. Some poblaciones, particularly those associated with the communist party, were also hotbeds of resistance to the dictatorship (Schneider 1995). Many pobladores participated in citywide strikes against the Pinochet regime, and most violent political conflicts took place in these areas. Oxhorn (1995) estimates that between economic and political activism, 15 percent of pobladores participated in some sort of popular sector organization during the dictatorship. As much as 80 percent of them were women (Molina 1986). wow

Oxhorn (1995) suggests that common experiences of marginalization and repression during the dictatorship led to the emergence of a new collective identity among pobladores. He emphasizes that the pobladores had common interests before the dictatorship, but their sense of commonality was heightened during this time as a result of the regime's complete disregard for their human rights. Oxhorn calls this emergent identity lo popular.[1] I outline it here because it provides a sense of what motivated the pobladores to engage in collective action during the dictatorship and also because it reflects the perspectives of many of the pobladoras represented in this book. Lo popular was a collective identity based on location, but it went beyond physical proximity to include common values like reciprocity and solidarity. Oxhorn argues that pobladores' sense of solidarity was an alternative to the military regime's emphasis on self-help, individual responsibility, and consumerism, but in my view, it is equally probable that solidarity and reciprocity were survival mechanisms in the face of political and socioeconomic insecurity.

Though Oxhorn does not classify them this way, the pobladores' common interests were based on interconnected economic, social, and political needs and demands. They included consumption needs related to housing, employment, nutrition, health care, and so on. The pobladores also shared the common desire to improve their life chances. Citing one of his respondents, who said, "It's horrible to be marginalized," Oxhorn suggests that the desire to improve life chances reflected a longing for integration into Chilean society. To the pobladores, integration meant being able to participate in and be consulted in deciding the future of Chile. These needs and desires were reflected in their definitions of human rights, which incorporated the right to live, freedom of expression, respect, consumption concerns, education, participation, and personal development. The pobladores sought an end to political oppression, but also to socioeconomic marginalization. Writes Oxhorn, "The realization of these rights would overcome the marginalization that characterized the popular sectors, not only under the military regime, but also during Chile's previous democratic regime, as well" (1995, 141).

As their common identity in the context of the dictatorship focused so strongly on socioeconomic marginalization, it corresponds that the pobladores would associate democracy with ending this marginalization. Writes Oxhorn (ibid., 154),

[T]hese people viewed political democracy as a mechanism for incorporating the popular sectors into society—as a way for the popular sectors to be heard and to ensure that the social costs associated with future policies would be shared more equitably within Chilean society. In this way, democracy would provide the popular sectors with the possibility of reasserting the dignity denied to them by the military regime. Only a return to democracy would allow the popular sectors to assume the role of protagonist in Chilean society—a role they had so far been denied under both the military and democratic regimes. As a collective identity, lo popular symbolizes this potential protagonism.

Despite the presence in the poblaciones of hundreds of economic survival, human rights, and other organizations, and the participation of many of them in mass mobilizations and protests, Oxhorn argues that they never formed a social movement, which in his view means going "beyond being an atomized conglomeration of markedly similar organizations linked by few organic ties" (1995, 21). A popular movement nearly emerged with the creation of the Comando Unitario de Pobladores (CUP, Unitary Pobladores' Command) in 1986 (Espinoza

1993; Oxhorn 1995). The Unitary Pobladores' Command was formed by three major poblador networks, and was intended to represent popular sector organizations from across Santiago as an interlocutor with the opposition parties. However, the emphasis of popular sector leaders on gaining political and socioeconomic integration on more equal terms "seemed to imply changes that are much greater than those actually realized during the transition in the late 1980s" (Oxhorn 1995, 172). Indeed, as the transition drew nearer, political parties, which were legalized in 1987, displaced popular organizations, which in turn became less relevant as political actors.

Part of the reason popular sectors were marginalized was that by 1986, the major opposition parties, then operating underground, had come to the conclusion that mass mobilization was an ineffective means for getting the regime to concede to a transition to democracy. The costs associated with military violence and middle-class resistance to mass mobilization had simply become too great (Oxhorn 1995). In 1986 a general strike as well as an assassination attempt on Pinochet took place, and both met with severe repression and loss of civilian lives. It became clear—at least to opposition elites—that the transition would have to take place within the framework established by the 1980 Constitution, which would be more palatable to the military regime because it implied a controlled transition in which the regime could exert significant influence. The opposition's new strategy was thus to insist on elections. This was tolerable to Pinochet supporters because they were confident he could win.

If mass mobilizations—a strategy in which pobladores were the most numerous participants—were to be deemphasized as a protest strategy, the relevance of popular sectors to the transition would be diminished. This is precisely what occurred. On top of this, direct popular sector participation in the opposition's decisions was purposely limited by the parties because of its potential to lead Pinochet and the rest of the right to reject the entire process (Oxhorn 1995, 282). Moreover, some popular sector leaders saw parties as the appropriate tool and focused their political energies through them even though the interests of popular sectors were not clearly articulated in party agendas. Eventually the Unitary Pobladores' Command became another instance for partisan posturing. As a result of all these factors, Chile's transition to democracy was totally dominated by party elites. Popular sectors were left without any organization that represented them directly. As De La Maza (1999, 391) notes, from the plebiscite forward pobladores were not invited to be part of the Concertación. Rather "they would only be considered as objects of social policies that aimed to palliate the most urgent social problems."

Today, lo popular does not have the same significance as a common identity that it had during the dictatorship. This is linked to the return to party politics as well as the cooptation of popular sector leaders. In addition, the return to democracy has made some of the common experiences upon which lo popular was based less readily apparent. Open political repression, for example, ended with the dictatorship (as shall be seen, this is not true in the Mapuche case). And as opportunities for employment improved, people became less interested in collective economic survival strategies and focused more intently on the prosperity of their own families. Participation in organizations declined across the board, including among women's organizations. However, even though their numbers have declined drastically, pobladora organizations are the one major sector of the incipient popular movement that remains visible today.[2]

I turn to my discussions with pobladoras to understand the extent to which lo popular serves as a source of common identity today. Lo popular is reflected in these women's discourse and in their self-identification as pobladoras. When I returned to Chile in the summer of 2001, I asked some leaders of REMOS, the Red de Mujeres de Organizaciones Sociales (which is composed of over forty pobladora organizations), how they wished to be identified in my written work: as pobladoras, leaders of social organizations, grassroots leaders, or in some other way. They agreed that any of these were fine, but they reflected at length about the word pobladora. One of the women observed that "pobladora" has an important connotation of historical struggle and involves a recuperation of popular sectors' own language.

The women went on to remark, though, that the history, language, and identity of which they feel so proud is fading in many poblaciones. Lucía Benvenuto, vice president of REMOS, commented, "With democracy, the pobladores have been losing their identity. We are from popular sectors, and we feel it; where we are from is part of our identity." Another woman suggested that this loss of identity has to do with consumerism and obsession with appearances. Now, under democracy, when there are more opportunities to get ahead, some women say, "I am not a pobladora anymore" (fieldnotes, August 2, 2001). Thus, it appears that the sense of solidarity, as part of lo popular, has diminished under democracy. Nevertheless, other aspects of lo popular are relevant to discussing poor and working-class people's demands today. As shall be discussed at greater length in the following chapter, pobladoras' demands continue to be associated with the effects of poverty and inequality. They reflect a desire for inclusion, integration into Chilean society, and an end to socioeconomic marginalization.

Demands for redistribution and integration are ultimately demands for social rights. Marshall defined social citizenship as including "the right to a modicum of economic welfare and security" as well as "the right to share to the full in the social heritage and to live the life of a civilized being according to the standards prevailing in the society" (1992, 8). Fraser and Gordon (1994, 91) note that social citizenship incorporates "liberal themes of (social) rights and equal respect; communitarian norms of solidarity and shared responsibility; and republican ideals of participation in public life (through use of 'public goods' and 'public services')."

Marshall conceptualized social citizenship as a way to temper the effects of capitalism and mitigate class conflict. During the dictatorship, however, the pobladores went beyond citizenship to envision social rights as human rights, standards which no human being should have to live without. Pobladora leaders continue to see them this way today. In the end, these demands reflect a longing to share in the benefits of the modern and economically advancing Chile, and thus a deep desire for the central basis for lo popular—class inequality—to disappear. As shall be seen in chapter 5, this point is of central importance, because it represents a marked difference between the urban poor and the Mapuche, who, through their demands for recognition, seek to maintain the aspects of their identity that differentiate them from the rest of Chilean society. In the next two sections of this chapter, I will evaluate the changes in how demands for social rights, redistribution, and integration have been received by the Chilean state over time.

NATIONAL DEVELOPMENT AND THE POOR

Social policy models reflect broader priorities related to national development. Social policy is also a key arena for evaluating any regime's commitment to social equality. Conducting such an evaluation requires knowledge of how the prevailing model of social policy has changed over time. In this section, I outline the three major social policy models in Chilean history. In doing so, I rely heavily on the work of Dagmar Raczynski, the main Chilean scholar to study social policy changes over time. I argue that changes in the social policy model implemented during the dictatorship and partially kept in place under the Concertación reflect a shift in paradigm from social policy as guarantor of universal rights and entitlement to social policy as generator of opportunities and access to the market.

Social Policy (1925–1973)

Prior to the Pinochet dictatorship, Chile was a benefactor state. Social spending on education, health care, and pensions, as well as the scope of coverage in these areas, expanded gradually from 1925 until 1973 and "the state assumed a growing role in the financing, management, and direct production of these services and programs" (Raczynski 1998, 6). Benefits were often employment related but price fixing and subsidies were also common. The range of beneficiaries expanded gradually as segments of the workforce organized and achieved concessions from the state. Organized workers were followed by the urban middle class, low-income urban sectors, and to a lesser extent, rural workers. "This dynamic led to a social policy system that had growing coverage (but was) internally fragmented and stratified" (Raczynski 1998, 6). Access to programs and social services was nominally universal, but aside from education, was conditioned upon whether and in what type of work an individual was employed. Moreover, because access was tied to participation in the labor market, given the sexual division of labor, most women were only guaranteed these rights insofar as their spouses were employed (Schild 2000). Coverage thus was not universal in terms of quality. Still, services such as health care, education, pensions, and housing were treated as social entitlements, or rights, by state and citizens alike. The very existence of social services generated an expectation that they would be delivered and a collective understanding that part of being a citizen was to have access to them.

Social Policy during the Dictatorship (1973–1989)

Like economic policy, social policy changed radically during the military regime. In fact, as Raczynski (1995) notes, during the dictatorship social policy was subordinated to economic policy. The military regime justified the changes by stating that it was necessary to "break with this apparent universality behind which profound inequalities were hidden, and that it should be assured that state action benefited only those persons and households that were not in the condition to attend to their most urgent basic needs on their own" (Raczynski and Cominetti 1994, 25).

Changes in social policy instituted under Pinochet included a variety of measures. First, as noted above, social policy was subordinated to economic requirements such as controlling inflation and maintaining macroeconomic equilibrium. Second, there was a drastic reduction of the resources designated for social spending—from 20–25 percent of gross domestic product in 1970 to 15 percent in 1980. This reduction affected the areas of housing, health care, and education in particular. Presumably in order to compensate for these cutbacks and to make the delivery of social services more efficient, the state established sectoral targeting. Mothers with children and the extremely poor were the targeted groups. The poor were (and continue to be) identified through a new poverty-measuring survey called the Ficha CAS (after the Comités de Asistencia Social, or Social Welfare Committees, initially organized in the 1970s). Focusing on mothers as a policy entry point to the rest of the family, on the other hand, was a method commonly used in previous administrations as well. Third, ministries and services were decentralized, and administrative responsibilities were transferred to the municipal level.[3] Fourth, certain functions were transferred to the private sector through direct privatization of some services, subcontracting of others, and the creation of private health and pension systems. Finally, demand was subsidized, which means that qualifying families received direct subsidies from the government and resources were allotted to providers based on the quantity of services provided (so schools would get x amount of money based on how many students were enrolled the previous year, and health clinics would likewise receive resources based on how many persons they had attended and what services were provided). Altogether, Raczynski and Cominetti (1994) refer to the changes that were implemented in social policy during the dictatorship as a shift from the benefactor state to the subsidizer state, one that would only intervene when the private sector could not adequately provide services.

Social Policy under the Concertación (1990–present)

When the center-left Concertación was elected into power in 1989, Chile's economy was growing at over 7 percent annually, yet almost 40 percent of the population was poor. Sustaining high levels of growth and simultaneously reducing poverty and inequality has been a goal of all three successive Concertación governments. This commitment to poverty and inequality reduction is reflected in the designation of development and equity as the pillars of Aylwin's growth strategy, Frei's creation of a special commission on poverty, and Lagos's campaign slogan, "To Grow with Equality." In the economic sphere, the Concertación's approach to achieving these goals has been largely consistent with strategies initiated during the Pinochet dictatorship. Creating incentives for international investment, eliminating trade barriers, flexibilizing labor, and maximizing exports—all part of Pinochet's neoliberal reforms—remain important elements in the Concertación's economic development strategy.

In terms of social policy, there have been changes as well as continuities under the Concertación. The most important changes are that the overall percentage of the national budget invested in social programs has increased, coverage has broadened somewhat, and social spending per capita rose by 51 percent between 1990 and 1996 (Raczynski 1998). Targeting continues to be a central strategy for social policy delivery, but youth, women, the aged, and indigenous peoples have been added to children and the poor as key "vulnerable sectors" and beneficiaries of social policy. Agencies such as SERNAM and the Corporación Nacional de Desarrollo Indígena (CONADI, National Corporation for Indigenous Development) were established to address the needs of those groups but are generally not authorized to fund or carry out their own programs. Rather, they are expected to coordinate monies and actions among other ministries and agencies as well as subcontractors. Privatization and subcontracting of services has not been reversed but, with limited success, attempts have been made to decentralize some decision making to the regional and municipal levels (Raczynski and Serrano 2001).

Raczynski (1995, 1998) suggests that under the Concertación, the state can be considered an integrator state because rather than being subordinated, social policy is integrated with and considered complementary to economic policy, and because its purpose is to integrate people into the country's development process. However, since economic policies have remained similar to those initiated under the dictatorship, the difference between the subsidizer state and the integrator state is sometimes difficult to distinguish.

Although substantial socioeconomic inequality existed under the benefactor state as well, an important discursive shift was initiated under Pinochet and remains in place under the Concertación: market principles, rather than universal social rights, now govern social policy in Chile. Raczynski (1998) maintains that the Concertación has strengthened social policies so as to guarantee "a basic level of citizenship for all the population: education, health, housing, social security, justice."[4] However, she also (1999, 131) suggests that the priority of social policy is different now. Rather than "giving help" to the poor, the Concertación seeks to "provide poor and vulnerable sectors with tools so that by their own effort they can overcome their situation. The purpose is to habilitate, generate capacities, and open opportunities so that poor sectors and vulnerable groups have a voice, organize, and participate in the solution to the problems that affect them." In the following section, I argue that despite its stated intent, the Concertación's focus on generating opportunities, developing human capital, and enhancing the individual capacity of members of targeted groups is more of a threat to universal social rights than a commitment to a common standard of citizenship. The Concertación's approach is problematic, I argue, because in the process of focusing on opportunities and human capital—without concomitantly focusing on rights—it legitimates the inequality produced by Chile's neoliberal economy policies.

FROM UNIVERSAL SOCIAL RIGHTS TO MARKET CITIZENSHIP: EVALUATING THE SOCIAL POLICY PARADIGM SHIFT

The change in social policy after the military took control is important because it represents a conceptual shift in the state's attitude toward social citizenship. Under the benefactor state, access to health care, education, pensions, and housing were considered rights to which all persons were entitled, simply because they were citizens of Chile. As noted above, this system was far from perfect. It was bureaucratic, unsustainable, overly centralized, benefits were pinned to workforce participation, and their quality varied widely according to which type of worker was receiving them. But the fact that these benefits were even nominally considered universal rights is important. By targeting some aspects of social policy and privatizing others, the Pinochet regime took rights out of the policy equation. The purpose of social policy was no longer to assure that all citizens had the right to "share to the full in the social heritage," as Marshall put it. Rather, it was to palliate the social effects of the crisis into which Chile was thrown as a result of the junta's economic measures. Today, despite the return to democracy and some progressive changes in the social policy arena (including a discursive commitment to equality and participation), social policy does not have the effect of assuring that all members of society share common social rights. I argue that this is in part due to the ways the Concertación goes about implementing social policies, but that it also has to do with the context set by its economic policies as well as an assumption that increasing individuals' access to the market will be sufficient to reduce social inequality.

The military regime's approach to social policy as a palliative measure as opposed to part of what people have rights to as citizens had several important implications. It did little to combat social inequality in quantitative or qualitative terms. Even though social spending was targeted at the poor during the dictatorship, overall social spending decreased, unemployment rose, and real salaries fell as a result of economic restructuring. Thus, the number of poor Chileans grew, as did the concentration of household income and the distance between the incomes of the richest households and those of the poorest ones (Raczynski 1998). Moreover, many people who did not qualify as beneficiaries of targeted policies could not afford to pay for services, particularly ones of good quality. Raczynski (ibid., 10) explains the exacerbation of social inequality in this manner:

> [T]he applied social strategy did not reduce poverty or the existing inequities in the social structure; on the contrary, it intensified them. The applied scheme, in addition, deepened social segregation tendencies. There was a restriction of the public spaces previously shared by the different levels in the social structure, such as public schools, clinics and hospitals, residential areas. The most dramatic expression of this situation was the *erradicación* of populations (forced removal to other locations) within the Metropolitan Region and also to the (other) regions.

In sum, inequality grew quantitatively as well as qualitatively during the dictatorship.

Have these tendencies changed under the Concertación? On one hand, the combination of high levels of growth and greater investment in social programs has had positive results: poverty was reduced from 38.6 percent in 1990 to 20.6 percent in 2000 (Krauss 2001). On the other hand, the already staggering level of inequality has worsened slightly. According to a 1996 World Bank study of sixty-five developing countries, Chile occupies the seventh worst position in terms of income distribution. In Latin America, only Brazil is more unequal (in Meller 1999). While in 1990, the richest quintile earned 14 times that of the poorest quintile, in 2000, the gap had grown to 15.3 ("Última Década" 2001).[5] These inequality figures represent a failure that the Concertación would prefer to de-emphasize. Indeed, the Ministry of Planning and Cooperation, which conducts the biannual CASEN income survey, initially released only the poverty figures. The inequality figures were only released approximately two weeks later, after significant criticism had been voiced by diverse sectors. After ten years of democratic power, and despite an expanding economy and increased social investment, the Concertación had been unable to reduce inequality in Chile.

As Meller (1999, 56) notes, inequality goes beyond income figures to include differences in quality of life, of which people are increasingly conscious and critical: "In effect, enormous differentials in the quality of health and education (housing, justice, insurance) contribute in a significant manner to the widespread perception of the existence of an increase in social inequalities." Income inequality in Chile today is exacerbated by a situation in which much of the population is lacking social entitlements and rights, which in turn intensifies perceptions of social exclusion.

I am arguing that the intensification of social inequality during the dictatorship, and now under the Concertación, is legitimated by the shift away from conceptualizing social policy in terms of universal social rights. As the campaign slogans cited above indicate, all three Concertación governments have given a lot of attention to reducing poverty and inequality while sustaining high levels of growth. References to paying back the "social debt" left behind by the Pinochet regime are commonplace in Concertación rhetoric. However, this does not represent an approach to social policy that focuses on universal social rights. Rather, as Schild (2000) argues, the Concertación's approach focuses heavily on increasing citizens' access to the market as a solution to poverty and social inequality—so heavily, that Schild calls potential policy beneficiaries "market citizens."[6] She explains (ibid., 286),

> The poor are defined as those excluded, because of lack of skills or opportunities, from effectively participating in the market and becoming masters of their own destiny. The thrust of social policy is therefore to help individuals and communities access the market. In other words, this framing of poverty considers the poor not as objects of charity, or as being personally deficient, or as subjects of universal rights, but as untrained, and unmarketable, and therefore as remediable.

In the remainder of this section, I will outline what I see as the central characteristics of this neoliberal or "market" approach to social policy. These include both discourses and practices: enhancing human capital, framing equality discourse in terms of opportunities rather than rights, targeting social policy at particularly vulnerable sectors, mandating the participation of beneficiaries in the delivery of social programs, and holding competitions for state funding among groups in civil society. After outlining these characteristics, I explain why this approach to social policy tends to be negative for the poor, particularly women, and does little to reduce social inequality and marginalization.

Lagos's campaign literature exhibited some of the characteristics of market citizenship. Many people on the left were very excited by the

Lagos platform. They were happy that finally a Socialist candidate, rather than a centrist Christian Democrat, was the Concertación's choice for president. And Lagos's platform was promising. Its central tenets included economic growth with more and better jobs, education, health care, "integration" of women, protecting individuals and families, protecting the environment, access to culture (fine arts, etc.) for all, security, decentralization and participation, and reforming the state and justice system such that democracy would be made "complete," including better treatment of indigenous peoples. Interestingly, these ideals represent a close match to many of the demands represented by lo popular collective identity.

A closer look at the campaign literature reveals a focus on modernity and growth as well as efforts to shift equality discourse from rights to opportunities. Lagos begins by proclaiming, "Ten years ago, we called all Chileans to a great event: the conquest of freedom. Today we invite you to achieve a second conquest: progress with equality" (1999, 1). He goes on to write that everyone should be equal and respected, regardless of income, sex, age, ethnicity, etc. However, he continues, "during this decade, Chile has grown as never before in history. Nevertheless, we have not managed to grow with the equality that would permit us to construct a just and human society." It is evident that progress and growth were central to Lagos's platform, but that so was a commitment to equality and justice.

What would be the route to that equality? The document goes on, "The equality of which we speak is that which seeks to create opportunities. . . . Chileans do not want gifts, but opportunities." These opportunities, which it is said will lead to greater individual capacity to succeed, include investments in human capital, such as education, job training, and support for small businesses. None of this is negative per se. However, it implies that given the right opportunities, individual Chileans will be able to work their way out of poverty, and that inequality can be lessened by targeting social programs at the worst off. As noted above, the combination of high growth rates and increased investment in social policy targeted at the poor has lowered the poverty rate significantly during the Concertación years. However, it has been totally ineffective in combating inequality. This is compounded by the fact that progressive and regressive taxes in Chile combine to have an almost null redistributive effect (1997 World Bank study cited by Meller 1999). The Concertación has tended to focus not on social rights (or their connection to human rights), which would imply a greater emphasis on redistribution, but on increasing opportunities for individual success.[7] This approach shifts the responsibility for reducing poverty and inequality from the state or even society as a whole to the individual.

There are several specific measures that contribute to this new approach to social policy. Insofar as it "shifts the meaning of deservedness away from notions of universal entitlements," targeting is a central part of this process (Schild 2000, 286). A second key policy in the shift from social rights to targeted policies, and from equal rights to equal opportunities, is the incorporation of the participation of beneficiaries into programs and projects sponsored by state agencies.

Because it is such a central part of the Concertación's social policy model, it is worth examining the roots of the concept of participation. Along with consciousness-raising and empowerment (inspired by Paolo Freire and his *Pedagogy of the Oppressed*), participation was an important part of the discourse and practice of non-governmental organization workers during the dictatorship. In the context of civil society, there is something that seems inherently democratic about the creation of opportunities for participation among the poor. The idea of Freirean non-governmental organization work was that the poor, working together, could improve their situation by building schools and health posts, but more importantly, in collective discussions of their condition, could come to realize that their oppression was not deserved, but rather, a key component of structural inequalities. Petras and Leiva (1994) and Schild (2000) point out that it was these non-governmental organization workers who brought participation and empowerment discourse to the state when they were hired to work for the national and local government after the dictatorship.

According to Raczynski, the rationale behind incorporating participation is to "give voice to beneficiaries" as well as to make social policy more efficient and effective. But what happens when a discourse of participation is appropriated by the state? In some limited cases, it can mean that beneficiaries participate in determining project priorities. In most cases, however, this does not occur. "Participation" usually amounts to self- and community-help initiatives—beneficiaries doing the work (without pay) necessary to implement the policy. Examples include building houses, schools, and clinics, conducting door-to-door public health campaigns, and even doing minor health care delivery. Paley, who devotes a chapter of her 2001 ethnography to what she calls the "paradox of participation," documents two types of participation that have been promoted by the Concertación in the health care sector: self-care (as in taking necessary steps to avoid the spread of diseases) and grassroots groups' participation in the delivery of services (such as distributing milk or picking up trash). In her examination of a community improvement program sponsored by the state agency Fondo de Solidaridad e Inversión Social (FOSIS, Social Solidarity and Investment Fund), Schild (2000) observed that "participation" entailed teaching market-friendly skills like self-help and individual responsibility. Few opportunities were provided for the generation of demands on the part of program participants. Rather, they were "guided" by project monitors into what were considered "appropriate" options for community improvements.

The appropriation of progressive participation discourses is a trend that goes beyond Chile. It is linked to the structural adjustment prerogatives of bi- and multilateral agencies, including the World Bank, the United States Agency for International Development (USAID), and the Inter-American Development Bank (IADB). As a part of adjustment packages, aid agencies have required governments to cut back on social welfare spending. As an alternative, they have advocated increasing citizens' participation, improving the social capital of the poor, and strengthening civil society such that it might become able to self-provide needed services. Thus, in the context of dismantling the state, organizations in civil society have been called upon to fulfill the role of the state in providing social rights. The Inter-American Development Bank's *Frame of Reference for the Modernization of the State and Strengthening Civil Society* is explicit about the relationship between restructuring the state and augmenting the role of organizations in civil society: "The change in the role of the state involves a transfer to citizens of responsibilities for production and services and for the control of and participation in public administration. Responsibilities divested by government may be assumed by either the private entrepreneurial sector or by civil society organizations" (p. 13, cited in Reilly 1996). Petras and Leiva (1994, 123) cite Concertación social policy expert Álvaro García, who in a similar vein, states that the regime sees the poor "as subjects of their own development, and in that sense, the role of the state is to complement and reinforce the effort that they [the poor] themselves carry out." This rhetoric sounds very progressive, but the conceptualization of state-as-complement not only has the effect of institutionalizing participation as part of social policy, but also justifies making the poor take on responsibilities that once belonged to the state.

The substance of state-advocated participation thus has little in common with the Freirean approach of years past. Establishing mechanisms by which the poor can help themselves fits well with the designs of structural adjustment—a process that Chile went through under the dictatorship, but whose general principles the Concertación has been unwilling to challenge. Defining participation in this way effectively shifts responsibility for the provision of social rights away from the state and onto civil society. This approach to participation has been problematic for non-governmental organizations as well. Many non-governmental organization workers have been absorbed into the government, and those who continue to work for non-governmental organizations are frequently subcontracted by the government to do service delivery, evaluations, or special projects. In the process, progressive discourses are coopted or "selectively appropriated" (Schild 1998). Moreover, non-governmental organizations may silence their critiques of government policy for fear that they will lose funds if they appear too oppositional.[8]

There are also inherent problems with the idea of the state "empowering" in a Freirean sense, because such empowerment involves questioning hegemonic interests, an activity the state is unlikely to sanction. Moreover, participation is one part of the state's strategy to "integrate" social and economic policy, and is thus framed by—and is likely to serve—hegemonic macroeconomic goals. This type of participation implies that the poor have a responsibility to work themselves out of poverty, while, of course, no mention is made of the responsibility of the rich to "participate" in economic redistribution. Participation, as Paley (2001, 146) puts it, thus becomes a mode of control. As shall be seen in chapter 4, the shortcomings of state-designed participation have particular impacts on women, who are usually the main "participants."[9]

Apart from self- and community-help initiatives, opportunities for participation have been created through the establishment of *concursos*, or competitions for state funding to carry out small-scale projects. State agencies establish thematic and administrative guidelines, and then publicly call non-governmental organizations, private consultants, municipalities, and/or grassroots groups (depending on the specific concurso) to present proposals and compete for the funds.[10] Municipalities sometimes hold their own concursos, as well. Since the end of the dictatorship, when much international funding for social programs was pulled out of Chile and redirected toward more "needy" countries, these concursos have been an increasingly important source of funding for non-governmental and grassroots organizations.

The concursos are problematic for a number of reasons. Grassroots organizations are often at a disadvantage when forced to compete with non-governmental organizations and private organizations whose employees have professional degrees and grant-writing experience.[11]

And as De La Maza (1999, 394) notes, these funds are problematic because they oblige organizations to compete among themselves for small amounts of money and "to formulate all social initiatives in the technical language of 'social projects.'" He adds that "the language of 'projects'—an efficient form of assigning resources and stimulating creativity—substitutes for the constitution of demands [by] local actors." In the end, market principles determine who is or is not a viable participant, leaving out vast numbers of people who have legitimate demands, and reframing those demands into a form of participation that individualizes social actors and pits them against one another.

While limiting the capacity of the poor to make demands is unlikely an explicit goal of the Concertación governments, it most certainly is a byproduct of poverty reduction strategies that target very specific sectors of the population. Valid social participation is either redefined as self-help or restricted to those who are lucky enough to qualify for programs or to win a project.

Raczynski calls the Concertación's approach to social policy the "integrator state." Insofar as it is supposed that making the poor "marketable" will integrate them into the economic system, this is an adequate portrayal of the state's intentions. It is clear, however, that this approach has not resulted in greater social or economic integration. In addition, left unanswered is the question of what happens after an individual goes through numerous efforts to make herself marketable, and she still is substantially worse off than other Chileans. Has she proved herself unredeemable? What is society's responsibility to such an individual? Taken to its logical extreme, this approach presumes that all individuals can succeed within a capitalist system, which is simply not feasible. Compensating for the ravages of the market is why social rights emerged as a value in many societies in the first place. But in Chile today, universal social rights have lost out to individual capacities and equal opportunities.

Why is this shift noteworthy? The 2000 CASEN household income survey (cited above) showed that the Concertación's approach to social policy has not been effective in reducing inequality or mitigating the effects of neoliberal economic policies on citizens' quality of life. What this approach does do is to make it difficult to talk about universal rights and deserving anything more than "opportunities" as a member of the nation. It thus in many cases exacerbates marginalization.

The repercussions of this shift are likely to be particularly harmful for women, since they are generally held responsible for household welfare. In addition, as Schild (2000) points out, social programs tend to assume gender neutrality, thus reinforcing the subordination of women, who are usually the main participants. Other times, gendered assumptions are built into the policy. Provoste (1997) provides an important example of this: the design of the primary health care system focuses on the involvement of mothers, and incorporates their participation in such a way as to require that they be stay-at-home mothers. "The poorer the families, the more time the women dedicate to the distinct services and social projects, frequently with an extraordinary burden in hours of activity, which they must add to their household duties (ibid., 56)." Meanwhile, working mothers find it difficult to access these services because they are not offered before or after working hours. The specific effects of the contemporary approach to social policy on women are at the root of some of the pobladoras' demands of SERNAM, which will be discussed in chapter 4.

Finally, applying market principles to citizenship stigmatizes the poor and counters any effort to enhance equality and social integration. Following political philosopher Hannah Arendt, Jelin and Hershberg (1996) emphasize that a sense of belonging and the possibility of interaction lie at the core of what it is to be human. Since extreme poverty serves to exclude and dehumanize the poor by forcing them to live on the margins of society, some provision of resources (i.e., guaranteeing social rights) is necessary to establish a sense of belonging as well as the ability to participate politically. When social rights are not universal and only targeted populations receive certain services, those who are not marginalized begin to see the poor as non-members of society.

Fraser and Gordon (1994) argue that in the United States, individual, property-oriented civil rights are privileged above rights related to socioeconomic welfare. Indeed, seldom if ever do we hear the term "social rights" in the United States. Fraser and Gordon note that a particularly problematic result of this is that social policy has come to be seen as a matter of goodwill and handouts from the state to its less fortunate citizens, rather than entitlements to which each citizen has a right and the state has a responsibility to provide. This is similar to what I describe in the Chilean case. Contractual and property rights gained pre-eminence during the dictatorship, and still today, social benefits are framed in terms of individuals' ability to exercise their civil rights. Though the purpose of social policy is discursively constructed in terms of social integration and reducing inequality, conceptualizing social policy in this way represents a limited view of what equality is (the right to have opportunities) and de-emphasizes the aspects of social rights that focus on public goods, solidarity, and shared responsibility.

CONCLUSION: DEMANDS FOR SOCIAL RIGHTS AND INCLUSION IN THE NEOLIBERAL CONTEXT

My goal in this chapter has been to show how social policy has changed over time, and how this affects the possibilities for poor and working-class people to mobilize around social rights. While collective action among pobladores has diminished since the dictatorship, Oxhorn's description of lo popular gives an indication of the types of demands made by poor and working-class citizens, and these are consistent with the demands discussed by the pobladoras I interviewed. These demands focus on redistribution, integration, an end to marginalization, and ultimately, the expansion of social rights.

While pobladores' demands have consistently been focused on redistribution, over time, the social policy environment has changed. Prior to the dictatorship, policy was guided by a paradigm that, however flawed and unsustainable, emphasized the expansion of social rights. After the coup in 1973, market principles were applied to social service delivery, a tendency that has continued under the Concertación. Today, official discourse portrays Chile as a modern and growing nation, and citizens likewise are called to be modern and integrate themselves into the new economic system. Social policy is oriented toward this goal. On a basic level, this coheres with pobladores' longings: to be included, to have a stake in the modern and democratic Chile. And yet the new policy model does little to actually work toward redistribution and greater equality. Altogether, the Concertación's focus on opportunities restricts the possibilities for the articulation of demands related to redistribution and universal social rights.

The context set up in this chapter is important for understanding the demands of organized pobladoras and their relationship with SERNAM, the municipal women's offices, and the rest of the women's policy machinery. This is the subject of the following chapter. State policy objectives place limits on what pobladoras can achieve. Their demands for inclusion get reframed or ignored, and their own efforts are often coopted. Moreover, the contemporary approach to ending poverty and inequality—reflected in SERNAM as well as other state agencies that pobladoras interact with—leaves little room for demand-making around citizenship rights. The information in this chapter also sets the context for SERNAM's approach to dealing with the issues faced by poor women. As a state agency, SERNAM's response to pobladoras' demands has to fit within state social policy objectives, which in turn reflect the state's economic priorities.

4

PARTICIPATION AND THE REPRESENTATION OF POBLADORAS IN THE STATE

Pobladora activists have an important place in recent Chilean history. They supported their families and communities during the dictatorship, not only by joining together to find common solutions to material needs, but also by raising their voices against the suffering and injustices that had become part of daily life. Through their experiences as activists, and encouraged by contact with feminists, many also came to recognize that women were oppressed in particular ways that were linked to but went beyond the authoritarian regime. During this period large numbers of women participated in organizations and received important financial and technical support from women's non-governmental organizations and international sympathizers.

Much has changed for pobladora activists since the return to democracy. Their numbers have dwindled, and their relationships with middle-class women activists have become strained. In this chapter, I explore the issues and conflicts involved in the relationship between the remaining pobladora activists and middle-class women who work for the state. The chapter is divided into two parts. In the first, I discuss how class and gender are manifest in pobladoras' identities, activism, demands, and proposals. In the second, I discuss the conflicts between pobladoras and the femocrats, which have centered on the concept of participation. Class differences among women come to the fore in these conflicts, as does the relationship of participation to the representation of women's interests.

In part, femocrats' conceptualizations of participation centralize femocrats themselves as the "representers" of women's interests in Chile today. To the extent that they desire pobladoras' participation, it is to reinforce the representation of women's interests that they have established and promoted. Pobladoras, on the other hand, conceptualize participation in terms of being present rather than merely being represented. [1] Thus, while participation for the pobladoras is frequently interpreted as a way to work toward redistribution-oriented goals, it is also centrally related to the recognition of their own skills, values, and contributions. Middle-class femocrats are reluctant to allow pobladoras to participate on their own terms, questioning their skills, demanding formal credentials, and often, appropriating their labor. State goals related to economic development further limit the content of participation—and also, of women's citizenship—in democratic Chile. The pobladora case demonstrates that despite a common history of struggle, women's substantive experience of citizenship rights in Chile today is differentiated on the basis of social class and access to political power.

CLASS AND GENDER IN POBLADORA DISCOURSE

In this section, I address the relevance of gender and class to how pobladora activists understand themselves, and to how they present themselves and their activism to others. Even as they began to focus on women's issues per se during the dictatorship, pobladora activists never abandoned class-based concerns. The centrality of class to how they define themselves and understand their activism has at times created tensions with middle-class feminists, and these tensions have become increasingly salient since the return to democracy. The purpose of this section is thus to delve more deeply into how class and gender come together in pobladoras' contemporary discourse. I suggest that while gender and class are both key factors in why these women have remained organized, their priorities and proposals vis-à-vis SERNAM and the Municipal Women's Offices are nonetheless linked to class-based inequalities among women. All women's gender interests are shaped by their social class, and pobladoras' lack of access to decision making around women's rights frequently leads them to express their concerns in terms of class difference.

In most cases, the pobladoras I interviewed cited gender as a central factor in explaining why they became activists. They organized in order to promote their rights and address other issues that were important to them as women. The organizations founded by pobladoras provided services to women in their communities in areas like personal development (self-esteem and empowerment), sexual education and reproductive health care, prevention of violence against women, elementary and high school degree completion programs, and the provision of child care.

However, women's rights and gender issues have not always been the motivation for pobladoras' activism. As noted in chapter 2, during the dictatorship, they initially organized around their roles as wives and mothers—the desire to protect and provide for their families. So how did gender issues and equality become a focus for these women? Caldeira (1990) suggests that in the case of women in Brazil, the very act of participating in organizations was a challenge to the patriarchal nature of their home lives and the association of women with the private sphere. Organizations were a place where women could talk about their problems, including domestic conflicts, birth control, and so on, and begin to see them—using C. Wright Mills's (1959) terms—as "public issues" rather than "private troubles."

Many Chilean pobladoras similarly described how participating in organizations changed the way they understood themselves. They were no longer submissive housewives, but women with a social vocation who could make a difference in the lives of others. Some suggested that the risks they took—in order to feed their families as well as to fight the dictatorship—helped them to recognize their value as individuals and grow as human beings. For example, Aída Moreno described how in the early years of the dictatorship, her family fell victim to political repression because her husband was a member of a small armed revolutionary group called the Movimiento Izquierdista Revolucionario (MIR, Leftist Revolutionary Movement). Before the coup, Moreno had dedicated herself solely to housework and raising her children. But in 1974 her home was raided by military police in search of evidence of her husband's association with MIR. Soon after, she was invited to participate in a church-based solidarity group. She quickly became a community leader, focusing on human rights and economic survival issues, and later joined the "popular feminist" Movimiento de Mujeres Pobladoras (MOMUPO, Pobladora Women's Movement), perhaps the most important network that brought together pobladora organizations during the dictatorship. Likely because of her outspoken critiques of the dictatorship, her home was burned down in 1987. She explained that her own strength grew out of adversity, which drove her to see beyond herself.

For me, having participated in the Movimiento de Mujeres Pobladoras also was a school where you grew, you grew and you grew, and you looked, and you saw everything at a broader level. Not just to look from my house in my población, but to look and fill myself with restlessness and knowledge (about) what was happening with so many things in those years. Suppose that one day we were going to a wake of a young person that they killed, then the next day they killed an adult . . . and all of them were well-known people, all were important people who worked for justice.

The repression experienced under the dictatorship, combined with the fact that so many of the participants in the oppositional movement were women, led her to understand the relationship between the injustices faced by women and their families in that specific authoritarian context to the subjugation of women throughout history. She continued: "And to feel that I myself needed that opportunity, because (it was like) I had opened my eyes, I had practically put on glasses to see that it was a life, that we women were leading, (filled) with so much injustice, because they had told us that we couldn't study, we couldn't leave the household, we had to be doing the things (we were told) and shut up about it." Through the experience of resisting the dictatorship, Moreno came to believe that women needed social spaces in which they could develop as individuals, acquire skills beyond cooking, washing, and ironing, and learn to look beyond themselves and work for social justice. This mixture of experiences—political repression, socioeconomic hardship, recognizing the specific effects of both on women, and coming to link them to women's subjugated position more generally—were what led Moreno to create a community women's center in Huamachuco, a población in Renca. Other pobladoras described the emergence of their gender consciousness in similar terms.

Another factor in pobladoras' growing focus on women's issues was their interactions with middle-class feminists during the dictatorship. Few pobladoras self-identify as feminist to this day and many dismiss feminism as bourgeois and extremist (comparing it to *machismo*). However, many of them attended personal development courses, antiviolence programs, women's health and sexuality programs, and a range of other activities run by feminists. As a result, feminist ideals and teachings often come through in pobladoras' discourse. María Chavez explained how a personal development workshop led her and other women to form their group, Mujeres Creando Futuro (Women Creating Future), after the return to democracy.

Well, above all, it was to get to know ourselves, to see what it is to be a woman, because a lot of times, it isn't clear to *us* what it is to be a woman. Because we thought that "woman" was housework, was worrying about the children. Being subjugated, that's what it meant to be a woman. And there (in a personal development workshop) we discovered that it wasn't about that. We also had to look out for ourselves, as a person, how to make ourselves feel good, and in the measure that we felt good, we would impart that to others, to our family, too. . . . So it was very beautiful, because we got to know ourselves as people, we discovered the worth that we have. . . . We discovered (this) and at the same time, got to know our friends, our neighbors . . . and we could let out everything that we had held in for many years . . . we could let out what was inside there, oppressed.

Mujeres Educadoras de Pudahuel is an organization of women that were originally brought together when they were young and pregnant by some Chilean and North American Quaker volunteers, who trained them to teach others about issues related to women's health, birth control, sexuality, and women's rights. I interviewed five of the women as a group at their center in Cerro Navia. When I asked how they had changed as a result of participating in their organization, they referred to things they initially learned through this training. Their conversation went as follows:

Margot: We can talk to the children without covering things up, because we learned here in the workshop that that is what you should do, not as we had been taught before, that everything had to be hidden. Now, no. Now we can have a conversation with our children without any problem.

Jessica: And also with the husband, that is, confront him, too.

Margot: And that is the same with the husband. No husband can yell at us. . . . It would be very different if we weren't organized. . . . I, with my husband, have the same right to go out that he does.

Author: And that is something that developed over time?

Margot: Here it developed slowly, because (men) also come from a machista family, and it is difficult for them, too, including for Titi, she couldn't stand in her doorway to have a conversation, because her husband would get mad.

Titi: Of course, (he said) I was a dyke.

Jessica: She was a dyke if she stood there.

Titi: And I was a whore, I couldn't get together with anyone, and now here I am, I'm the one who gives orders.

Andrea: She learned.

(Unidentified):   Poor Marcelo.

Titi: I learned to defend myself, yes.

Jessica: She learned to know her rights, to know our rights, and to learn that a partner is a partner, and that he has the same responsibility to take care of the kids, to educate the kids.

Contact with feminist perspectives gave many pobladoras the tools necessary to challenge inequities in their daily relationships.

Nevertheless, the class issues that were the initial impetus for many pobladoras' activism continue to be relevant today. When I asked them to talk about their demands of the state, all of the pobladoras referred to the socioeconomic need in their communities. Their demands were associated with the effects of poverty and inequality: more and better jobs, better education and health care, access to decent housing, more security in the poblaciones, opportunities for women and young people, and participation in how policies and programs are designed and operated. All of these demands are linked to redistribution. Even the demand for participation, which will be discussed in great detail in the following section, is based in part on the idea that the pobladoras themselves could develop policies and programs more effective in improving the living conditions and life chances of the poor. As Oxhorn noted in his description of lo popular, such demands reflect a desire for inclusion, integration into Chilean society, and an end to socioeconomic marginalization.

While most of the pobladora organizations whose leaders were interviewed for this study combined class and gender concerns, a few focused primarily on class-related issues. For instance, Rayen Mahuida (in Mapudungun, Flower of the Mountain) was a women's organization that started as an economic survival organization during the dictatorship and has had loose contact with SERNAM and the Women's Office in Cerro Navia. The organization's main activities involved running a child care center and an activities program for children and teenagers in the community. Likewise, the Casa de la Mujer Huamachuco (Huamachuco Women's Center) was established as a center for women, and was run entirely by women. However, in 2000, it was billing itself as a "family center." In addition to courses in personal development and women's sexuality, the Casa's activities included administering the World Vision program (an international non-governmental organization that benefits children), creating three local libraries, establishing an onsite child care center, and offering computer classes, a beautician course, and psychological services. Many of these services were available to men and children of the población as well as women.

Despite the central place of social class in their demands and activities, most pobladora activists recognized the importance of SERNAM's issues. For instance, when asked what the state's priorities should be, Lucía Benvenuto of the Casa de la Mujer Laura Rodríguez in La Pintana said, "In relation to women, I think that here there is a serious problem in health, for example, in work, in housing." She went on to explain the ways that several general issues faced by the poor affect women in specific ways: housing shortages mean that adult children and their families live with their parents, restricting the mother's freedom; financial need in the household is likely to mean that girls, rather than boys, are pulled out of school in order to take care of younger siblings while the mother looks for work. She also cited teenage pregnancy as a central issue that needed to be addressed. Her response indicated that—as is the case for all women—both class and gender enter into pobladoras' definition of their needs and priorities. The issue was generally not that pobladoras felt that SERNAM's focus was irrelevant to their lives, but that their particular identities and needs as women whose daily lives are shaped by being poor and working class were not prioritized by SERNAM.

The demands and proposals that pobladoras have presented in written form reflect their overlapping class and gender interests. Women from REMOS as well as municipal level women's assemblies in El Bosque and Renca have issued proposals that center solely on social class, such as improving education and health services, guaranteeing mental health care coverage in the poblaciones, and training health care providers to treat población residents with greater dignity. But they have also made gender-based proposals, or ones that address both class and gender issues. These have included establishing child care services in municipal buildings so women could more easily take advantage of available training programs and participate in municipal meetings; designing education completion programs with class-appropriate, non-sexist content and changing class schedules so working pobladoras could actually attend them; offering scholarships for poor women to attend college or technical school; establishing equal access for women to sports and recreational facilities; increasing resources for the prevention and prosecution of domestic violence; and providing free birth control programs and information (Oficina de la Mujer el Bosque 1996; Orrego and Martínez 1999; REMOS n.d.).

Sometimes, pobladoras prioritized issues similar to those of middle-class feminists, but even then, they tended to interpret them in a way that reflected the class differences between the two groups. For example, in a conversation with the leaders of REMOS, one of the women explained that REMOS had been involved in a campaign, along with women's non-governmental organizations, which involved collecting signatures in favor of legalizing divorce. She explained that legalizing divorce would make better relationships possible among family members, and would force the country to acknowledge the reality that there are many women heads of household, most of whom do not have the financial support of their spouses even though they are married to them. Lucía Benvenuto added, "We (women) are adults, we are women who can make decisions," whether the issue at hand is divorce, abortion, or the day-after pill. She maintained that people with power in Chile fear women making their own decisions, and therefore withhold information and rights from them. There is a need for complete and objective information, she explained, so that women can make their own informed decisions. Interestingly, these pobladoras' discourse around this issue seemed quite similar to that of middle-class feminists.

However, the women added that for them, divorce was not just a women's issue, but a poor women's issue in particular. In Chile, legal annulment (as opposed to ecclesiastic annulment) is the only way to legally end a marriage (though this will obviously change when a divorce law is passed, as is expected to happen before the end of 2004). In order to acquire a legal annulment, the parties involved must prove that their marriage in effect never existed. Both the husband and the wife must agree to do so, and the process entails paying expensive legal fees and acquiring two witnesses to say that some detail of the marriage certificate—most commonly the address of residence at time of marriage—is incorrect. Once any detail is proved to be inaccurate, the entire marriage certificate is deemed invalid, which means the marriage never existed in a legal sense.

Why is legalizing divorce important for poor and working-class women? The women asserted that legal annulment is only for the rich, since the poor cannot afford it. Benvenuto added that some state actors have a "double discourse" on the issue: the senators, deputies, and other authorities who oppose divorce often end their own marriages by paying for an annulment. She went on to say that the women of REMOS are in favor of a "good" divorce law—one that does not leave women destitute—because it would benefit women of scarce resources, who upon separating from their husbands—whether or not they can afford an annulment—currently face an unregulated situation in which determining alimony, property, and child care rights and responsibilities is extremely difficult (fieldnotes, August 2, 2001). These women provided a poignant example of how pobladoras' identities and concerns as members of the poor and working class and as women come together in how they explain and understand their activism.

Corresponding to their class-based analysis of gender issues, pobladora activists often found it difficult to talk about SERNAM's equal opportunities discourse without referring to Chile's extreme socioeconomic inequality. Many said that they would like SERNAM to work to resolve the concrete problems faced by pobladoras: lack of work, education and health care of poor quality, and so on. While it was clear to them that the role of SERNAM was not to resolve problems in all of these areas, the women suggested that these needs had to be prioritized before it would be possible to talk about equality of opportunities. Jessica Vergara of Mujeres Educadoras de Pudahuel focused on the irony of discussing gender equality without recognizing the limitations imposed by poverty.

> It is laughable. It makes me angry and it makes me laugh, the equality that they've made here in the comuna. I think that the first equality that we have seen is that of the woman with the shovel and pick, same as the man, in the streets. There's your equality. But that equality, I think, none of us want. Because I feel this is the last straw. It is what we saw in the dictatorship, because it was then that this issue started, of women sweeping in the plazas, with the shovel, with the pick, same as the men. Women can do it, we aren't saying we can't do it, but we find that we are discriminated against in this way, or that we are denigrated in this way. I believe that in Cerro Navia, this is the equality that we've seen up to this point.

To Vergara, without a simultaneous focus on class inequality, achieving gender equality translated into achieving equally bad conditions as men. She was responding in part to SERNAM's focus on women's employment as essential to their liberation, and implied that this approach falls short because it does not include an analysis of what employment opportunities are actually available to women depending on their social class. Interestingly, she associated the current approach with the job programs for indigent women created during the dictatorship, suggesting that not much has changed in the employment opportunity structure for poor women in Cerro Navia.

Several of the femocrats I interviewed criticized the pobladoras for focusing on economic survival and ignoring the broader gendered implications of their daily lives and activities. This critique reflects feminist debates over Molyneux's (1986) distinction between practical and strategic gender interests. Pobladoras, in contrast, suggested that the strategic issues that SERNAM focuses on are important, but cannot be separated from practical needs rooted in class inequality. They asserted that in order for it to be possible to talk about equal opportunities, the socioeconomic conditions that prevent some women—as well as some men—from being able to take advantage of those opportunities also have to be addressed.

Some pobladora activists, as well as some employees of Women's Offices in poorer municipalities, said that even when SERNAM's work has relevance in their communities and women are aware of their rights, the practical means to put SERNAM's goals and plans into action are lacking. An example from Aída Moreno, director of the Casa de la Mujer Huamachuco in Renca elucidates the connection between economic resources and putting equal opportunities for women into practice. While Moreno evaluated her relationship with SERNAM as positive, she explained that when she applied for a grant from SERNAM's Civil Society Fund in 1998 (which she eventually received), she decided to submit a project for child care, so that women could participate in anti-violence workshops offered by the Casa without being interrupted by their kids. She said that in a conversation with Valeria Ambrosio, who was then regional director of SERNAM, she explained the relationship between child care and equal opportunities.

> I told Valeria, "I don't see equal opportunities in my neighborhood. . . . I can't give a battered woman a document, and say 'Go read this. Look, SERNAM exists.' So that woman is vulnerable. She needs, first of all, a place where she can put her children, while she goes, accompanied by another person, to press charges. Then we are doing everything that should be done. I don't see," I told her, "how I am to go to the women and call them to come hear pure talk. Because we are in Huamachuco, in a neighborhood where there aren't nannies to take care of the children. As such, I want to use this project so that children can be taken care of by someone while the woman participates in a workshop, or in order to have the option to work."

The lack of resources to assure that women in poor communities are able to exercise their rights is an example of the different issues faced by distinct groups of women. While in this case, the pobladoras involved identified with the work SERNAM was promoting, they were restricted in their ability to promote women's rights and opportunities because they lacked the necessary resources.

In another example, women from Rayen Mahuida in Cerro Navia criticized SERNAM for the lack of "direct support" given to women and women's organizations. In the area of domestic violence, for instance, they said SERNAM gives talks about women's legal rights and the procedures involved with prosecuting batterers. They complained, however, that they lacked the ability to ensure that the police follow the proper procedure when women make domestic violence complaints and that judges actually enforce the law. Despite the fact that police personnel and judges have received domestic violence training, in the pobladoras' experience public servants continue to insinuate that women have done something to deserve the violence, and some judges encourage reconciliation regardless of the gravity of the case. According to the women of Rayen Mahuida, this makes encouraging women to make legal complaints against their batterers difficult. While they valued the existence of the law, they suggested that its proper enforcement depended upon having a representative of SERNAM in the comuna who could accompany women in their dealings with the police and work in conjunction with the court system. Interestingly, Mapuche women in Santiago who attended leadership workshops held by the non-governmental organization Centro de Estudios de Desarrollo Económico y Social (Cedesco, Center for Economic and Social Development Studies) made similar comments. They observed that only wealthy women were likely to be able to afford to hire a lawyer to guide them through the process. For poor women, they said, it was often better not to issue a formal complaint, not only because they did not have access to legal assistance, but also because they often did not have the financial means or external support to live anywhere but with their batterers until the process was concluded (fieldnotes, January 13, 2001).

These problems were recognized by femocrats. They are rooted not in SERNAM's ignorance of what needs to be done, but in the fact that the law was passed with little funding for implementation. Two central issues are involved. First, SERNAM is operating in a contested political context in which support for women's rights is often limited by conservative political forces. It does not have the funds to follow up on or enforce laws in order to ensure that women's rights are guaranteed in practice. Second, the effects of this equivocal support for women's rights are felt disproportionately by poor women. In the end, a well-intentioned law designed to guarantee a basic human right of all women—the security of their own physical persons—is likely to have a more positive impact on those women who can afford to pay for it.

Gender and class are both relevant to pobladoras' activism. Like any group of women (including the rich and the middle class as well as the poor), how they define their gender interests is shaped by their class interests. Moreover, as shall be seen in the following section, pobladoras asserted that within the democratic context, they were excluded from the work of SERNAM, the Municipal Women's Offices, and feminist non-governmental organizations. They associated this exclusion with class differences. Pobladoras sought inclusion and recognition on the basis of the unique contributions and special perspectives they have provided as poor and working-class women who are active around women's issues in the poblaciones. At the same time, their demands also reflected a desire for inclusion, integration and redistribution, and an end to the socioeconomic inequality that is the source of their "difference" with other women. Resolving these differences would entail a commitment to redistribution, not only among women, as I shall argue, but within Chilean society as a whole. It would also entail recognition of pobladoras' skills, contributions, values, and desires. Both of these issues are central to debates over the concept of participation, the subject of the remainder of this chapter.

COMPETING DEFINITIONS OF PARTICIPATION AMONG POBLADORAS AND FEMOCRATS

The historical relationship among pobladoras, middle-class members of the women's movement, and many of the women who came to staff the state women's policy machinery led many to think that SERNAM would be a highly participative institution, one that would solicit the opinions and participation of diverse women in the process of creating plans and policy objectives. But the concept of participation has been interpreted differently by pobladoras and femocrats, leading to conflicts among them. In this section, I delineate pobladoras' and femocrats' competing definitions of participation. I then review the ways femocrats and pobladoras understand and explain the exclusion of pobladoras from decision making around women's rights. I argue that the exclusion is related to power differences among women. Women with power in the state construct pobladoras as invalid participants, fail to communicate with them, and require that the major participants in the formulation of policy around women's rights have formal academic credentials. All of these factors are related to the appropriation of pobladoras' social labor. I also suggest that pobladoras' exclusion is reinforced by state policies and goals that privilege development above both women's rights and socioeconomic redistribution.

Pobladoras' accounts of their relationship with SERNAM, the Municipal Women's Offices, and women's non-governmental organizations frequently included assertions of exclusion, which they linked to class inequalities among women. While few would claim that power discrepancies among women were non-existent during the dictatorship, pobladoras' history of inclusion within the women's movement made their sense that they had been abandoned by their middle-class

counterparts particularly acute. While some found they had greater freedom to determine their own agendas under democracy, most pobladora
activists missed working in conjunction with feminist and middle-class
women. From a practical perspective, by the late 1990s, it had become
difficult to survive without the institutional support that had been available to them during the dictatorship. More importantly, pobladoras felt
they still had something positive to contribute to the advancement of
women's rights. They wanted to hold authorities accountable for the
rights of women and the poor, but they also wanted to be consulted
in the various stages of social policy: diagnosing needs, establishing priorities, designing, carrying out, and evaluating programs. However, they
were rarely afforded the opportunity to do so under democracy.

Femocrats, in contrast, expressed conflicted feelings about their relationship with pobladoras (and also with middle-class women's non-
governmental organizations). For many, their past experiences in the
women's movement led to a sort of hybrid understanding of self: insofar as they continued to sympathize with women's demands and priorities, they were part of the movement. But insofar as they were
confronted by bureaucratic limitations and priorities that were not always the same as those of women's organizations, they were part of
the state. This hybridity was also reflected in the marginality of SERNAM
within the state and the Women's Offices within most municipalities.
Alicia Monsálvez and Lilian Medina, who worked in the Women's Office in Cerro Navia, suggested that the position of these offices in the
state is similar to that of women in society in general. According to
Medina, many women in the municipalities struggled to institutionalize the legitimacy of a gender perspective and to be considered a permanent part of government. To the extent that they were all looking
for the material and symbolic resources to satisfy women's demands
and to work toward equality, Monsálvez said, the women in her office
were the "coconspirators" of pobladora activists. In her view, the state
was a site of struggle over women's rights, a struggle faced by women
on the inside as much as those on the outside. And yet, even though
many femocrats identified with the struggles of poor and middle-class
women activists who remained outside the state, their interpretation
of their relationship with pobladora activists differed substantially from
that of the pobladoras themselves. They suggested that if pobladoras
were excluded, it was because their organizations were too weak and
dependent upon femocrats and middle-class non-governmental organizations to be valid participants in dialogue with the state. Some

femocrats asserted, furthermore, that pobladoras exaggerated the extent of their exclusion.

The debate between pobladoras and femocrats is essentially a conflict over who gets to participate in defining the content of women's citizenship and in deciding how women's interests will be represented. Indeed, both pobladoras and femocrats often expressed their differences in terms of "participation." Yet the meanings assigned to this word differed substantially for the two groups.

In chapter 3, I noted that in neoliberal-democratic Latin America participation is a highly contested concept, one that has very real consequences for the lives of the poor and the content of democratic practice. I argued that how participation is implemented by the Concertación has the potential to coopt poor and working-class activists. This is largely because participation has been operationalized mostly in terms of beneficiaries' carrying out projects and delivering services rather than being involved with establishing priorities, policy objectives, or project design and evaluation. Simply assigning cooptation as the state's intent, however, is an overly simplistic interpretation of the Concertación's focus on participation. Part of its stated purpose—to make policies more efficient and effective—meshes well with international efforts to shrink Latin American states. Another aspect, however, involves giving beneficiaries (though not necessarily all citizens) a voice in the policy process. I suggest that while the cooptation of dissenting views may be the ultimate result of the state's participation discourse, it is not necessarily the deliberate intent of Concertación bureaucrats, and more specifically, of the femocrats.[2]

The idea of giving voice to citizens resonates throughout femocrats' discourse. The values of consciousness-raising, solidarity, empowerment, questioning hierarchy, and participation that were endorsed by many who opposed the dictatorship were especially promoted by the women's movement. The women's movement participants who went on to work in the women's policy machinery brought these ideals with them, and with the possible exception of CONADI, where participation has been the subject of contentious debate, participation appears to be taken more seriously in SERNAM than in any other state agency. However, femocrats' motivations are complex, and while they may use the same terminology ("participation") as pobladoras, they often mean something very different by it. Understanding these contrasting meanings, as well as their effects, requires careful examination of how femocrats and pobladoras talk about participation.

In my conversations with femocrats, few of them actually mentioned efficiency or policy effectiveness as reasons to support pobladoras' participation. This does not mean that they did not actually incorporate participation components that have this objective into their programs. Rather, efficiency was simply not part of how they explained the importance of participation. The femocrats talked about participation in two main ways.

The first involved institutionalizing women's formal participation in power structures and decision making in the public sphere. It was generally understood among femocrats that part of SERNAM's responsibility was to improve women's participation in these areas, and this was among the central objectives of the Equal Opportunities Plan. Specifically, this has meant working to increase the number of women in positions of power, such as judges, ministers, local and national politicians, and union and political party leaders. For example, SERNAM has encouraged the use of quotas by political parties. In the Plan and some of its programs, SERNAM also associated increasing women's formal political participation with strengthening organizations, informing women of their rights and improving their capacity to hold government accountable for them, encouraging women's participation in matters of public debate at the local and regional levels, and training them in leadership skills. For instance, SERNAM's program for temporeras, the seasonal agricultural workers, includes workshops on leadership, and collective organization and negotiation. Finally, in the Plan, SERNAM explicitly links women's formal participation to the unequal distribution of household labor that often prohibits women from engaging in politics.

Because of their past role as part of the women's movement, many femocrats felt a great deal of responsibility toward women's organizations. Cecilia Fernández, who worked in SERNAM's regional office in the Araucanía (and actually did not participate in the women's movement), went so far as to say that SERNAM's work would have no meaning if women's organizations were not given the opportunity to organize, make demands, and evaluate SERNAM's work. She, like many other femocrats, saw part of SERNAM's role as strengthening women's organizations to fulfill this task. Femocrats associated strengthening organizations with women becoming aware of their rights and eventually becoming a counterpart or a complement to the work of SERNAM. This complementary vision is the second (and more prevalent) meaning femocrats assigned to participation. Femocrats explained that women's organizations' responsibilities as counterparts included being sounding boards and coconspirators and holding SERNAM and other state agencies accountable for women's rights. A notable example of complementary participation was a series of *cabildos*, in which women's representatives from diverse sectors of society (including academia, non-governmental organizations, politics, program beneficiaries, and grassroots groups) were invited by SERNAM to evaluate the first Equal Opportunities Plan.

Thus, some femocrats seem to have a "feminist conscience" that leads them to at least consider less hierarchical state-society relations than those that exist in other parts of the state. Valeria Ambrosio explained her idea of what the complementary relationship should ultimately look like: "I think the social organizations should be independent with respect to the state. If they have certain demands, they should come here and we should listen to them and say, 'Look, in this we are in agreement. We can do it together and we are going to implement it. And in these other areas, we don't agree. We can't do it together because of a, b, c, and you are going to have to do it somewhere else.' I feel our role should be of independence with the social organizations, and of negotiation." Most pobladoras would agree with Ambrosio's comments. They would point out, though, that the opportunities that she refers to—to make demands or to negotiate with the state—generally do not exist. Aside from the cabildos, the measures that were taken to strengthen women's organizations' ability to perform a complementary role tended to be much more restrictive. They included the creation of the competitive Civil Society Fund for non-governmental organizations and pobladora organizations to receive small grants for projects related to the Equal Opportunities Plan and a 2000 "Woman Citizen, Woman with Rights" campaign that aimed to inform women about their rights through public workshops and the distribution of accessibly written pamphlets about women's rights.

For pobladoras, participation also had two central meanings. Both of these were distinct, however, from those of the femocrats. The first is an oppositional conception of participation. The central idea is that it takes place among citizens in civil society, standing in opposition to the state. Esteva (1997, 4) argues that the "common denominator" of participation in popular organizations or movements "is the autonomy of the organizations constituting civil society, their independence from the state, and their antagonism towards it." In this view, participation is conceptualized in terms of citizens who band together in organizations and create a sense of community by working together and carrying out tasks and services important to the functioning of the group as a whole. More crucially, they make demands for what they perceive as their rights, and hold the state accountable for them. As noted elsewhere, in Chile this oppositional conception of participation is rooted in the Freirean empowerment, consciousness-raising, and anti-authoritarian activism that started in the late 1960s and took hold during the Pinochet dictatorship. Many pobladoras have continued to see a relevant place for oppositional participation under democracy, particularly insofar as it involves holding the government accountable, making demands for rights, and denouncing official practices and policies that have harmed poor and working-class women and their families (Paley [2001] also identifies these as key concerns of popular sector organizations).

Pobladoras' stance on participation was not entirely oppositional, however. In fact, the predominant meaning they assigned to participation had more to do with being included in the state than with standing in opposition to it. Pobladoras demanded inclusion in decision making about program design, the establishment of institutional priorities, and the content of official documents, such as Chile's Beijing agenda or the Equal Opportunities Plan.[3] Indeed, one of their central demands was that they be consulted as "experts" about issues faced by poor and working-class women in the creation of policies and programs. Why did pobladoras consider this "inclusive participation" so important? Maria Molina, leader of the Coordinadora de Mujeres Luisa Toledo (Luisa Toledo Women's Coordinating Network), a pobladora organization in La Pintana, echoed many of the pobladoras when she remarked that not involving them in this process was a serious problem because the middle-class professional women who make the decisions have not lived the experience of pobladoras, and so cannot adequately represent them.

The notion that the voices of pobladoras must be directly present in decision making around women's issues is also reflected in written documents produced by pobladoras. For example, proposals for SERNAM in REMOS's (n.d.) written analysis of the first Equal Opportunities Plan included formally certifying the pobladoras who had been providing health care services in their communities since the dictatorship, establishing dialogue and consultation with pobladoras who work in mental health and family violence in the process of carrying out government programs, and maintaining permanent contact with pobladora organizations as a line of communication with poor and working-class sectors more generally. All of these proposals involve recognizing pobladora activists for the work they have done as experts on women's issues in poor and working-class areas. By demanding inclusive participation, pobladoras argued that they must have a direct voice and hand in decisions that affect them in order to be adequately represented. But demands for inclusion are also ultimately related to pobladoras' longing for redistribution and socioeconomic integration.

Time and again, pobladoras contrasted their demands for participation with what they complained had not been "real" opportunities to participate in the past. Lucía Benvenuto described a time that SERNAM came to La Pintana to discuss the content of the second Equal Opportunities Plan. Over the course of the meeting, it became clear to Benvenuto that the Plan was essentially finished, and that rather than participation, SERNAM simply wanted a seal of approval. She asked, "What do we get out of doing it if you've brought it already done? Why do you ask that we work with something that you have *sagrado y sacramentado,* finished already? Come here when you want an opinion: 'What do you, as an organization, want to be part of the Equality Plan?'"

Pobladoras' frustration was also directed at the Municipal Women's Offices. While some Women's Offices (like Renca's, until the end of 2000) were praised by pobladora organizations for working hard to develop opportunities for participation, others were criticized for providing only superficial opportunities. Pobladoras felt that their opinions were not considered in things that mattered, like how money was spent, what issues received attention, and what kinds of programs were created. On the other hand, they were often invited to "participate" when it seemed like it would benefit municipal officials. Jessica Vergara explained: "Sometimes they call us to meetings, as if to demonstrate that the comuna has a lot of organizations. The thing is, there are a lot of meetings or workshops that they've invited us to where we don't fit in." The women in Vergara's organization, who called themselves popular educators, used theatre to communicate with women and young people about HIV, sexuality, and other health-related issues. They had been invited by the Women's Office and other municipal authorities to attend several activities such as an assembly of the Single Women Heads of Households program. This struck them as strange, because they were not invited to perform or share their skills, but simply to attend, and no one in the organization was eligible for the program because they were married and over the age of thirty-five, the upper limit for participation. Vergara explained how they understood this type of invitation: "We take it . . . as if they want to reach a quota or get a lot of people to show up, so that people (specifically, the authorities who are often in attendance at such events) see that there are people, that people are organized." Thus, participation is sometimes reduced to a public relations opportunity for government officials.

On the surface, the oppositional and inclusive meanings that pobladoras assign to participation seem to contradict one another. However, I think they are more closely related than they seem. Oppositional participation is a strategy that focuses on voicing dissent about state policies and contesting official conceptions of participation. Using Hirshman's (1970) exit, loyalty, and voice schema, I suggest that pobladora activists are unwilling or unable to completely disengage or exit their relationship with the Chilean state. They are loyal to the Concertación's ideals of instituting a more participative form of democracy and reducing poverty and inequality. At the same time, they are critical of the limited way the Concertación has gone about meeting these goals, and so they voice their dissent. Unlike the opposition to the dictatorship, in the context of democracy pobladoras' oppositional stance is not generally a complete rejection of the system but rather a demand for changes that need to be made in order to achieve greater social inclusion (which pobladoras had imagined would be a part of democracy once it was returned). Conversely, in a context in which it is denied, demanding inclusion is a way of voicing opposition.

The women who are most likely to be afforded participation along the lines pobladoras demand are not necessarily members of organizations. Rather, they are the direct beneficiaries of government programs. This includes SERNAM's "high impact programs," which center on specific, targeted populations: victims of domestic violence, pregnant teens, single women heads of households, and seasonal workers. In the programs for heads of households and seasonal workers in particular, SERNAM has incorporated evaluation workshops at the local and national levels, during which program participants are able to share their experiences and opinions of the program and make proposals for future changes.[4] Natacha Molina, former deputy director of SERNAM, contrasted this "beneficiaries' participation" with what she considered "citizens' participation," which would involve opening up the institution to the critiques and opinions of citizens more generally. This, of course, is more along the lines of what pobladoras propose: a type of participation that would include them, as citizens interested in changing the way the women's policy machinery operates. But such participation is incorporated only reluctantly, Molina reasoned, because "neither in SERNAM nor in any ministry do they like to be told that they are doing things badly." In the following section, I discuss in greater depth the reasons femocrats gave for not acceding to pobladoras' demands for greater participation.

The purpose of this section has been to contrast the meanings femocrats and pobladoras assigned to participation. Femocrats' ideas about participation differed somewhat from those promoted by the Concertación governments. Most femocrats were committed to participation in a way that went far beyond increasing the efficiency of policies and programs. They wanted to improve women's understandings of their rights and strengthen their organizations so they would be better able to participate in the public sphere and also, be able to play a role as SERNAM's counterpart in civil society. At the same time, as shall be discussed below, they argued that the state's role in creating opportunities for participation should be limited and that proposals for change needed to come from civil society and to be issued in a way that complemented, rather than opposed, the work of the women's policy machinery. The femocrats' two approaches to participation focused on increasing the presence of women in the public sphere, a goal that is not completely out of touch with pobladora understandings of the concept. Nevertheless, neither involved creating opportunities for pobladoras to exert influence in SERNAM. Pobladoras maintained that space for "real" participation, in either its oppositional or inclusive form, was virtually non-existent in the women's policy machinery as well as other parts of the state. They did not have access to participating in defining women's rights, interests, or even the concept of participation, and their demands for change were rarely heard or acted upon by the femocrats.

In the following three sections, I address how these different conceptualizations of participation came into conflict with one another. In the first, I argue that femocrats not only defined participation differently than pobladoras, but also were reluctant to incorporate participation along the lines pobladoras desired because they considered them organizationally weak and incapable of negotiating in a democratic setting. In the second, I look at how pobladoras responded to these assertions. They maintained that femocrats did not openly communicate with them and that opportunities for participation were only availed to those with formal academic credentials. The perspectives of both groups demonstrate that how participation is put into effect can end up reinforcing existing power inequalities. In the third section, I suggest that regardless of femocrats' personal dedication to participation, institutional and political limitations placed on the women's policy machinery preclude the inclusion of pobladoras. Thus, conflicts over women's citizenship can only be understood by placing them in the wider context of state economic and ideological goals.

Constructing the Invalid Participant,
Contesting Pobladoras' Democratic Know-How

In my discussions with femocrats, they often remarked that pobladoras were ill-equipped to participate in a democratic setting. By this, they seemed to mean several things. The predominant issue was that pobladoras were organizationally weak and dependent on femocrats to provide opportunities for their participation. Femocrats also believed that pobladoras lacked clarity on what the role of SERNAM and the Women's Offices actually was. They also suggested that pobladoras were overly oppositional, and failed to recognize the commonalities that actually existed between what they wanted and what SERNAM could provide. All of these explanations reflect the different meanings femocrats and pobladoras assigned to participation. Pobladoras opposed the government (and the women's machinery's) stance on participation because they desired to be included in decision making about issues that affected them. For femocrats, pobladoras were not supposed to be oppositional; they were supposed to provide a complementary working partner within civil society. And even if they acknowledged they had a role in strengthening women's organizations, femocrats' participation discourse did not embrace the idea that once they were strengthened, they would be included in decision making.

Femocrats were critical of what they perceived as women's organizations'—pobladora as well as middle-class feminist ones—dependence on the state. Valeria Ambrosio, SERNAM's director of programs, associated this dependence with SERNAM's need for a counterpart in civil society.

> Because, what happens? The organizations are very weak now, and they don't have the ability to negotiate. So the point is, until what point should or should not the state be a facilitator of women's participation and sociability? So there we sometimes fall into ambiguities. On the one hand, you know, we realize that we shouldn't get involved, and on the other hand, we feel that as the state we should be facilitators of the social organizations. Because one could say, "Well, you don't have the ability? Too bad. I wash my hands of this." But if we are a women's institution and we want to develop the potential of this, how are we going to do it already? So there we've tried to do some work strengthening the associations, but at the same time, hopefully to transmit that they have to be independent and that their role is more of *control* and holding us accountable.

According to Ambrosio, women's organizations have not shown themselves capable of taking an independent position vis-à-vis the women's policy machinery. Similarly, many femocrats lamented the absence of a strong women's movement that could exercise *control ciudadano*. Control ciudadano is a reference to the international watchdog network of non-governmental organizations known as Social Watch in English, whose members engage in advocacy, information campaigns, and monitoring in order to hold governments, international agencies, and the United Nations system accountable for fulfilling their commitments related to eradicating poverty, promoting human rights, and ending socioeconomic and gender inequality (Social Watch 2001). The network was created in the context of the World Summit for Social Development and the Beijing World Conference on Women. (Grupo Iniciativa [Women's Initiative Group], the network of feminist non-governmental organizations originally set up to monitor Chile's progress on its Beijing commitments, is probably the group most responsible for bringing the concept of control ciudadano to Chile.) By questioning pobladoras' capacity for exercising control ciudadano, femocrats cast doubt on their ability to participate in decision making around women's rights.

Yet at the same time many of them were conflicted about this stance, as reflected in their belief that they had a role to play in strengthening the organizations. From a bureaucratic point of view, it seems strange that femocrats would invite women's organizations to exercise control ciudadano at all. It would seem more logical for them to prefer separate and defined roles for the two actors. Yet the fact that many femocrats were previously women's movement actors means that their expectations for what the relationship between the women's movement and SERNAM would be like under democracy were similar to those of movement actors who remained outside of the state. After all, SERNAM was created in response to women's movement demands. This generated, among many femocrats, the feeling that their work was inherently tied to the women's movement.

Others were not so conflicted about pobladoras' lack of participation and saw very little reason to increase it in any form. These women's priorities shifted once they entered the state, and they now wanted more definite separate roles for SERNAM and the movement. An anonymous SERNAM employee in the Metropolitan Region insisted that women's organizations needed to understand that women in SERNAM were no longer part of the movement. She was critical of pobladora demands to be consultants, and questioned the extent to which the state had the responsibility to strengthen organizations in civil society at all.

Others simply felt that pobladoras did not understand what

SERNAM's role was intended to be. Valeria Ambrosio suggested that women knew what their demands were, but did not necessarily know where in the state to address them, and looked upon SERNAM as the agency responsible for resolving all their problems. Pobladoras as well as non-governmental organizations "point their darts" at SERNAM when solutions are not forthcoming, she said, rather than holding the housing authority responsible for housing issues, the ministry of education for educational issues, and so forth. She linked this issue with the lack of democratic know-how, saying that aside from Grupo Iniciativa, "there is no capacity to organize, to object. The . . . concept of exercising rights and being a citizen is not there."

Natacha Molina explained another concern related to SERNAM's role. Having worked for women's rights both within and outside of the state, Molina spoke from a dual perspective. She had participated actively in SERNAM's creation and was deputy director of SERNAM for part of Frei's government. After Lagos was elected, she returned to the Instituto de la Mujer, the feminist non-governmental organization she cofounded and where she had also worked before her stint at SERNAM. To some extent, she sympathized with pobladoras' claims of exclusion. At the same time, when I asked her to respond to pobladora critiques that there were not enough opportunities for them to participate or have their opinions taken into account in SERNAM, she reminded me that SERNAM *by design* was intended to be a policy-coordinating agency. "SERNAM's central task is to convince the other ministries to do things for women in terms of equality. The issue of participation comes in against the grain, you realize, since there is not a direct means of dialogue. That is the design." Molina suggested that given this structure, it makes sense that pobladoras don't feel included. In other models for women's policy machineries, such as that of Brazil, where women's organizations participate in a presidential council, pobladoras might feel more included.

> SERNAM never had that design. It didn't have a participatory design or a council that represented distinct groups, and by not having it, it frustrated the expectations of all the women, but above all, those of the pobladoras. That whole movement that was growing, that brought down the dictatorship, and that was grand, glorious, etc., in which all of their expectations were concentrated, of which (they said), "In democracy, we are going to participate, we are going to be part of it," but that didn't happen. So there, there is a complaint, and there is a complaint . . . that has a piece of truth and a piece of resentment that you will eternally find in any human group.

Molina explained that one of the main reasons SERNAM was created without some kind of commission to gather the opinions of distinct sectors of women was that the women who wrote the initial proposal wanted the emphasis of SERNAM to be on transforming the state. Rather than simply establishing a relationship between the women's movement and a particular government that would change as soon as that government was voted out of office, the goal was to institutionalize a gender perspective in the state. While this is certainly a sensible strategy, it also reflects power differences among women: because they already had access to decision making, the middle-class women who were active in the creation of SERNAM were less concerned about giving voice to the women's organizations than were the pobladoras who ended up being excluded from the process.

Femocrats also sometimes criticized the remaining activists for appearing to be more interested in making adversarial demands than in working together. Women, in their view, were to support the efforts of SERNAM as well as the Concertación more generally. To some extent, to be critical of SERNAM was to betray the struggle of the women's movement. Likewise, to be critical was sometimes portrayed by government officials as anti-democratic. Paley (2001, 166–167) provides the poignant example of Hernán Rojo, a Christian Democrat parliamentary representative who participated in a public assembly in San Ramón in 1991. Upon hearing pobladores criticize (among other things) inadequate public housing, unpaved roads, and neglected garbage dumps, Rojo complained, "What is lacking here is knowledge of how to operate in democracy." He went on to say that the state could no longer be held responsible for meeting these needs, and that from now on, pobladores would be expected to establish and carry out projects like cleaning up the dumps and paving the streets.

The Concertación has continued to make efforts to squelch visible displays of dissent. President Lagos and others often discourage public protest by insisting that "the doors to the Moneda are always open." In the case of the Mapuche, public protests are likewise frequently delegitimized by calls for dialogue as the only acceptable way to voice discontent. This tendency is indicative of a very limited conception of participation in which performing a role that is complementary to the government's goals is acceptable but opposition and dissent are tantamount to disloyalty. Saying that pobladoras do not know how to operate in democracy fits with an overall participation discourse that implies that "good" democratic citizens do not voice dissent, make demands, or hold government accountable (regardless of the extent to which femocrats say this is part of their conception of participation), but rather provide for themselves and cooperate with the government.

Femocrats at all levels also noted that pobladora organizations like those discussed in this chapter are a minority among women's organizations, and that most of the requests they receive are not for participation, but for funding for supplies or to rent a headquarters. Even among the pobladoras with more organizational skills, funding was often a central demand. Many femocrats considered such demands a sign of pobladoras' organizational immaturity. Natacha Molina explained,

> When you are (in the state), of course you have to have an open attitude about listening, but you also have to think that what we call civil society is very weak in our country, and that there are very few voices. And there is still a very strong dose of reliance on handouts (*asistencialismo*) and paternalism, where they wait for you to give to them, instead of demanding. If there were a stronger civil society, that took initiative, that asked for meetings, that pressured public authorities, *then* if they were denied, the complaint is valid, but the truth is that often, the complaint is "No, (SERNAM) hasn't done anything. They haven't come around here."

As a former femocrat who now strongly identified with her role as a feminist in civil society, Molina expressed more support for oppositional participation than most femocrats. Yet she also echoed femocrats' criticism that pobladoras were overly reliant on the state to create opportunities for them to express their demands (or in essence, to "participate"). Femocrats' participation discourse did not fully reflect the state's focus on efficiency or getting beneficiaries to deliver services. Rather, it centered on women's organizations fulfilling a role as femocrats' complement in civil society. Nevertheless, by suggesting that they did not have the capacity to function in a democratic setting, femocrats put the responsibility for pobladoras' exclusion on their own shoulders and constructed them as invalid participants in decision making around women's rights.

Pobladora Understandings of their Exclusion

Are femocrats' claims about pobladoras' democratic know-how legitimate to any extent? How do pobladoras respond to them? In the years I conducted my fieldwork, there were substantial differences across Santiago's comunas in the quantity of pobladora organizations that were still active as well as in the quality of their political presence and linkages with femocrats and other government officials. In Renca, for example, women's organizations persevered and, with the help of the

Municipal Women's Program and the Programa de Desarrollo de la Mujer (PRODEMU, Women's Development Program), created a women's network that worked closely with municipal authorities until a rightist mayor was elected at the end of 2000 (see chapter 2). Cerro Navia, which had been home to significant resistance against the dictatorship, represented the opposite extreme. By 2000, few organizations remained activist around women's issues and no formal means had been established for them to communicate with one another or the Municipal Office.

With the return to democracy, the overall number of women who participated in organizations diminished dramatically. I frequently heard pobladora activists and femocrats alike lamenting the fact that women had "returned to their homes since the end of the dictatorship" and most questioned whether a women's movement even existed in democratic Chile—much less a pobladora women's movement. Some women—in the state as well as in non-governmental organizations and pobladora organizations—almost seemed to look back with a sense of nostalgia to the dictatorship when more women participated in organizations and there was a greater sense of cross-class social solidarity. Lilian Medina, who directed the Women's Office in Cerro Navia, associated the decrease in participation with what she felt was a general cultural objective of the dictatorship: the destruction of any sense of the collective. She observed that the Women's Offices' relationship with women of the comuna had very little to do with the solidarity of the past. "The women's relationship with us is like a supermarket. They say, 'What do you have for us this year?'" (fieldnotes, July 27, 2000).

Pobladoras themselves attributed the drop in participation to a number of factors. The loss of funding and support from non-governmental organizations was a major factor, and their exclusion from the process of incorporating women's demands into democracy, creating SERNAM, and establishing its priorities was demotivating. Pobladora activists also regretted what they perceived as a growth of individualism, reflected in many women's reluctance to identify themselves as pobladoras. In addition, since the end of the dictatorship, there had been more opportunities for women (particularly young ones) to work for pay, and women took these opportunities because of economic need as well as increasing materialism. But pobladoras also said that many women had lost a sense of urgency about participating in organizations. During the dictatorship, economic need and political oppression gave women clear reasons to participate. With the return to democracy and the ousting of Pinochet, many pobladoras felt their reason-for-being as activists had run its course. In the absence of a clearly defined common enemy, it became difficult to articulate concrete reasons to organize around gender issues. Many women preferred to invest their energy in their homes, families, and jobs. Others simply wanted to rest after so many years of struggle. It is likely that all of these factors have combined to lead to the decrease in participation in pobladora organizations.

Pobladoras reacted in several ways to suggestions that some of the responsibility for their exclusion lay on their shoulders. Some acknowledged that these claims had some legitimacy. Several members of REMOS, the national network of pobladora organizations, admitted that they had yet to become widely recognized as a representative of pobladoras at the national level or even to give public voice to their concerns.[5] Aída Moreno, who was REMOS's first president, suggested that one of the network's shortcomings was failing to make clear what the contributions and long-term purposes and goals of women's social organizations were. She noted that rather than taking advantage of the potential force of the network and acting as "a bridge between the social organizations and the state" on big issues like domestic violence and divorce, REMOS had simply reproduced much of the same work that the organizations themselves had been doing for years, such as conducting personal development workshops. The limitation, according to Moreno, was not that pobladoras did not know how to behave under democracy, that they were overly dependent or adversarial. Rather, the problem was that they did not know how to assume the public presence and political role that they rightfully deserved based on their representativeness.

A Mapuche woman, communist, and human rights activist whose husband was imprisoned and daughter detained during the dictatorship, Ana Pichulmán has chosen to focus her activism in democratic Chile on women's issues. At the time I met her, she worked as a domestic servant, headed a local-level women's collective, and was also president of REMOS. She included achieving a critical public role as one of REMOS's goals, but cautioned that learning to participate in a bigger, more public context was a frightening task for many pobladora leaders. Most pobladoras were wives and mothers before becoming activists, and many still shunned politics and were not party members. They perceived their activism largely as an extension of those roles, or as a social vocation, which, in their minds, was separate from the political. They were strong leaders, skilled at getting things done with limited resources, but not very experienced in setting concrete agendas and negotiating. Moreover, while most pobladoras resisted total dependence on non-governmental organizations and the Church and insisted on some level of organizational autonomy during the dictatorship, much of their activism developed in the context of their relationships with middle-class women. This may have made the development of an autonomous movement and agenda in democratic Chile more difficult. To some extent, Moreno and Pichulmán seemed to agree with femocrats' claim that pobladoras lacked some of the political skills necessary for working under democracy. On the other hand, pobladoras and femocrats meant somewhat different things by saying this: pobladoras felt they needed to learn the skills and find the emotional resources to take a more public role. Femocrats would agree with that, as they often criticized pobladoras for their dependence, but many would also say that pobladoras needed to lose their oppositional stance in order to participate productively under democracy. As much as they desired inclusion, pobladoras, in turn, would identify an oppositional stance as essential to holding government accountable.

Several pobladoras also placed the blame for their lack of participation directly on the femocrats, asserting that they had little access to information about the policies and programs of the state that pertain to women. The language used to talk about women's interests and rights was often inaccessible to pobladoras who lacked higher education (REMOS n.d.). Insufficient communication between SERNAM, the Women's Offices, and pobladora organizations further limited the possibility that pobladoras could participate, or even perceive that their interests were represented in the priorities of the state. When I asked if they identified with the priorities of state agencies that focused on women, some noted that this was a difficult question because they lacked information about what these priorities actually were. This problem was not entirely unrecognized by femocrats. It was the realization that many women had no idea what the Equal Opportunities Plan was that led SERNAM to initiate the "Woman Citizen, Woman with Rights" informational campaign in 2000.

Pobladoras also complained of a lack of communication and opportunities to participate at the municipal level, an indictment that went beyond femocrats to include municipal employees as a group. Pobladoras sometimes responded to this problem by attempting to participate anyway. These decisions were often justified by Concertación rhetoric that encouraged people to make proposals and enter into dialogue with the government rather than engaging in the more oppositional tactics of the past. An example given by one anonymous leader shows the limits of participating, even when it is done along these officially promoted lines. She explained that, with money they were awarded from SERNAM's Civil Society Fund, her collective was able to hold a series of workshops for women in their comuna to learn about the Equal Opportunities Plan. The women who attended the workshops came up with a number of proposals for how the municipal government could better implement the Plan. The collective presented the proposals to the mayor, who was a member of the Partido por la Democracia (Party for Democracy), one of the leftist parties in the Concertación. The mayor accepted the proposals, but none of them were ever implemented. The pobladora remarked, "Some say they don't have any money, what do I know? But sometimes it seems like there's not much will, either, to do things (that would benefit women)." While it should be expected that some municipal governments would be more open to proposals and participation than others, examples such as this lend credence to the argument that participation is simply a mode of coopting dissent.

In the one instance I was told of in which SERNAM took action in response to pobladora proposals, it curiously did not acknowledge pobladoras as the impetus behind the changes that were implemented. According to two feminist non-governmental organization workers, SERNAM instituted two proposals made by REMOS in their evaluation of the first Equal Opportunities Plan. These were the creation of a SERNAM newsletter directed at pobladoras and the establishment of affirmative action within the Civil Society Fund such that some funds would be reserved specifically for grassroots organizations so they would not be obliged to compete directly with non-governmental organizations and professional consultants (fieldnotes, July 23, 1999). Proposals like these show that pobladoras are indeed capable of contributing to the democratic process. That SERNAM took up these suggestions was a positive step, but it represented only half the battle. By not acknowledging that the ideas came from pobladoras, SERNAM perpetuated the marginalization of pobladoras' knowledge and skills.

While many middle-class feminists became femocrats after the return to democracy, only a handful of pobladoras were able to do so. These women possessed a hybrid perspective, in the sense that they often continued to personally identify strongly with pobladoras, but found themselves professionally identified with the state. Their views on the relationship between femocrats and pobladoras reflected both identifications, and were instructive in clarifying some of the problems involved. Olivia González was one of these women. During the dictatorship, she participated in clandestine women's organizations in the comuna of San Bernardo and eventually became a volunteer for the Vicaría Sur (Southern Vicariate, part of the Catholic Church's social arm), working in the *ollas comunes* and as an *arpillerista*. At the time of our interview, she was the territorial coordinator for the Women's Office in La Pintana, where she had worked since 1992. She was critical of the absence of a visible, cohesive popular women's movement but she acknowledged that the dictatorship was a different era, in which "we were all fighting for a cause, and that was democracy." She argued, though, that there were plenty of causes for women to organize around under democracy, listing better jobs and better education as two among many.

González said that poor communication, which she attributed to lack of time and resources, was her Office's major shortcoming. She indicated that this was a problem that extended beyond the state women's machinery to the remaining feminist non-governmental organizations. She had recently attended a forum about sexual and reproductive rights organized by an international funding agency, and noted that academic women, professional women, and femocrats were all in attendance. However, "the woman from the grassroots, the woman of the people who represents what she knows, what the people feel, wasn't there." When I asked her why she thought pobladoras do not attend these conferences, González reflected, "I think they don't go because they are not invited." González's comments suggest that the frustrations of both groups were understandable, yet she notably did not suggest that pobladoras lacked the capacity to participate in a democratic setting.

Pobladoras frequently linked their exclusion to the simple fact that they do not have money. Much of the international funding that had been available to Chilean non-governmental organizations was redirected to other parts of the world at the end of the dictatorship.[6] As a result, many non-governmental organizations were forced to shut down or to greatly reduce the scope of their activities. Many religious volunteers who worked in support of pobladora organizations also moved on to other countries or went home when the dictatorship ended. The consequences of this for pobladora organizations cannot be underestimated, as the majority of their activities depended on the financial and organizational support of Chilean or international non-governmental organizations and religious organizations. Thus, the end of the dictatorship meant a major withdrawal of resources for pobladoras, which continued to be felt by the organizations that remained. They functioned mostly on the basis of small project grants from state agencies and municipalities, some private connections with international sources, minor support from a few remaining non-governmental organizations, and money from pobladoras' own pockets. Over ten years after the return to democracy, one of the main needs cited by pobladoras was financial resources to carry out their activities.

A cofounder of the anti-dictatorship popular feminist organization Las Domitilas, which was established in 1980 and named in homage to Bolivian miners' rights activist Domitila Barrios de Chungara, Caty Orellana was working as a provincial director at PRODEMU and seeking a degree in public administration when we spoke. Like González, she believed that changes in pobladoras' relationship to middle-class women activists had a lot to do with the debilitation of their movement. She explained that Las Domitilas had been one of the most vibrant pobladora organizations, at one point reaching a membership of 100 women. However, the organization lasted only until 1990, when several of its leaders (many of whom had been young women whose studies were suspended when the dictatorship hit) took jobs in the state or in other institutions. She also emphasized the importance of the support they had had from non-governmental organizations and other institutions during the dictatorship, saying, "If we wouldn't have had the support, we would have done things, but not at the level that we did." She wondered aloud what things would be like today if institutions that could help to construct and support a popular women's movement still existed.

From her perspective as a pobladora, Orellana understood how important resources and support were to taking action. Because of this understanding, she was able to contextualize what most femocrats considered symptoms of pobladoras' organizational weakness: their focus on resources and their dependence on middle-class women. The loss of external support was disastrous for middle-class-run non-governmental organizations, though most of the women who worked in them still had relatively more access to decision making around women's rights than pobladoras. For poor women to lose their financial backing as well as their regular communication with middle-class feminists was surely even more devastating. It may be that the relative political isolation and marginalization pobladora organizations have faced since the return to democracy is a bigger part of the problem than their supposed lack of skills. Thus, while I do not deny the possibility that pobladoras would benefit from political training, I do want to suggest that femocrats' insistence that pobladora organizations need to be taught how to function under democracy may be somewhat misguided.

In addition to communication issues, a number of the pobladoras also linked their exclusion to their lack of academic training and officially endorsed credentials. They suggested that they are not taken seriously as participants or consultants because they do not have formal degrees. Explained Gloria from Rayen Mahuida,

> So much fighting for a democracy . . . but it's not what we wanted. That is, it's not really what we women were fighting for during all that time. The actual participation of women in democracy . . . took studies into account. That is, the people who had a profession were taken into account. But unfortunately, the people who fought to have democracy weren't taken into account anymore. And it was because there wasn't the opportunity to study at that time. We were twenty-five or twenty-six years old, and perfectly, we could have studied, but we didn't have the means. Nevertheless, there were people who didn't risk it all, who didn't fight, and they were able to get a degree in the exterior, I don't know, or in an institute. They had the means to do it and (now) they are taken into account wherever they go. You could say that it is not that way for us, the pobladoras, or for the pobladores, because the guys who, the (men) of my age who also risked it all during that time, the guys now are working in construction or working in something else because they didn't have the opportunity, either.

Gloria went on to say that if they were "-ologists," meaning psychologists, sociologists, etc., they might have more success in getting a response from the municipality or SERNAM, but as it is, "They don't respect pobladoras," or recognize their expertise in the areas they have worked in for years. She added that Rayen Mahuida, with twenty-one years of experience as a social organization, has never been consulted by SERNAM about the needs of women in their sector.

Middle-class women with better access to formal education are more likely to have access to positions of power and decision making about issues related to women. This is the case of women who are employed in the women's policy machinery, who determine institutional priorities, and in essence define the priorities of women citizens (which has included establishing the institutionalization of a gender perspective in the state as a priority above involving diverse groups of women's participation in this process). It is true as well of middle-class women who work in non-governmental organizations. Though these women also express frustration about the way femocrats go about making decisions in isolation from women's activists, they are more likely to win projects and work as subcontracted consultants with SERNAM, as Schild (1998) points out, and have been more successful than pobladoras in demanding that SERNAM open lines of communication (there is an academic council, for example). Paley (2001) associates credentialism as part of how knowledge is legitimated throughout democratic Chile. In this case, the knowledge of pobladoras, who often lack formal education and credentials, is constructed as less legitimate.

The focus on formal credentials is compounded, as well, by the use of concursos, or "competitive funds" as the principal inlet for citizen participation. As noted in chapter 3, pobladoras complained that the proposal forms are complex and hard to fill out, and that they are at a systematic disadvantage compared to middle-class non-governmental organization employees with university degrees. Education is an important source of differentiation among women, and this differentiation seems to be felt more strongly by pobladoras under democracy, when women with more education have greater opportunities to not only be paid for working on women's issues, but also to have their opinions taken into account.

Several of the women suggested that the focus on formal credentials in combination with the absence of opportunities for consultation or effective channels of communication meant that the opportunities for participation that were availed resulted in the appropriation of their labor. The women did not necessarily hold SERNAM responsible for the actual appropriation, but they did identify it as an issue of particular concern to them that the women's policy machinery had not expressed much interest in addressing. They argued that they provided important resources that the municipalities often did not provide, and yet received no pay. This social labor, an important investment of time and resources in their communities, was viewed by the state (particularly at the municipal level) as a voluntary contribution, a way of "participating" in the new democracy.

Sometimes this appropriation was quite explicit. An anonymous leader and member of REMOS explained that her organization, which focuses on women's rights and sexuality, tried to work with their municipality on various occasions, but with little success. At one point, municipal authorities asked the organization to do some vaguely defined "community action" for women in the comuna. The organization agreed to conduct some workshops, but they soon found out that the authorities had absolutely no plans or objectives for the project. The organization concluded that the municipality, one of only a few in Santiago without a Women's Office, only asked them to participate in order to say that they were doing "something" for women. In addition, they were to do the workshops for free; not even their photocopies were paid for. She explained the group's reaction,

[W]e thought: What are we going to do? We are going to do their work for them. And they are working with a salary . . . while on the other hand, the reality is that we are pobladoras, with slim means. We have to give our work away, because that is the mentality. I, lately, have a different mentality: our work is worth something. All morning I have been crazy, doing—or trying to do—a project (proposal) to send off. And we have had to learn as we go along, computer skills or what have you, and learn so many things that we didn't know before. And all of this stresses you out, it tires you, and we don't receive anything for this, not for administration, or a secretary. All of this we have to do. According to our possibilities, we contribute what we can. Last year we sent a solicitation to the municipality for a subsidy that they say they give to organizations. . . . It was last February, but they still haven't responded (in April of the following year).

María Molina explained that in her experience, not just the municipality but also professionals from some non-governmental organizations take advantage of the voluntary work of the pobladoras.

You see, all of the professionals come to us: "Look! I won money to do a project about child abuse, but I need fifty women. Get them for me so we can do a workshop in such-and-such place." I am going to run around all afternoon, getting those fifty women, transporting them there, bringing them, but it's the professionals who receive the money. And we do all the work, doing the posters, going to the market and handing out pamphlets to the people who pass by. And well, there has to be some recognition if we are the ones carrying out the project.

When I asked Molina if she identified with the work of SERNAM, she said no. In addition, she linked her ideas about what belonged in the Equal Opportunities Plan to the issue of appropriation, saying that pobladoras had a right to their own way of thinking, different from that of the professionals who run SERNAM, the Women's Offices, and the non-governmental organizations. She implied that professionals rely on pobladoras not only for their free labor, but also because their careers are built around the existence of the pobladoras. If there were no pobladoras, professional women could not write grants to create programs for them, and in turn, would have no salary. While pobladoras did not expect to get paid for their social labor during the dictatorship, seeing professional women make the transition from being activists to getting paid for working on women's issues has led some to question why they are not being paid, too, or at the very least recognized for the social labor they invest in their communities.

While many of the women expressed resentment that they were not paid for their social labor, they also talked about their work as a vocation. In this sense, they sought *recognition* that they were providing important services to the community. For example, the anonymous leader cited above stated that her organization's main demand of the state would be "that the state value all of the things that we do, that they value our work, the role that we are filling in the organization, in our sectors." And in a REMOS workshop that took place in November 2000, a conversation took place about domestic violence prevention training that was being offered by the municipality of San Joaquín. To enthusiastic applause, Hilda Muñoz of Mikempai, an organization that focuses on domestic violence prevention, pronounced that although she was happy to see young women getting involved in this type of work, older women with many years of experience wanted to be recognized by the municipalities for their work and valued for their experience. That the municipality would train new women without recognizing the experience of those who had worked for many years against domestic violence was perceived as an insult by Muñoz and many of the other women, as well as a waste of the human resources that already existed in these comunas. It also demonstrates how the focus on formal credentials can, intentionally or not, lead both to the exclusion of organized pobladoras from participating in government programs and to the continued appropriation of their labor (fieldnotes, November 2, 2000).

The focus on credentials and the appropriation of pobladoras' labor demonstrate that these conflicts over participation are both gendered and classed.[7] To the extent that they involve a shifting distinction between the public and the private, they are gendered. Where women's work is performed continues to affect its value in the eyes of the government as well as much of society. However, the distinction between private and public has been redrawn to define the work of some women—middle-class non-governmental organization workers and the femocrats—as "public" (and therefore paid) while the work of other women—pobladoras, who continue to perform social labor in their communities—remains "private" (and therefore unpaid). The feminist movement succeeded in getting professional women's activities accepted as legitimate "work" and thus part of the public sphere, but the pobladoras' work remains outside of that realm, and thus, devalued. That it is poorer women's work that continues to be devalued, and that this is reinforced by power differences among women themselves, demonstrates that changing gender politics do not necessarily represent gains for women of all social classes. As shall be seen in the remaining section, these changing definitions of participation, the public, and the private also serve to reinforce hegemonic economic development goals.

Pobladoras' and femocrats' explanations of their conflicts over participation reveal power differences among women. Middle-class women are more likely to have had access to the education necessary for them to become femocrats to begin with. Speaking from a position of greater (albeit contested) social authority, femocrats are able to discursively construct pobladoras as invalid participants by pointing out the shortcomings in their political skills. And once they are on the inside, it is femocrats who have the power to decide what information they will communicate to pobladoras and under what circumstances. The point is not necessarily that femocrats intentionally exclude pobladoras or that their perspectives are invalid, but simply that power differences among women often result in the exclusion of certain groups' views. Because only limited political space has been allotted to women by the state, the women with power within the women's policy machinery are more likely to preserve it for themselves than to share it with pobladoras. Likewise, while femocrats may dedicate resources to resolving the concerns of poor and working-class women as they see them, they are less likely to spend resources on incorporating those women into the decision-making process.

Contextualizing the Women's Policy Machinery as Part of the State

Power differences alone cannot fully explain the exclusion of pobladoras from decision making around women's rights. The conflicts between pobladoras and femocrats can only be understood within the wider political context. By this I mean two things. First, part of the reason femocrats' conceptualizations of participation are so disconnected from those of pobladoras may be related to the significant institutional and political limitations on what they can do to represent *women's* interests, much less represent differences among women. In a sense, the creation of the state women's machinery represents a successful struggle from below. But at the same time, the limitations put on SERNAM and the Women's Offices from above demonstrate that women's access to full citizenship is still contested in Chile. And second, regardless of their personal priorities, femocrats *are* part of the state. The context of state priorities related to the issues of growth, poverty, and inequality is thus important to the discussion of the representation of pobladoras' priorities because SERNAM's approach to dealing with the issues faced by poor women has to fit within state social planning objectives and design. And of course, the neoliberal approach to social policy leaves little room for making claims related to the expansion of citizenship rights. Both of these issues contribute to the exclusion of pobladoras' perspectives from the women's policy machinery.

The contested character of the struggle for women's rights was reflected in the legislative process around the creation of SERNAM, discussed in chapter 2. The proposed law did designate a "space" for SERNAM to interact with women's organizations, but this was taken out of the law in parliamentary discussions. Natacha Molina took this to mean that, on some level, some politicians did not want SERNAM to have a close relationship with the women's movement. That is, certain elite interests continued to be resistant to efforts to promote women's equality. But because they had less access to the women's policy machinery than middle-class women (who were more likely to work there as femocrats or work in non-governmental organizations and do subcontracted work for it), pobladoras in particular suffered from the removal of this part of the bill.

In addition, as part of the state, SERNAM cannot contradict official goals. Its approach to dealing with the issues faced by poor women has to fit within state social planning objectives and design. Its policy focus has reflected the Concertación's priority of poverty reduction as well as the strategy of targeting policy initiatives at particularly vulnerable groups. One of SERNAM's four "thematic axes" under the Lagos government is "Women's Economic Autonomy and Overcoming Poverty." Its stated goal is the "improvement of the conditions of women's economic participation, especially those (women) of scarce resources, promoting their complete insertion into the economic and social development of the country" (SERNAM 2001). As noted in chapter 2, the Chilean state has a dual interest in increasing women's employment: it might promote women's equality, but it will also help improve Chile's position in the global marketplace. Little mention is made of the ways that the workplace can constitute an additional site of exploitation for women, particularly those of scarce resources.

Its focus on poverty is also seen in the special programs SERNAM coordinates and targets at particular groups of women, such as woman heads of households and temporeras. These programs provide important benefits to the women who qualify for them, and opportunities for critical participation are incorporated into their design. But pobladora activists, who have traditionally represented one of the most active sectors of civil society, generally do not qualify for these programs, and few additional opportunities for them to participate are provided.

Thus, targeting as a social policy strategy not only shifts the debate away from social rights, but it also effectively restricts the field of valid critical social actors to those who qualify to participate in the programs.

Appropriation of pobladora activists' labor is an additional byproduct of efforts to make social policy more effective and efficient. This occurs in three main ways, the first of which I discussed above: pobladora organizations provide important services, such as violence counseling, and reproductive health and sexual education, which could legitimately be considered rights to which all citizens are entitled, and which the state should therefore provide or subsidize. On the contrary, pobladora organizations are often the only providers of these services, and they perform the work for free. Second, as Schild (2000) notes, targeted programs often include a built-in element of "participation," which generally amounts to self-help schemes. Poor and working-class women who participate in state-run programs end up providing services to their families and communities that range from child care and health care to milk delivery, garbage clean-up and disease prevention. And third, organizations with significant political skills are frequently invited to participate in ways that de-emphasize their oppositional role while contributing to the efficiency objectives of the state. For example, the Grupo de Salud Llareta (Llareta Health Group) has worked in the area of community health in the población La Bandera since 1984, focusing on the relationship among poverty, environment, and public health as well as the importance of preventative care. (This group was also at the center of Paley's 2001 ethnography.) Members have made numerous public efforts to hold the government accountable for health in their comuna, but have also expressed willingness to participate in diagnosis of needs, planning, and the analysis of programs that are implemented. The government's invitations for them to participate, however, have mostly been limited to service delivery, such as distributing milk within their comuna (Grupo de Salud Llareta 2001). All three types of appropriation are tantamount to what Petras and Leiva (1994, 125) describe as the institutionalization of women's unpaid productive labor at the household and community levels, made even more egregious because it is almost exclusively poor women who end up performing this labor. The reduction of citizen participation to the appropriation of labor or self-help may be an efficient way to save money and time in policy initiatives, but it also coopts the possibility of demand-making on the part of social actors, and implies that the poor are somehow responsible for their condition.

The limits to the market-oriented approach to social policy are also evident in the area of "competitive funds," discussed at length in chapter 3. Unlike many other state agencies SERNAM responded to pobladoras' proposal that an affirmative action mechanism in benefit of pobladora organizations be inserted into its Civil Society Fund, but because market principles determine who is or is not a viable participant, vast numbers of people who have legitimate demands are left out, and demands are reframed into a form of participation that individualizes social actors and pits them against one another.

CONCLUSION

Pobladora activists provided important services in their communities, and, aside from the better Women's Offices, were the main voices defending women's rights in the poblaciones. The reasons for pobladoras' lack of a broader public voice are linked in part to the fact that they were not considered viable participants in setting priorities under democracy. There simply did not exist the discursive space for pobladora activists to be a part of determining the substance of women's citizenship. Moreover, many pobladora activists themselves struggled to frame their activism as a movement that was taken seriously by state actors and by others in civil society.

In the first part of this chapter, I described how pobladoras' gender and class identities entered into how they explained and understood their activism, demands, and proposals. In the second, I discussed the conflicts in the relations between pobladora activists and the femocrats. Pobladora activists asserted that their priorities were not represented and that they were excluded from decision making in the women's policy machinery. They linked this exclusion to class differences. Femocrats were conflicted about their relationship with pobladoras, sympathizing with them based on a shared history of activism, but finding that, as part of the state, their priorities were often different. Conflicts between the two groups emerged along several lines, most of which were related to distinct conceptualizations of participation.

Pobladoras looked at participation in terms of voicing opposition or dissent, and especially in terms of achieving inclusion in decision making around women's rights. Femocrats noted that institutional strictures placed limits on what they could do for pobladoras. At the same time, they made choices about who could participate and what form that participation would take. They envisioned a complementary role for the pobladoras, principally as supporters and sounding boards outside of the operations of the women's policy machinery. They suggested, moreover, that if pobladoras were not included, it was because their organizations were too weak and dependent to be valid participants in dialogue with the state. Ultimately this amounts to a very conditional approach to participation. "Yes, the pobladoras can participate, but only if they do it on our terms." "Yes, the pobladoras could participate, if they understood democracy." "Yes the pobladoras could be consultants, but only if they had the necessary credentials."

That pobladora activists were excluded from determining priorities around women's rights cannot be denied. Despite their dedication to issues important to the pobladoras, the femocrats' approach to participation ultimately functioned, in Paley's (2001) words, as a mode of control. Femocrats, who had power in the state, constructed pobladoras as invalid participants, failed to communicate with them, and required that the major participants in the formulation of women's rights policy have formal academic credentials. All of these measures served to silence pobladoras' dissent and to reinforce power differences among women. Moreover, by allowing it to be defined as part of the private (and unskilled) sphere, femocrats facilitated the appropriation of pobladoras' social labor. At their essence, these conflicts over participation are struggles over who has the right to define the content of women's citizenship, and femocrats seemed to be saying that pobladoras did not share in this privilege. Being denied this privilege made it difficult for pobladoras to convey their priorities and interests to the femocrats. Moreover, insofar as the act of participation is itself an affirmation of citizenship, denying them the right to be present (rather than merely represented) was a way of denying pobladoras' citizenship.[8]

Hegemonic socioeconomic priorities reinforce pobladoras' exclusion. State policies and goals privilege development above both women's rights and socioeconomic redistribution. This includes those policies or laws that limit the scope of efforts to promote women's rights, those that restrict access to programs that would promote socioeconomic equality, and those that conceptualize participation in terms of using citizens' labor to substitute for state delivery of social welfare services. Participation in particular is constructed in such a way as to further contribute to the appropriation of pobladoras' labor and to silence their dissent.

Pobladoras' assertions of difference and exclusion encompass both recognition- and redistribution-based claims. They maintain that poverty and socioeconomic inequality make it so that their needs are not identical to those of other women, pointing to a need for redistribution and socioeconomic integration. They also say that their specific contributions to advancing women's interests are not recognized by femocrats. While these assertions involve a desire for recognition of class differences, they ultimately reflect a desire for inclusion, integration and redistribution, and an end to the socioeconomic inequality that is the source of their "difference" with other women. The pobladoras do not just want to be recognized as different, they want to be integrated into planning and policy making around women's interests on equal footing with the middle-class women who are already there. (Whether or not the inclusive participation pobladoras seek would actually lead to the recognition, integration, and redistribution they desire is, of course, another question altogether. It is just as likely to lead to further cooptation of social movement goals and leaders on the part of the state.)

In the following chapters, I move on to the Mapuche case. In chapter 5, I outline some of the specific ways that the Mapuche are affected by Chilean social and economic policy. With high rates of poverty, many Mapuche face similar issues to the Chilean poor and working class. (Indeed, many of them are poor and working class.) Yet their history of invasion and exploitation at the hands of the Spanish and then the Chileans has meant that their relationship with the state is distinct. In addition, economic policy decisions often have very specific effects on their way of life. As a result of these factors, some of their demands focus on redistribution. However, in contrast to the pobladores, recognition of their status as a people is at the root of most Mapuche demands. Moreover, a national identity discourse that says all Chileans are one people is employed by the state against the Mapuche in order to justify national development goals as beneficial for the nation as a whole and to delegitimate claims for autonomy. While distinct from that of the pobladoras, the situation faced by the Mapuche results in similar limitations for Mapuche women activists. This is the subject of chapter 6. Power differences among women have meant that femocrats ignore or don't understand Mapuche women's claims. Moreover, SERNAM is unlikely to stray from policy guidelines set up by the state in attempting to address Mapuche women's concerns.

5

STATE GOALS, NATIONAL IDENTITY, AND THE MAPUCHE

Mapuche women consistently link their priorities as women to the struggle against the exploitation of the Mapuche people as a whole; their gender identity is mediated by being indigenous. Furthermore, SERNAM is part of the state. Thus, in order to understand Mapuche women's viewpoints as well as their relationship with SERNAM, it is necessary to understand the relationship between the Mapuche and the Chilean state more generally.

Throughout history, the Mapuche have been profoundly affected by the Chilean state's national identity and national development goals. In this chapter, I use media clippings, official speeches and documents, and secondary sources to explore the state's discourse and practices around national identity and development as they relate to the Mapuche. I provide a brief history of the relationship between the Mapuche people and the Chilean state. I describe the commitments made by Chile to the Mapuche at the return to democracy, and demonstrate that many of them have been broken in the name of national development. I then explore how a national identity discourse based on a unitary notion of "Chilean people" is used to reinforce and justify national development goals. I go on to summarize the state's policy initiatives in light of the tension between seeking to improve Chile's position in the global economy and desiring legitimacy vis-à-vis indigenous people and the international community. These initiatives, which involve deflecting attention from recognition as a basis for Mapuche demands and reframing them in terms of integration, diversity, and redistribution, reflect the interconnected and mutually reinforcing goals of strengthening Chile's position in the global market and maintaining a unitary Chilean national identity. I conclude the chapter by discussing what this means for the Mapuche struggle for cultural rights. I also preview the relevance of this chapter to my findings specific to the representation of Mapuche women in the state women's policy machinery.

A BRIEF HISTORY OF THE RELATIONSHIP BETWEEN THE MAPUCHE AND THE STATE

Understanding the contemporary relationship between the Mapuche and the state requires knowledge of how the Mapuche came to be subsumed into Chile. Lauded as excellent tactical warriors and skilled horsemen, the Mapuche were never defeated by Spain, with whom they had their first confrontation in 1546. The Mapuche were the only South American people with whom the Spanish crown was forced to sign treaties, the most important of which were signed in 1641 and 1803, establishing the Bío-Bío river as the border between Spanish and Mapuche territory.

Through their social and biological roles, women played an important part in Mapuche efforts to keep the Spanish from conquering their territory. Before the Spanish arrived, the extended family represented the extent of political structure among the Mapuche. Family groups were usually led by a male *lonko* (in Mapudungun, head). (Shamans/ spiritual leaders, known as *machi*, could be male or female, though since the mid-eighteenth century, most have been women [Bacigalupo 2003b].) Defending themselves against the Spanish required the creation of alliances among families. These alliances were generally sealed by marriage, and as Mapuche culture was patriarchal and patrilocal, women were the ones to relocate to another community. Polygamy likewise was used as a wartime strategy to increase the Mapuche population. Some feminist scholars have suggested these practices are evidence of the sexist nature of Mapuche traditional culture (Valenzuela 1987), but other scholars argue that polygamy in particular was a survival strategy of the Mapuche in the face of direct threats to their existence.

Partially because their treaties were generally respected, most Mapuche leaders sided with Spain during Chile's war of independence (1810–1818). The new Chilean nation had designs on Mapuche territory, much of which was prime farmland. By the 1850s, when the California gold rush increased demand for Chilean wheat, Chile had begun serious colonization and usurpation of Mapuche territory. In 1869, Chile initiated the War of Extermination, which was also known euphemistically as the "Pacification of the Araucanía." The Mapuche were ultimately defeated in 1881, when they were overpowered in their last attempt at a general uprising. Chilean military and civilians, who had already occupied much of the Araucanía, continued to attack and burn houses, kill animals, and murder Mapuche people long after the uprising had finished. Dispossessed of their land, thousands of Mapuche died of starvation, epidemics, and lack of shelter after the war had ended. "Indigenous groups wandered around the outside of the forts and during almost twenty years, the army fed thousands of Mapuche who, defeated, could not procure their own sustenance" (Bengoa 1985, 329).

In a process that was not completed until 1920, the Mapuche were relegated to what was then a total of 3,000 small parcels of land called "reductions," or "communities." Mapuche lands were reduced to just 510,000 hectares, or 6.4 percent of their original territory (Aylwin 1998). The reductions were a far cry from the expanses of land that the Mapuche had used for ranching horses and gathering provisions. They were forced to become peasants, a way of life to which they were unaccustomed. Unused to subsisting on small-scale agriculture, many Mapuche continued to starve on these lands. Moreover, the Chileans did not respect the traditional extended family basis for Mapuche communities and often grouped together more than one extended family in the same reduction. In many cases, this resulted in internal conflicts. Lynching, brandings, and other violence continued to be committed against the Mapuche well into the twentieth century.

Today, the Mapuche make up between around 4 and 10 percent of the Chilean population.[1] The majority of the rural Mapuche continue to reside in their families' communities, which are located in what are now Regions VIII, IX, and X of the country. Approximately 60 percent of the Mapuche population, however, now resides in urban areas, including Santiago. They have migrated for a number of reasons, all rooted in the historical invasion and appropriation of Mapuche territory. The small plots cannot sustain families that grow through the generations. And, over time, additional land has been stolen from the Mapuche through the practice of "running fences," fraudulent land titles, and ever-changing and contradictory laws regarding ownership of Mapuche lands. Finally, nationally and internationally owned forestry plantations near Mapuche communities leach the soil of water and nutrients, making even subsistence agriculture unsustainable.

Policy toward the Mapuche under recent regimes has varied. The

Mapuche benefited from agrarian reform, which was begun under Frei Sr. (1964–1970) and intensified under Allende. However, the Mapuche were treated as peasants, not indigenous peoples, by both administrations. Aylwin (2001, 65) observes that although the quantity of land and support given to the Mapuche during the Allende era was significant, the reform had a *campesinista* bias.

> It is clear that the actions impelled by the authorities of that brief epoch were oriented toward incorporating the Mapuche into a political project—in this case, socialist—based on a class analysis and not an ethnic-cultural one. As some analysts that supported the agrarian reform have recognized, the Mapuche demonstrated their rejection of collective or cooperative forms of land tenancy which were promoted by the government. The will of the Mapuche was not always respected when decisions were made about these important issues.

Some positive initiatives were undertaken toward indigenous peoples during the Allende government. In 1972, parliament passed (with modifications) a law that had been proposed in 1970 by indigenous organizations. This law represented the first time that indigenous people were legally recognized as existing independent of their lands (Comisión Asesora 1999). The law also created an Institute of Indigenous Development. All of this became inoperable, however, upon the military coup the following year.

The Mapuche were harshly victimized during the Pinochet regime, suffering the death, disappearance, or exile of many leaders and the loss of lands that had been handed over to them during the Allende administration. Ironically, the Pinochet regime mandated that these lands be returned because they had been "usurped" from their rightful *latifundista* owners during Allende's Agrarian Reform. In 1978, the regime enacted a decree-law that aimed to divide communal lands, thereby instituting private ownership and making these lands more saleable to non-indigenous individuals. The lands could be divided at the solicitation of just one community resident, Mapuche or not. These legal changes, combined in many cases with the intimidation of community residents, resulted in the division of 1,739 Mapuche communities, or almost 60 percent of the total, between 1979 and 1986 (Comisión Asesora 1999). Most importantly, the decree mandated that "the parcels resulting from the division of the reserves will no longer be considered indigenous lands, nor indigenous their owners and residents" (ibid.). That is, upon division of their lands, the Mapuche would no longer be Mapuche; they would be *campesinos* like any other. Although this decree was eventually modified, it "was considered by Mapuche organizations to be a clear attempt to promote the legal destruction of their people" (Aylwin 1998, note 11). Many Mapuche organized in resistance to this decree, and Mapuche organizations, particularly the Centros Culturales Mapuches (Mapuche Cultural Centers), and their successor Ad Mapu,[2] played an important part in the movement to bring about an end to the dictatorship. While both men and women participated in these organizations, men predominated in leadership and decision-making positions, as they continue to do to this day. Gender dynamics within Mapuche organizations are addressed in greater detail in the following chapter.

The return to democracy represented a political opening for many marginalized sectors of Chilean society, including the Mapuche. In 1989, Mapuche and other indigenous leaders signed a pact, known as the Nueva Imperial Agreement for the city in which it was signed, with then candidate Patricio Aylwin of the Concertación. In the agreement, Aylwin promised that, once elected, he would work toward the constitutional recognition of indigenous peoples, the establishment of a special commission which would draft an indigenous law, and the creation of a governmental agency for indigenous affairs.[3] Although political opposition has precluded constitutional recognition, the Indigenous Law was passed in 1993. In addition to establishing means for the protection and expansion of land and water rights, the law created the National Corporation for Indigenous Development, CONADI, a state agency dependent on the Ministry of Planning and Cooperation. Although it was seriously modified before it was passed, most Mapuche leaders were hopeful that the law signaled a new era in their relations with the state.

The contemporary Mapuche movement is made up of a diversity of actors. The creation of CONADI and the Indigenous Law led to a proliferation of Mapuche organizations. There are over 60 associations in Santiago, and about 175 associations and between 1,500 and 2,000 communities in Region IX, in addition to many more in Regions VIII and X.[4] With such a considerable number of actors, it is difficult to make generalizations about the movement. First, of course, not all movement actors privilege the same demands and there is often politically charged conflict among them as to which strategies and goals are most important (Reuque Paillalef 2002). Many focus on issues of redistribution or access, and their demands are commonly referred to by critical actors within the Mapuche movement as "integrationist" because they are demands for inclusion in the state, and thus, for the expansion of citizenship in redistributive terms. Examples include demands for education, health care, housing, agricultural training, and development programs. Even demanding land per se does not directly challenge the state or the idea of the nation.

Poverty is a central factor in many of these demands. According to the 2000 CASEN national household income survey, more indigenous people in Chile are poor—30 percent in urban areas and 36 percent in rural areas, compared to 20 percent and 22 percent of non-indigenous people. It makes sense, then, that many of their demands are not very different from those of other poor people. In difference with pobladores' demands, however, most of these so-called integrationist demands involve incorporating issues of identity—and recognition of cultural difference—into state programs. Such is the case with bilingual education, intercultural health programs, and culturally adequate housing. A second difference is that access has been restricted to the Mapuche because of the poverty and discrimination that have resulted from a history of colonialism and denial of their status as an autonomous people.

A second current of Mapuche claims is made up of what are referred to as "autonomy demands." These demands go beyond claims for the expansion of citizenship to assert the basis for an independent nation, including such elements as independent territory, self-determination, and autonomous self-government. Satisfaction of these demands, it is argued, would do more to redress historical wrongs against the Mapuche, ultimately resulting in a more significant redistribution of power and resources. Marcos Valdés (n.d.) points out, though, that autonomy and integration are not just types of demands, but philosophies of interaction with non-Mapuches and the state, and that both have been present throughout Mapuche history. He also maintains that rather than representing a linear progression from integration to autonomy, the two currents function dialectically and respond to particular historical junctures.

While different actors emphasize different demands, for most Mapuche even demands that seem integrationist are built on the principle of recognition of their status as a people. Most women told me that satisfaction of their demands with regard to integration or redistribution meant little if Mapuche status as a people was not recognized. However, the relationship between redistributive claims and those based on recognition is not always made explicit at the moment demands are issued. Mapuche scholar Victor Toledo (1998, 78) argues that this is problematic as far as broader movement objectives are concerned. Without a firm basis in the legitimacy of being a "people with inherent rights," he suggests, demands that focus on redistribution, access, or reforming public policies alone could lead toward assimilation. In this sense, such demands may warrant the "integrationist" title.

However, it would be a mistake to elide substantial differences in priorities, goals, and strategies among the Mapuche themselves. For example, Mapuche in Santiago sometimes have different priorities than those in the south. And even though I argue that recognition is at the core of almost all Mapuche claims, explicit demands for autonomous territory and self-government are nowhere near universal, even within ancestral Mapuche territory. Moreover, competition over limited resources and ties to political parties often result in bitter debate over which goals are most crucial and which strategies are best suited to meet them. Suspicion about the motives and political connections of those who receive funds is also common. Gender differences occasionally emerge, as well, as some women identify concerns that are specific to being Mapuche and women. These concerns, addressed in chapter 6, are sometimes brushed off as divisive by other Mapuche men and women. Finally, some Mapuche—women and men and urban and rural residents among them—simply feel that material concerns are not only the most immediate, but also the most important to improving the condition in which many of them live. Interests and priorities are not unitary among the Mapuche. As shall be seen, the existence of a diversity of demands is a key issue in how the state responds to Mapuche claims. It opens up the opportunity for the state to respond to demands that foster integration while downplaying or delegitimating more radical claims for recognition and autonomy.

The principle of peoplehood has specific meaning and implications. Like indigenous movements throughout the world, the Mapuche claim that they are a "people," in the sense in which this term has been used by the United Nations to describe the rights of colonized populations, particularly in Africa and Asia. The term is favored by indigenous movements because it implies a degree of sovereignty and the right to self-government. For instance, ARTICLE 1.1 of the International Covenant on Civil and Political Rights declares, "All peoples have the right of self-determination. By virtue of that right they freely determine their political status and freely pursue their economic, social, and cultural development."[5] The covenant goes on to pronounce that all peoples have the right to "freely dispose of their natural wealth and resources," and that state parties must promote the rights of peoples to self-determination, including in non-self-governing and trust territories. Being considered "peoples" per international law would give the indigenous the legal backing for demands for collective rights such as self-government and control over natural resources.

The international community has made clear that this definition of people does not apply to indigenous peoples. For instance, the International Labor Organization's Convention 169: Indigenous and Tribal Peoples (1989), which is the most important international agreement dealing with these issues, emphasizes in ARTICLE 1.3 that "The use of the term peoples in this Convention shall not be construed as having any implications as regards the rights which may attach to the term under international law." Similarly, the declaration of the World Conference on Racism held in Durban, South Africa in 2001 refers to the indigenous as peoples but holds that indigenous peoples' rights cannot interfere with states' sovereign rights (Díaz 2001). Nevertheless, many indigenous movements throughout the world consider recognition as peoples an important step toward gaining cultural and collective rights.

NATIONAL DEVELOPMENT VERSUS THE MAPUCHE

As noted in the preceding sections, many Mapuche looked on the return to democracy with great hope, believing that the Agreement of Nueva Imperial signified the beginning of a new treatment of indigenous peoples in Chile. Nevertheless, guarded optimism soon gave way to disillusionment and open frustration, as the Chilean state demonstrated that indigenous rights are not a priority when national development is at stake. An emblematic example is the construction of the Ralco hydroelectric plant, and it is worth discussing in some detail. Ralco is the second in a series of dams planned for construction along the Bío-Bío river in Pehuenche (a branch of the Mapuche who live in the cordillera) territory by the Empresa Nacional de Electricidad, Sociedad Autónoma (ENDESA, National Electric Company), the Chilean utility that was bought out by a Spanish corporation in 1999. Ralco's construction was announced in 1994. It soon became apparent that it would entail the relocation of ninety-one Pehuenche families, the flooding of their ancestral lands, and the destruction of sacred cemeteries and other religious sites. The dam's construction was opposed from the start by the Mapuche on cultural, economic, and environmental grounds. Moreover, the project's environmental impact statement was initially rejected because of possible negative social and cultural consequences. However, the Comisión Nacional del Medio Ambiente (CONAMA, the National Environment Commission), authorized construction in 1997.[6]

Construction of Ralco appears to violate several aspects of the Indigenous Law. First, the law mandates that the government consult with and consider the opinions of indigenous peoples before making decisions that will impact them. Second, the law stipulates that indigenous lands cannot be sold outright to non-indigenous individuals or corporations, but must be exchanged for land equal in quality and value. In addition, not only must the indigenous residents of the land agree to relocate, but CONADI's National Council must authorize the exchange. This turned out to be a key factor in the debate over Ralco.

Fifty percent of the sixteen-member CONADI council is constituted by elected indigenous representatives. The other eight counselors include representatives of various state agencies and three presidential designees. CONADI's national director also votes on council decisions, and in the case of a fifty-fifty tie, would cast the deciding vote. Mapuche activist Mauricio Huenchulaf was CONADI's first director. He was vocal about his opposition to the project, and it became clear that the land swaps would not be approved under his authority. In April 1997, President Frei forced him to resign, and removed two other members of the council. Meanwhile, ENDESA had begun to arrange individual resettlement packages with the families (a strategy of questionable legality) and sweetened the deal by offering houses with plumbing and electricity, jobs, tools, and other amenities. Eventually eighty-four of the Pehuenche families agreed to be relocated, many of them moving to their new homes even before the land swaps had been approved.

Huenchulaf was replaced by Domingo Namuncura, a human rights activist of Mapuche descent who, it was widely believed, would approve the land swaps. However, Namuncura visited the relocated Pehuenche and found their new land inadequate for agriculture or animal husbandry. In addition, many told him that they had agreed to the relocation because they were under the impression that they had no choice in the matter. It soon became apparent that Namuncura would not approve the land swaps, either. On August 5, 1998, he, too, was forced to resign (along with two other council members). This was one day before the council was scheduled to vote on the land swaps. The following director of CONADI, Rodrigo González, was non-indigenous and under his power in 1999 the council approved the majority of the swaps.

In the meantime, ENDESA had initiated work on the dam, while a handful of families, led by elderly Pehuenche sisters Berta and Nicolasa

Quintreman, continued to resist pressure from ENDESA and the government to abandon their lands. In March 2000, just hours before leaving office, Frei signed the final electric concessions needed by ENDESA to carry through with the project. In January 2002, the Supreme Court ruled on a suit filed by the Quintreman sisters to detain completion of the dam. The court concluded that construction could legally continue, but reiterated that ENDESA must complete the remaining land swaps before flooding the affected territory ("Suprema dio" 2002). In December 2002, six remaining families brought a complaint against the Chilean state before the Inter-American Human Rights Commission (IAHRC). That same month, however, Nicolasa Quintreman accepted ENDESA's compensation offer, reportedly out of concern for the health of her son, who has a spinal disorder ("Spanish Energy" 2003). Her brother followed suit, leaving just four families. In February of 2003, the Inter-American Human Rights Commission ruled that the state and Pehuenche families must work toward an amicable solution and that the state must work to protect indigenous rights in the process. Negotiations between ENDESA, the government, and the remaining Pehuenche families were renewed, and in September 2003, the families agreed to leave their lands for 77 hectares and 200 million pesos (about 285,000 dollars) a piece, the same amount Nicolasa Quintreman had settled for in December 2002. The decision was mourned by those who opposed construction of the dam on the grounds that it contributed to the ethnocide of the Pehuenche people, reduced the collective rights issues of indigenous territory and cultural survival to an individual-level monetary solution, and further demonstrated the priority conferred to national development over indigenous rights.

The forestry industry provides another example of how the state privileges national development above Mapuche rights, and also of the continuities between the dictatorship and democracy. Today in ancestral Mapuche territory (Regions VIII, IX, and X), national and international forestry companies possess three times the land recognized by the state as belonging to the Mapuche (Aylwin 2001). According to Aylwin, this situation is due in large part to a state subsidy for forestry companies established under Pinochet in 1974 and later renewed by Frei. The subsidy frees forestry companies from paying taxes, returns 75 percent of costs to owners, and covers management and administration costs. The forestry companies are a demoralizing symbol of the privileged position of national development above Mapuche rights, and they also have important material impacts on Mapuche livelihood, particularly as they substitute native old growth forests with quick growing pine and eucalyptus which leech the surrounding soil of water and nutrients. The forestry companies have been a significant target of Mapuche protests in the form of written demands that the companies be removed from Mapuche territory as well as direct actions, particularly on the part of groups associated with the radical organization Coordinadora Arauko Malleko (Arauko Malleko Coordinating Network). These actions have included occupying plantations, cutting or burning down trees on disputed lands, blocking roads, and sabotaging equipment.

The state has similarly granted mining and water rights to national and international corporations. As of 1996, the state had granted 1,357 concessions for mining exploration or exploitation in ancestral Mapuche territory, 104 of these actually in Mapuche land. Seventy-five percent of possible water rights in the same territory had been granted by 1996; only 2 percent of these were granted to Mapuche individuals (Toledo 1997). While the proposed Indigenous Law included guarantees for water and subsoil rights for indigenous communities, Congress removed these provisions from the final law (Aylwin 2001). Another case of privileging national development above indigenous rights involves the construction of highways through Mapuche land in order to facilitate the forestry and tourism industries.

Today, many Mapuche feel deceived by the Chilean state. They argue that CONADI, which was supposed to have been an instance of co-governance between the state and indigenous peoples, has turned out to be a tool of the state, under-funded, bureaucratic, and inefficient. The situation has become increasingly uneasy, as direct actions continue and the state insists that it will not negotiate with people who, they argue, violate the rule of law and threaten national security. Dozens of Mapuche individuals involved in the conflicts over the forestry industry have been jailed; they are widely considered political prisoners by others in the movement. Meanwhile, Region IX is the most heavily militarized in the country, and military police repress even peaceful Mapuche protests with tear gas and billy clubs. A 2001 march against the violent police raid of the Consejo de Todas las Tierras' (Council of All Lands, another of the more radical organizations) headquarters in Temuco, resulted in the detention of 125 persons, as protestors countered police violence with violence of their own. An altercation between police and Mapuche in November 2002 led to the first fatality from the conflicts; seventeen-year-old Alex Lemun died of a bullet wound to the head inflicted by a police officer. Overall, the hope and promise felt by many Mapuche since the signing of the Nueva Imperial Agreement has almost completely disappeared, as indigenous rights are neglected in favor of national development.

IDEOLOGY AND ECONOMICS: UNITARY NATIONAL IDENTITY AS DEVELOPMENT'S DEFENDER

Behind the actions that privilege national development above Mapuche rights is a national identity discourse that says there is only one people that inhabits Chilean territory. Up until very recently in Chile, "indigenous peoples" rarely appeared in common parlance or in official state discourse. *Etnia*, best translated as "ethnic group," was the preferred term. Chilean historian José Bengoa (1999) points out that this is problematic because in international law, the rights of ethnic groups are held by individual members of those groups, whereas the rights of peoples are collective. "People," writes Bengoa, "indicates a more profound, more historic relation of a human group, it implies an everyday life that has been lived for a long time" (ibid., 201). Today, "people" is almost never used by the political right to refer to the Mapuche, and "indigenous people" and "ethnic group" are often used interchangeably by members of the Concertación, serving to diminish the significance of Mapuche claims for "peoplehood."

This is not to say that the appropriate term has not been debated in recent years. Per the Nueva Imperial Agreement, in 1991 President Aylwin sent to Congress his proposal to amend the first article of the Constitution in order to recognize the "indigenous peoples" that form part of the nation. However, in congressional discussions and consultations with constitutional experts, the amendment was opposed on the grounds that it violated the Constitution, in which the concept of "people" is univocal. It was thus argued that two or more peoples cannot fit into the idea of the Chilean nation (Bengoa 1999). As a result, the amendment project was archived. It was revived in 1999, and the reform came to a vote in the House of Deputies in 2000. The lack of success in passing this measure in the past had been attributed to conservative sectors of Congress. This occasion painted a somewhat different picture: while no Concertación deputies voted against the reform, and a number of rightist party deputies actually voted for it, seventeen Concertación deputies did not show up to vote. (Some were in a budgetary committee meeting, others claimed a truckers' strike prevented them from arriving in time for the vote.) As a result, the reform failed to garner the two-thirds majority necessary for it to pass. Several Mapuche movement actors depicted the situation as evidence of continuing racism in Chile, while others, such as Consejo de Todas las Tierras spokesman Aucan Huilcaman, said the language of the reform was so generic that even if it had been passed, it would have made little difference in the struggle for autonomy and self-determination (Rossel 2000). In another attempt to revive the amendment in 2002, the Senate's Constitution Committee again expressed concern about the concept of "people," opting instead to recommend to the full Senate recognition of "indigenous populations" within Chilean territory ("Acuerdo en Senado" 2002). Two proposed amendments did come to a vote in the Senate in April 2003—one using the word "peoples" and the other "populations"—but once again both failed to pass, mostly due to rightist opposition. It is important to emphasize that the reform does have the support of the Executive Branch, representatives of which have publicly noted that constitutional recognition of indigenous peoples in other countries has not led to "divisions of the state" or secession ("Gobierno reinstala" 2002). In fact representatives of the Concertación often discursively link constitutional recognition to the "integration" of Chile's indigenous peoples (see Senado de Chile 2003; Comisión de Constitución 2003). Overall, this case demonstrates the lack of monolithic interests within the state itself.

Unlike several other countries in Latin America, Chile has yet to ratify the International Labor Organization's Convention 169, either.[7] Ratification has been approved by the House of Deputies, but few analysts believe there is much hope it will ever pass in the Senate, where passing progressive legislation is often difficult, partially because of the existence of nine designated "institutional senators," a provision worked into the Constitution by Pinochet. The failure to establish constitutional recognition of indigenous peoples, as Aylwin (2000) notes, reflects the historical denial of the multicultural and pluri-ethnic character of Chilean society. Failing to ratify the International Labor Organization's Convention 169, meanwhile, serves to limit the extent to which indigenous peoples can achieve their demands for cultural and collective rights.

Usually, officials who are strong advocates of unitary national identity couch their concerns in terms of national sovereignty. This is especially true of representatives of the political right. On occasion, though, some officials draw a more direct link between unitary national identity and national development. For example, during a 1999 Senate discussion about the "Indigenous Situation," Institutional Senator Julio Canessa gave a speech in which he suggested that by establishing the Nueva Imperial Agreement and the Indigenous Law, the Concertación had put an end to the tradition of treating Mapuche individuals "like any other Chilean." Recognizing the Mapuche as somehow different, he maintained, led to their segregation from the national community, and, as a result, to greater marginalization and poverty. He went on to contend that CONADI was stimulating nationalist consciousness among the Mapuche and that the Concertación's indigenous policy was the source of the political violence in the south. He considered the violence a hazard for economic development, noting that if the violence escalated "it could seriously affect two or more regions that up until a short time ago we considered very prosperous. The stability of this productive region is being threatened" (Senado de Chile 1999b). The causal chain in Canessa's argument is thus: recognizing the Mapuche as different leads to the development of specific indigenous policies, which in turn leads to political violence that threatens economic development. Other Senators, including Sergio Diéz from the Renovación Nacional (National Renovation Party), drew a link between failing to uphold a unitary national identity and ethnic strife along the lines of what has occurred in Kosovo, Kashmir, and Pakistan (Senado de Chile 1999a). Unitary national identity was thus rhetorically linked by the Senators to national development and economic and political stability.

While the right's rhetoric is certainly more virulent on this issue, a second example linking national development and unitary national identity comes from Lagos's 2001 presidential address. In his discussion of a "New Impulse for Growth," Lagos made no direct reference to the Mapuche, but said, "Seen from the world, seen from history, we are Chileans, simply Chileans. We are not one or the other, we are inevitably one family confronted with the challenges of a global world, everyday more present in our lives." To imply that Lagos was referring to the Mapuche conflicts in this passage is probably incorrect. It is much more likely that he was referring to political conflicts over economic strategy. Yet the absence of any mention of indigenous peoples in this part of the address is perplexing, considering the central place that conflicts between the Mapuche, private interests, and the state over forestry plantations and construction of highways and hydroelectric dams in Mapuche territory had played in the months leading up to the speech.

In the address, Lagos went on to discuss the need to adapt to the world's new economic order, necessary capital market reforms, and new opportunities for private/public sector cooperation. Lagos called "all social and political actors, businessmen, workers, professionals, unions, academics, students, political parties, to join this strategy which will permit (Chile) to compete with success and give a new impulse to growth." He talked about the need to strengthen ties with other Latin American countries because "common history, territory, language, and culture unite us." The absence of any mention of indigenous peoples in these passages leads one to wonder: Do the impacts of national development policy on indigenous peoples or cultural rights simply not cross the minds of Chilean leaders when they establish economic policy? Or is not mentioning indigenous peoples a deliberate omission? In any case, official state discourse today is a far cry from what it was in 1989, as democracy was about to return to the country and Patricio Aylwin signed the Nueva Imperial Agreement, which was to signify the beginning of a new treatment of indigenous peoples in Chile. As one Mapuche leader expressed at a presentation of my work in Temuco, "Under the Concertación the Mapuche are experiencing repression only slightly less than during the dictatorship."

MAINTAINING LEGITIMACY

In this chapter thus far, I have shown that the state's vision of what "Chile" represents as a nation, and what its future will be, does not include the cultural or collective rights of indigenous peoples. In some sense, this seems like the rational response for a state attempting to secure its position in the global economy. Recognizing the rights of indigenous people would likely put limits on state and private development initiatives, particularly as they involve land and other natural resources on or near indigenous lands. Yet even as they do not recognize Chile as multiethnic or multinational, for a number of reasons Chilean leaders cannot—and do not—totally ignore the demands of the indigenous peoples that reside within Chilean borders. To begin with, the development of an international movement around the rights of indigenous peoples has led to the commitment of international law-creating bodies to some form of recognition of collective and cultural rights. Chile cannot completely violate indigenous rights without losing legitimacy as a democratic state in the eyes of the international community. Indigenous organizations, moreover, were able to take advantage of the political opportunity opened up at the end of the dictatorship to get the state to establish land and water and development funds through the Indigenous Law, and to commit to working toward constitutional recognition of indigenous peoples. The Concertación-controlled state cannot renege on its commitments to indigenous peoples without breaking the law or totally losing the political support of indigenous leaders. Finally, growing and sometimes violent protest to situations in which Chile *has* reneged on those commitments (such as Ralco) has created a situation in which the state finds itself obligated to respond in some way to the anger and frustration felt by many Mapuche, for fear that more radical groups that sponsor land reclamations and violent acts against forestry companies will grow in popularity.

LEGITIMATE, ILLEGITIMATE, AND ILLEGAL DEMANDS

The Concertación-run state's position is clearly more progressive than that of Pinochet, whose legalization of the division of Mapuche lands was interpreted by many as an attempt to eliminate the Mapuche altogether. It is an advance, as well, over the "peasantization" of the Mapuche under the initial creation of the reductions and later agrarian reforms. Yet despite the progress reflected in the establishment of the Indigenous Law and CONADI, Chile has sought to address Mapuche demands without sacrificing national goals. In the following section, I argue that the policy response since the democratic transition has had three main aspects. First, some recognition claims are reframed as demands for (the less politically charged) diversity. Second, those recognition demands that directly challenge state ideological and economic goals are declared illegal or illegitimate. And third, redistribution claims that can be framed in terms of socioeconomic integration and development rather than historically based cultural rights are directly addressed by state policies. Altogether, this policy response serves to remove the political content from Mapuche claims.

Reducing Recognition to Diversity

Demands that cohere with the concept of diversity fit well within the parameters set by state goals, and calls for diversity are common in official Chilean rhetoric. This can be seen in one of two lights. On the one hand, recognizing diversity is a step forward in Chile, where up until the 1992 Census (the first that asked questions about indigenous identification) many citizens would tell you that there were no Indians in the country at all. On the other hand, focusing on diversity has long been criticized by indigenous peoples throughout the world as a discourse that, much like mestizaje discourses, justifies integrationist state policies, rather than leading toward the recognition of cultural or autonomy-linked rights.[8]

Sometimes the link between diversity and integration is plain. In his first presidential address (2000), Lagos described "integrating Chile" as one of the main tasks faced by his administration. By this he said he meant two things: decentralizing the country and enhancing the cultural, social and economic contributions of the various regions, and "the recognition of our diversity through the complete incorporation of the *pueblos originarios* (first nations/peoples)." He went on to say,

> I want to propose to our pueblos originarios that we (incorporate knowledge of) their values, customs, art, and spirituality. I do it for them and for all Chile. Dealing with the issue of the *etnias originarias* is not just about them, it is an issue that has to do with all Chile, with our richness which is our diversity as a nation. . . . Here, to our land, people have arrived from distinct places. After the discovery of America, after many other places, Catholics and Protestants, Jews and free thinkers have arrived here; all have found a way of understanding that Chilean society takes them in, in all of their broadness. Chilean society also has to take in and respect the culture of our *etnias originarias* to preserve the diversity of Chile, because if we preserve this diversity, we preserve the richness of the country.

Lagos's speech highlighted some of the ways that official state discourse works against recognition of the rights of the Mapuche as a people. While the majority of Mapuche people consider themselves both Mapuche and Chilean, and would agree that having the respect of non-indigenous Chileans is important, they insist that they are a different people, with a culture different from the dominant Chilean one. Canadian liberal theorist Will Kymlicka (1995, 22, 60) identifies the limits of logic like that revealed in Lagos's speech in these terms: rather than recognizing indigenous peoples as distinct nations or "peoples with their own cultures and communities" it assumes "they are a disadvantaged 'racial minority' or 'ethnic group' for whom progress requires integration into the mainstream of society." Implicit in such logic is a perception that indigenous cultures are inferior and need to be changed or at least integrated.

Lagos's speech also demonstrated ambiguity toward the term "people." By linguistically fusing the concepts first nations/people and ethnic group, he diminished the more radical meaning of "people." Gaining status as a people is important precisely because a people have rights as such and cannot be integrated away through diversity-oriented policies. Kymlicka (1995) points out that defending group-differentiated rights on the basis of diversity appeals to the interests of the majority (in contrast to arguments based on the obligation to adhere to historical agreements or a need to ensure equality). This comes through in Lagos's speech, in which the incorporation of indigenous peoples was framed entirely in terms of its benefits for Chileans. In my interview with her, Mapuche leader Isolde Reuque called this type of discourse "folklorizing" rhetoric, because it has the effect of converting living people into pieces of folklore: indigenous people are the "richness of the country" that needs to be "preserved" rather than subjects of rights that may sometimes conflict with elite or state interests. In the process, "recognition" is reduced to a more palatable "diversity."

Of course, for a diversity discourse to matter, the state must generate support for it among Chileans, and particularly among the Mapuche. The call for diversity must be presented as a measure considered positive by Mapuche leaders themselves. An effort to generate such support took place in 1999, when after a summer filled with protests, land occupations, and other direct action in the south, the Frei government established the Advisory Commission in Issues of Indigenous Development, which created a "Pact for Citizen Respect." The pact was signed by Mapuche representatives, government officials, and other high profile Chileans, and stated that "Peace, respect and the celebration of diversity should eradicate ignorance, violence, and discrimination" (in Aylwin 2000). Frei presented the pact, along with a package of development-oriented measures intended to alleviate the conflicts, at an event held at the Moneda, attended by the lonkos of 1,000 communities and blessed by machi. Such ceremonies are considered problematic by some observers. For example, Bacigalupo (n.d.) contends that the democratic regimes have involved machi in their ceremonies in order to symbolically differentiate themselves from the dictatorship, but that when coupled by measures that effectively result in the destruction of indigenous culture, this amounts to little more than the ideological incorporation of "indigenous culture into national culture in order to legitimate (the state's) domination in the name of the people."

The priority given to diversity is reflected in the types of programs promoted by the Concertación. Both Frei and Lagos increased funding for programs that present little challenge to national goals and identity. In Santiago, pro-diversity programs like intercultural health care and pilot bilingual education programs made up the extent of state policies targeted at the Mapuche at the time of my fieldwork. In the south, these programs were also common, in addition to more general development initiatives (which are the subject of a later section). To the extent that they respond to some demands of the Mapuche movement, such programs are important. Through the intercultural health program in Santiago, the Ministry of Health made money available to organizations in the sectors of the city with high Mapuche populations to work in concert with local health clinics. Their projects included sensitization programs for health care professionals, co-care programs between machi and western-style doctors, and first aid training for members of

Mapuche organizations. In the south, the Amul Dungun health program basically consisted of providing bilingual assistants who could translate for Mapuche patients who were not comfortable speaking in Spanish. Intercultural education programs in Santiago involved training Mapuche leaders to enter classrooms and teach about Mapuche history and culture. No money was set aside to pay these individuals, however. In the south, some schools offered limited bilingual education.

Such programs were given a lot of publicity, as examples of positive things the government was doing for the Mapuche. This was a complex situation for Mapuche leaders who advocated or participated in the programs. Many were pleased to see the programs funded, and recognized that they benefited some of the Mapuche and represented progress toward answering some of their demands. However, they had mixed feelings about how they were publicized, noting that the programs were under-funded and, particularly in the case of the health programs, often ended up being less about combining aspects of Mapuche healing practices with western-style medicine than about providing Mapuche communities with access to mainstream medical care. Nor were the programs generally connected to recognition of the historical basis for Mapuche demands or their status as a people. Leaders who participated were caught between wanting to take advantage of any resources being made available to their communities or organizations and the criticisms of autonomist movement actors who accused them of selling out to the state.

The government, meanwhile, took advantage of these positive interactions to improve its image. Former head of MIDEPLAN Alejandra Krauss appeared in a piece on the agency's website visiting with women and children at a Santiago organization whose children's singing group made a compact disc that was funded by a grant they won through the government's anti-drug agency. "During the meeting," the article announces, "The Secretary of State confirmed the approval of their proposal to expand their meeting place, which they presented (for funding) to CONADI" (MIDEPLAN 2000). This was presented as an upbeat occasion, which it was. But the organization was held up as an example of one that was happy with government policy toward the Mapuche, which is more problematic. When I interviewed members of this organization a few days before this event, they were very happy that their CD had been released, and were pleased that their proposal to expand their meeting place had been approved. But at the same time, they were highly critical of the construction of the Ralco dam and other development initiatives that threaten Mapuche communities in the south, and were equally frustrated with the state's focus on diversity and integration of the Mapuche into Chilean society. The event served the purpose, however, of demonstrating the state's willingness to respond to Mapuche demands.

Projecting an image of a government that recognizes and appreciates diversity is part of managing the Mapuche conflicts. While the focus on diversity is mainly a discursive strategy to integrate the Mapuche into the image of the Chilean state, it has important effects on what kinds of programs are actually funded. Responding to demands that fit into diversity discourse is also a way to answer some demands while deflecting attention from those recognition-related demands, like autonomy, territory, and self-determination, which would result in a more radical redistribution of power and resources.

Illegitimate and Illegal Demands

The flip side of the state's willingness to address diversity involves defining claims related to autonomy as the illegitimate and illegal actions of small groups of individuals acting without the support of the majority of the Mapuche. Lagos made his position clear in the context of talking about diversity and the incorporation of indigenous peoples in his first presidential address when he stated, "Our willingness for recognition and reparations toward these peoples should not be confused with infinite concessions to small groups that upset public order or threaten the rule of law." Indeed, as alluded to above, numerous Mapuche individuals associated with the Coordinadora Arauko Malleko and other radical organizations, who have allegedly participated in occupations of forestry plantations and privately owned estates in Mapuche territory or violent incidences therein, have been jailed on the assertion that their actions threaten national security. State representatives define not only these actions as illegitimate, but the demands that are behind them, as well. They often contrast legal and legitimate "integrationist" demands with the recognition-related illegal and illegitimate claims of more radical groups. When asked by a journalist to explain the government's view of the Mapuche conflict, Minister of the Interior Insulza responded (Bell 2001),

> The government has always considered that behind the Mapuche conflict, there is a quantity of unresolved problems in the Araucanía Region that have to do with land. They are not ancestral *reivindicaciones* but rather land problems that occurred in the last three decades. Above all, problems with development and poverty, access to education, to health, etc. In addition, there is a very substantial increase in

ethnic consciousness, which implies that the issue of cultural, political, and social recognition is also important. This is why constitutional reform that recognizes them and the adhesion of Chile to the ILO 169 agreement is so important to us. Our view is that behind this, extremist actions, violent actions, etc. will always take place, but in essence, the Mapuche conflict is not a violent conflict.

Insulza's insistence that these are not claims with a basis in historical injustice but socioeconomic problems basically created by the dictatorship denies the historical and cultural nature of the Mapuche conflict. The scarcity of land is an issue that goes back at least to the creation of the reductions. Poverty, lack of education and health care, and other associated difficulties, while exacerbated by present export-oriented macroeconomic policies, are linked to the history of invasion, cultural depredation, and expropriation suffered by the Mapuche. Insulza's de-emphasis of the historical and cultural basis for Mapuche claims suggests an understanding of the threat that acknowledging that basis entails for hegemonic socioeconomic goals. Such discourse conjures up an image of "good Indians" who want to develop themselves and be part of the diversity of Chile and "bad Indians" who are antisocial and intent on violating the rule of law.[9]

"Legitimate" Demands and Development-Oriented Solutions

The Mapuche movement's success in taking advantage of the political opportunity provided by the return to democracy, growing activism around indigenous rights at the international level, and the increasing intensity of the conflicts in Mapuche territory have nonetheless led to a situation in which the state must make some effort to address Mapuche claims. I described above how the state reframes some recognition demands in terms of diversity, and in turn funds programs that foster integration. A related approach involves framing the Mapuche struggle not as historical claims for rights, but as socioeconomic problems easily eradicated by development-oriented solutions that focus on access to land subsidies, education, and agricultural training. As is the case with bilingual education and intercultural health care, the point is not that development is an unimportant part of Mapuche demands. Indeed, many observe that the problem with CONADI's land fund (which provides subsidies to individuals and communities and also purchases and hands over to the Mapuche lands whose ownership they are disputing) is that it does not provide the training and resources necessary for beneficiaries to make effective use of those lands. The point is, rather, that these diversity and development programs effectively take emphasis away from the political and historical basis for Mapuche claims and dilute demands for recognition of Mapuche status as a people with all the rights that status entails.

Two major examples of the state's emphasis on socioeconomic development rather than the political-historical aspect of Mapuche claims occurred over the course of my fieldwork. In 1999, in response to rising violence and tension over the Mapuche problem, the Frei government instituted a series of communal dialogues, in which officials from MIDEPLAN and CONADI met with leaders of more than 1,000 communities in Regions VIII, IX, and X. The dialogues were assembly-style conversations, but MIDEPLAN compiled the results into proportion-based statistics, claiming that while only 15 percent of the demands were sociopolitical, 40 percent focused on infrastructure and services, 32 percent on economic and productive issues, and 12 percent on land (MIDEPLAN in Lavanchy 1999).

In response to the demands issued in the dialogues, Frei announced the designation of 140 billion pesos to address Mapuche demands in the south. The measures outlined included infrastructure improvements, technical support to communities, housing subsidies, improvements in land buybacks and dispute resolution, more land subsidies for young Mapuche families, more indigenous scholarships, wider-reaching intercultural health and education programs, and the establishment of two new Areas de Desarrollo Indígena (ADIs, Indigenous Development Areas)—all development-oriented solutions. In addition, according to former director of CONADI Domingo Namuncura, as much as 75 percent of the 140 billion pesos had already been designated prior to the dialogues, and all of the measures Frei announced were included in the CONADI council's 1997 three-year plan ("Critican Soluciones" 1999).

The results of the communal dialogues, as Lavanchy (1999) points out, seem to indicate that political issues do not really have much to do with the demands of the Mapuche living in rural communities. Some scholars have questioned the methodology used in conducting these dialogues, however, and in the presentation of their results. According to Mapuche sociologist Marcos Valdés (2000), the government sought to lower the profile of groups involved with "territorial recovery," and marginalize them from the process, so as to diminish the political character of the Mapuche conflicts. He asserts that the government's main goal in initiating the process was to "impede the qualitative leap from economic demands to political demands." He argues that this is clearly the goal because the Ministry of Planning, as opposed to a more political ministry, such as the Ministry of the Interior or the secretary general, led the dialogues. Moreover, some communities and organizations, particularly those linked to the Coordinadora Arauko Malleko, may have distanced themselves from the dialogues. That the government proceeded to present Mapuche demands as predominantly development-oriented is thus misleading, because the most radical sectors did not participate in the process.

Valdés also notes that attention was drawn away from the political quality of the demands through the methodology used in presenting the results. Even though the dialogues were qualitative, the results were presented as a typology of measures, which allowed for the presentation of economic development and sociopolitical demands as mutually exclusive categories. This method simply cannot capture the idea that the two types of demands are linked or that over the course of the dialogue, the same person demanding self-governance might also be saying that the Mapuche need better access to land, education, and agricultural training.

The Lagos administration used a slightly different tactic, but with similar results. Shortly after taking office in March 2000, Lagos created the national-level Working Group for Indigenous Peoples, which incorporated a broad range of representatives from indigenous movements, business, and the government. The working group divided into several commissions; each commission held several meetings and prepared a report for the main working group. A final report was created, and Lagos responded with sixteen measures intended as steps toward resolving the conflicts. The initiatives addressed demands in the areas of land, training, intercultural education and health care, and constitutional recognition, but notably did not address what are considered to be more radical demands, such as autonomous territory, self-government, or even collective political representation. In addition, the higher profile "autonomist" organizations did not participate in this working group, some, like Consejo de Todas las Tierras, by choice, and others, like the Coordinadora Arauko Malleko, by deliberate exclusion, as the state had accused that organization of activities that violate the National Security Law.

It is interesting to note that in Lagos's 2001 presidential address (the same speech in which he made no mention of indigenous peoples in the context of talking about national development) indigenous people were mentioned only in a section dedicated to "Policies for Equity," which also addressed women's issues and unemployment. Lagos stated, "Today I can affirm with tranquility and happiness that we have achieved greater protection of (the needy) and that we are recognizing indigenous peoples in all of their dignity, opening new opportunities for development." He went on to mention the Comisión de Verdad y Nuevo Trato (Truth and New Treatment Commission) established as part of his sixteen measures and a US$140 million Inter-American Development Bank loan to be used for development programs for indigenous peoples. All of this was framed by introductory comments about the need to "integrate the country, equalizing opportunities for all Chileans (male and female), regardless of their ethnic, social, or geographic origin." Like the preceding Frei administration, the Lagos government chose to address Mapuche demands fundamentally in terms of development and by "creating the conditions for equality," ultimately avoiding the recognition of cultural rights.

In addition, debates over the meaning of participation have pervaded conflicts related to the administration of the state's development-oriented solutions. As noted in chapter 3, participation has been a central tenet of Concertación social policy since the return to democracy. As noted in chapter 3, participation in the creation, management, carrying out, and evaluation of plans and policies was a demand heard from many sectors of society at that time, including the Mapuche movement. Active indigenous participation in the Comisión Especial para los Pueblos Indígenas (CEPI, Special Commission for Indigenous Peoples) which would eventually create the proposed Indigenous Law, in CONADI, and in a proposed "ethno-development fund," was all written into the Nueva Imperial Agreement. The creation of the proposed law was very participative, as Mapuche leaders discussed and debated its content with all Mapuche communities as well as in urban areas. But once the proposal was submitted to Congress, it was out of indigenous leaders' hands. It was a strange experience for the Mapuche, as Bengoa (1999) notes, to have a law about them, and which they wrote, being debated and decided on while they—and their legitimate authorities—ultimately had no say in the final product. Indeed, significant changes were made to the proposal. In the proposed law, Indigenous Development Areas were intended to be instances of indigenous territoriality and of co-governance and management. The territoriality provisions were taken out of the law by conservative sectors of Congress, for fear that they would result in the fragmentation of the Chilean nation state (Aylwin 2001). However, Article 35 of the Indigenous Law stipulates that state organisms should consider indigenous participation in the management and use of protected wildlife areas found within the Indigenous Development Areas, which has not occurred. Likewise, absolutely no Mapuche input was solicited in the drafting of the proposal for the US$140 million Inter-American Development Bank loan, and, according to Alejandro Herrera, director of the Instituto de Estudios Indígenas (Institute of Indigenous Studies) in Temuco, the projects funded through the loan are unlikely to be sustained after its 2008 completion date. Despite the fact that this loan represents Chile's most important investment in Mapuche development ever, it has thus been widely interpreted as a strategy to neutralize conflict (cited in Muga 2002). These instances, on top of Ralco, suggest that Mapuche participation is no longer considered convenient to Concertación democracy.

CONCLUSION: WHERE DOES THIS LEAVE MAPUCHE ACTIVISM AND CULTURAL RIGHTS?

In this chapter, I have shown that the state's priorities in the global marketplace influence how it responds to Mapuche demands. State responses reflect the interconnected and mutually reinforcing goals of strengthening Chile's economic position and maintaining a unitary national identity. By framing Mapuche demands in terms that foster integration and dilute their relationship to recognition of Mapuche status as a people, the Concertación-run state demonstrates its reluctance to incorporate cultural rights (beyond diversity) into its citizenship regime. This has important implications for Mapuche movement actors. In the end, the state responds favorably only to demands that fit well within its paradigm of national identity and development. Mapuche social worker and cofounder of the non-governmental organization Aukiñko Domo (in Mapudungun, Voice of the Woman) Carolina Manque objects to the injustice of this strategy.

> The Chilean state has a historical debt with our people, for having taken from us, by force of death and guns, our territory and independence. It's obvious that all the public policies the state generates for the Mapuche population are going to act vis-à-vis the 'effects' of a colonialist state: poverty, illiteracy, lack of economic, educational, etc. opportunities, but always thinking of us as a vulnerable and poor sector. . . . In the current situation of oppression and colonialism from the state toward our Mapuche people, the path of public policies, like the laws, has served until now to seek "integrationism" or dependency. Now, in terms of the issue of public policies and Mapuche women, as a doubly or triply discriminated sector of society, what role is there for the state? [Email correspondence with author]

As the leaders of many local-level organizations, women are implicated in the state's strategy of incorporating diversity and development-related demands, while de-emphasizing the historical and political

content of all Mapuche demands. Because they are traditionally responsible for the day-to-day welfare of the family as well as perpetuating
cultural values and traditions, women often respond positively to state
policies that could potentially help them fulfill their roles. Nevertheless, many male leaders emphasize similar concerns and it would be
erroneous to associate women alone with redistributive concerns. For
all of these leaders, engaging with the state and participating in these
processes without permitting the state to dilute the content of their demands is extremely difficult.

The context presented in this chapter is essential for understanding the representation of Mapuche women's interests in the state, and
in SERNAM in particular. Mapuche women position their activism not
within a separate indigenous women's movement, but as part of the
Mapuche movement. Thus, to a large extent, the demands of the movement are women's demands, and as such the state's response to the
movement is the state's response to women. In addition, this wider context sets the stage for how far SERNAM—as a representative of the
state—is able to go in responding to Mapuche women's demands. In
the following chapter, I will show that despite their insistence that their
demands are coterminous with those of the movement, Mapuche
women sometimes make demands directly of SERNAM. I will demonstrate that power differences among women represent a central factor
in explaining why Mapuche women have so little success in gaining
representation in the women's policy machinery. In addition, however,
I will show that as part of the state, SERNAM necessarily follows the
state strategy vis-à-vis the Mapuche: it avoids conceiving Mapuche
women's demands as claims for cultural rights, relying instead on an
additive approach to "ethnicity" and a loose treatment of diversity.

6

VISIÓN DE PUEBLO AND THE REPRESENTATION OF MAPUCHE WOMEN IN THE STATE

Mapuche women have often played a prominent role in conflicts between the state and the Mapuche people. Some were said to have fought alongside men against the Spanish and the Chileans, and women also had an important presence in resisting Pinochet's *desalojos*, the attempts to remove the Mapuche from the lands returned to them through Allende's agrarian reform. Sisters Berta and Nicolasa Quintreman led the struggle against the construction of the Ralco hydroelectric plant and the flooding of their lands. Women also have been visible participants in land recuperations and the occupation of government buildings, and, upon occasion, have literally pummeled Chilean male authorities who they perceive do not respect Mapuche rights. Such actions on the part of Mapuche women do not cohere with Chilean gender norms. Mapuche women assert, moreover, that their cause, gender ideology, and experiences of discrimination are distinct from those of other women.

Nevertheless, some Mapuche women leaders interact with SERNAM and other parts of the state women's policy machinery, issuing demands and proposals for programs which would better meet the concerns and priorities of Mapuche women. In this chapter, I examine the issues, contradictions, and conflicts involved in these interactions. The chapter is divided into two parts. In the first, I discuss how indigenous identification and gender are manifest in Mapuche women's identities, activism, demands, and proposals. I address three interrelated topics: the content of Mapuche women's gender-related demands and proposals, the context in which they make them, and how they make sense of their claims and justify them to others. In the second section, I examine how SERNAM represents Mapuche women's concerns, and show that SERNAM's and Mapuche women's discourses often come into conflict with one another. I suggest that SERNAM's representation of Mapuche women's interests is inadequate. Power differences among women result in restricted access for indigenous women to decision making about the content of women's citizenship as well as policy and program objectives. In addition, SERNAM's actions are framed by the context of the Chilean state, which, as seen in chapter 5, is reluctant to recognize cultural rights. The case of Mapuche women shows that access to full citizenship in Chile is differentiated not only along gender and racial/ethnic lines, but also *among* women themselves. Moreover, it compellingly demonstrates the difficulty of fighting for the inclusion of cultural rights as part of citizenship.

INDIGENOUS IDENTIFICATION AND GENDER IN MAPUCHE WOMEN'S IDENTITIES AND ACTIVISM

The Mapuche women leaders in this study are not a homogenous group. Leaders from Santiago and the Araucanía differed in some important ways, and even within each of these groups, the women varied in terms of their political and religious views, the types of demands they emphasized, their rural or urban backgrounds, and the extent of their interactions with the state. These issues are described more extensively in the appendix, and I highlight them where relevant throughout this chapter. For all of their internal diversity, however, Mapuche women leaders in Santiago and the Araucanía tended to share similar views on two key points: the centrality of the Mapuche struggle to their own activism and the differences that existed between them and non-Mapuche women.

All of the Mapuche women I interviewed identified themselves not as members of an autonomous women's movement, but as part of the general struggle of the Mapuche people. Women's issues were not their central focus. Nevertheless, they sometimes made demands specifically as Mapuche women, which entailed interacting with the national and international women's movements, as well as with SERNAM. [1]

"Difference" is a key element of Mapuche women's discourse as they confront the representation of women, and of the Mapuche, in the Chilean state. In this section, I explore how indigenous identification and gender come together in Mapuche women's identities and activism by looking at how they explain themselves and their activism to other people. In laying out the various aspects of Mapuche women's discourse, I address three interrelated questions: What claims and demands do Mapuche women make? How do Mapuche women make sense of their claims and justify them to others? And what is the context in which they make them? I show that even when they are issuing gender-based demands, Mapuche women's discourse focuses principally on recognition of their differences with non-indigenous women, and ultimately, recognition of the people as a whole.

The Context for Talking about Gender among Mapuche Women

For Mapuche women, talking about women's issues is complex. This is true for two main reasons, which frequently have been confronted by indigenous women and women of color throughout the world (among others, see Collins 1991; Fernández 1994; Nelson 1999; Royal Commission 1996) as well as by women participants in nationalist movements (Jayawardena 1986; Seidman 1999). First, there are some within the Mapuche movement—both women and men—who question the motives of talking about "Mapuche women." They say that dealing with the topic of "woman" or "gender" is to import western concepts and "compartmentalize" women in a manner inconsistent with the Mapuche worldview, which emphasizes the complementary nature of women and men's roles. They also suggest that talking about women only serves to divide the people and distracts from historically based *reivindicaciones*. Their basic argument is that women's rights contradict cultural and collective rights. Women who focus on gender issues and women's rights risk losing the respect and confidence of others in the movement.

According to Ana Llao, the women who formed the Coordinadora de Mujeres Mapuches (Mapuche Women's Coordinating Network) in Temuco in the early 1990s faced significant opposition. These women had diverse reasons for creating a women's coalition. Some did not identify with what were being portrayed as Chilean women's concerns in SERNAM or in the preparations for the Beijing Conference and wanted to have an indigenous voice in this process. Others wanted to address what they felt was women's triple work load in the communities and discrimination against women in Mapuche organizations. Still others wanted to develop women's potential in support of Mapuche culture and to recover traditional values of gender balance. Regardless of their reasons, Llao, who is a former president of Ad Mapu and was a member of the Coordinadora, said that they "were criticized in the region," and "looked down upon in the Mapuche world." Insofar as their activities were seen as involving work exclusively with women, they were considered to be out of sync with the Mapuche worldview. Both men and women within the movement issued hurtful accusations of Coordinadora participants: they were "lesbians," "manlike," were "betraying their culture," or "needed a man." According to some of the women, it was partially because of these criticisms that the Coordinadora had largely ceased operating by the late 1990s.

On the other hand, to directly address women's issues also carries the opposite risk that Mapuche women's priorities and discourse will be appropriated or distorted by non-indigenous women who are active in the women's movement or working in SERNAM. Many Mapuche women perceived that feminists and femocrats were overly insistent in their efforts to fit them into a monolithic "women's cause," and they associated this with the state's general efforts at assimilation. For example, when I asked her about discussing Mapuche women's perspectives with SERNAM, one young leader from the Araucanía explained: "It hasn't been talked about, this is only starting recently. But generally before, they talked about the issue of gender, and that doesn't fit, because the relations between men and women in Western culture is one, and within Mapuche culture, it's another. Our way of relating with men is different. So long as they don't recognize us as a people, they are always going to try to assimilate us, so that we will be the same as the Chileans, except for the folkloric thing." This woman perceived that SERNAM wants Mapuche women to concede that they face the same issues as non-Mapuche women. SERNAM, she said, only wants to appreciate Mapuche women's difference in a folkloric sense, as a part of Chile's culturally rich distant past, rather than admitting the possibility that there are contemporary differences in gender relations among the two peoples. Isolde Reuque, cofounder of the Mapuche Cultural Centers, a member of the Coordinadora de Mujeres Mapuches, and a special advisor to President Lagos on indigenous issues, was the most openly feminist of the Mapuche women I interviewed, and yet she was also critical of the women's movement's treatment of indigenous women. She agreed with Ana Llao that dealing with women's concerns within Mapuche organizations has been difficult, and added that this has also been true of campesino organizations, urban organizations, and non-indigenous women's organizations. She spent some time explaining to me the issues faced in dealing with the women's movement.

It's been difficult . . . with women who are not indigenous who generally want you, as an indigenous woman, to submit to the canons that they have, to their forms of organization, their structure, their vision. And they don't realize that we are a distinct people. . . . It's been difficult . . . with the intellectual women's organizations that look at you sometimes like, "These poor indigenous women, we have to help them, we have to do this, we have to do that." So they look at you like someone for whom they have to go and do something, and tell you what to do. They don't see you as distinct, and as someone who can contribute. I'm telling you that this is very hard.

The women I interviewed who dealt with women's issues and interacted with SERNAM responded to both of these debates. While Mapuche women leaders consistently came down in favor of indigenous rights, their reflections are instructive as to the intersections between cultural and women's rights.

Several external factors have shaped the development of Mapuche women's gender-related demands. First, the international human rights movement and international development industry have been very influential. The preparations surrounding the Fourth Annual World Women's Conference held in Beijing in September of 1995 gave special attention to issues affecting indigenous women (Grupo Iniciativa 1994, 1997). In Chile, Mapuche women leaders participated in the preparatory process for the Beijing conference and some attended the conference itself. Indigenous women's conferences held in Temuco and Santiago in 1995 took place in this context.

Second, focusing on gender as a specific program area has become a prominent trend in project and funding opportunities within the international development community. International and bilateral agencies like the United Nations, World Bank, the United States Agency for International Development and its European counterparts, the Inter-American Development Bank, and international non-governmental organizations have all placed increasing emphasis on gender in their own programs as well as in the requirements for funding that they make available to non-governmental organizations and governments in recipient countries. Governments and local non-governmental organizations, in turn, frequently make program participation or local-level project funding dependent upon a gender perspective. This means that in order for grassroots groups and local non-governmental organizations to gain access to funds, they have to focus on gender, which usually amounts to focusing on "women's issues." This trend is most likely an indirect result of the United Nations's Decade for Women. As noted in chapter 2, the existence of SERNAM and the creation of funds and special programs for women in other Chilean ministries are partially a product of this international context as well. Mapuche activists recognized that one way to get resources for their communities and organizations was to focus on the particular needs of women.

The extent to which the funding agencies' focus coheres with the priorities of Mapuche women is questionable. Employees of Cedesco, a Chilean non-governmental organization that received funds from a European agency, told me that their program for urban Mapuche organizations originally divided its activities into thematic subject areas, including "women," "youth," "the aged," and "children," because that was what appealed to the funder. It did not, they said, necessarily reflect Mapuche worldview or the wishes of program participants, who wanted programs that acknowledged the "integral" character of Mapuche community life and the reality of their organizations, which were usually multigenerational and composed of men as well as women. Cedesco eventually changed its programs to reflect this reality (fieldnotes, February 25, 2000 and March 3, 2000). Moreover, Mapuche women occasionally suggested to me that they would look for resources anywhere, and if focusing on gender meant that they could receive funds and services to meet their own needs and provide support to their communities and families, they would do so.

Some Mapuche women leaders saw SERNAM as a potential ally in getting access to other parts of the state. In discussing the proposals made to SERNAM through the Urban Mapuche Women's Working Group,[2] Mapuche activist and former advisor to CONADI Beatriz Painequeo commented that the women's main idea in making the proposals was for SERNAM to "help us to open spaces, because for us, it's not so easy to open spaces in other public services . . . because in reality we don't have the spaces to rely upon, but for them it should be somewhat easier." Achieving access for women by assuring that state ministries incorporate a gender perspective is the institutional purpose of SERNAM. Beatriz's comment is interesting because she included Mapuche women among the people toward whom SERNAM has a responsibility. She, and others who shared her views, reformulated SERNAM's discourse to demand that state ministries not only eliminate their gender bias, but their ethnic bias, as well.

A final factor shaping Mapuche women's gender demands is the Chilean women's movement, particularly in the Araucanía. As noted in chapter 2, some feminist non-governmental organizations, namely CEDEM (and its predecessor PEMCI), initiated interactions with Mapuche women in the Araucanía during the dictatorship. Perhaps the most visible outcome of CEDEM's outreach to Mapuche women was the creation of the Casa de la Mujer Mapuche in Temuco. It was also active in encouraging the involvement of Mapuche women in the Beijing process and in the creation of the Mesa Rural, a working group that aimed to incorporate rural and indigenous women's issues into SERNAM's agenda. In addition, since 1998, several Mapuche women's organizations have participated in the National Association of Rural and Indigenous Women, which has ties to the women's movement. Clearly, then, a variety of factors—both internal and external to the Mapuche people—are involved as Mapuche women leaders articulate their views on women's issues.

Mapuche Women's Discourse of Difference

My purpose in the remainder of this section is to examine how Mapuche women make sense of their identities as Mapuche and as women, and how they justify making claims for rights as such. In contrast to SERNAM's equality-based gender discourse, Mapuche women's discourse is rooted in difference, or in the idea that in order for there to be justice, equal treatment for all women, or for all persons, is not enough. That is, in discussing their demands vis-à-vis SERNAM, or their relationship with other organized women, Mapuche women emphasized how their own struggles, interests, and demands are distinct.

Sociologists have long insisted that identity is socially constructed— the self is produced and maintained through interactions with others (Blumer 1986; Cooley 1902; Mead 1934). More recently, and drawing from postmodern and poststructuralist perspectives, feminist scholars have emphasized that identity is shifting and context-driven (Bordo 1993; Butler 1990). They stress that all forms of knowledge are "situated," contextualized by the social location of those who are producing them and the power relations that entails (Haraway 1988). Women of color and third world feminists in particular have contributed to this body of knowledge (Anzaldúa 1987; Collins 1991; Mohanty et al. 1991; Sandoval 2000; Spivak 1994). In their analyses of indigenous women's issues, Nelson (1999), Bacigalupo (2003a), and Stephen (2001) remind us of these fluid aspects of identity. Bacigalupo emphasizes that "identity and gender are . . . defined by individuals as they interact with local and global systems of meaning." Stephen suggests that especially in the context of social movements, identities are necessarily constructed in terms of internal sameness and difference with the external—rendering certain characteristics or ways of being as "other." Like all women, Mapuche women define themselves and their gender identities differently in distinct contexts. The "discourse of difference" discussed here is Mapuche women's gender discourse vis-à-vis the Chilean women's movement and SERNAM. This is not necessarily the same way they present themselves and their interests vis-à-vis Mapuche men. While extremely important, this second issue is somewhat peripheral to the subject of this chapter, and will be dealt with in only a limited manner.

In discussing difference, Mapuche women subverted and appropriated the discourse of equal rights and opportunities. By "subversion" I mean playing on the word "equal," which contains a sense of both "fairness" and "sameness." Mapuche women argued that they are not the same and that this is precisely the point: any equal opportunities plan or other government strategy that does not take account of their difference will not result in justice for the Mapuche people. By "appropriation," I mean adopting a discourse that calls for an expansion of the concept of equal opportunities to include the priorities of Mapuche women, who do not feel represented by SERNAM.

Difference was asserted by Mapuche women along three main lines, which reflect this subversion and appropriation. First, Mapuche women asserted that their central struggle is that of the Mapuche people as a whole. Even when they make gender-based claims, they insisted, their goal is to contribute to the wider struggle. Second, they contended that cultural differences mean that gender relations are not the same in Mapuche society as in dominant Chilean society. And third, they suggested that the discrimination experienced by Mapuche women is different from that experienced by other women, and often, is perpetrated by non-Mapuche women.

Gender issues are not usually the central focus of Mapuche women's activism. Mapuche women's struggle has primarily occurred in the context of the general Mapuche movement, and not as a separate, autonomous women's movement. As such, the central tenet of Mapuche women's gender discourse is what many of them refer to as *visión de pueblo*. For example, when asked how Mapuche women's gender discourse differed from that of non-Mapuche women, Mapuche activist Elisa Avendaño answered: "The principal difference is that we women struggle as a people, we have a visión de pueblo. We women assert as a people that we have to be recognized, we want autonomy, and we are not going to achieve autonomy as women, we are going to achieve it as a people" (in Calfio 1997, 105). This visión de pueblo was reflected in the written documents I collected from Mapuche women's organizations as well as in my own interviews. For example, when I asked

Mapuche women what their demands were as women, they usually first mentioned demands that were not specific to being women, but rather, related to recognition of their status as a people, including demands for land, intercultural education and health care, constitutional recognition, autonomy, and so on. Written records of Mapuche women's demands suggest a similar focus on the demands of the people as a whole. Several women referred to the Primer Encuentro de la Mujer Rural (First Meeting of Rural Women) held in Punta de Tralca in July 1986 as an example of an early instance in which they had issued demands specific to being Mapuche women. Both indigenous and non-indigenous women attended this meeting, and they recorded their demands in a document called *La demanda de la mujer rural*. The document contained demands for the return to democracy, and for guarantees for women's rights related to organization and participation, equal protection under the law, work and social security, land, health care, housing, education and training, leisure activities, and maternity and child protections. Indigenous women's demands, however, were listed separately in the document, and all were related to the general claims of the Mapuche movement, ranging from respecting indigenous people's autonomy and restoring Mapuche land rights, to various issues involving the preservation and development of Mapuche culture.

When Mapuche women do issue gender-specific demands, they are nearly always inflected by their indigenous identities. This is reflected in several ways. As suggested in the previous paragraph, Mapuche women's discussions of gender-related demands tend to be interspersed with the demands of the people (see Coordinadora de Mujeres de Organizaciones e Instituciones Mapuches 1995; Flores et al. 1995). In addition, when the women I interviewed spoke of gender differences or inequality, they made it very clear that their principal struggle, their reason for being organized, was to bring about justice for the people as a whole. Thus, women who advocated training and organizing women stressed that these activities were a support to the Mapuche struggle more generally. For example, while clarifying that her organization, Aukiñko Domo, did not wish to "separate" women from men, Carolina Manque noted that, "to the extent that the women can be on better footing, more valued, more recognized, it will be a benefit for women and for the (Mapuche) people. For a people that is oppressed and needs to rise up and needs to speak out—as a people." Isolde Reuque agreed, "There is an idea inside of me that is like that challenge to say, 'I am capable . . . and I want to support this challenge of the people, on the one hand, (and) of women, on the other, in what we want to arrive at:

the autonomy of the Mapuche people.'" Their activism as women, even when they are dealing explicitly with "women's issues," is ultimately linked to being Mapuche.

Finally, when Mapuche women make gender-related demands, they do so not just as women, but as *Mapuche* women with specific experiences that are different than those of non-Mapuche women. For instance, at the National Meeting of Indigenous Women in 1995, proposals included guaranteeing indigenous women's access to agricultural training and animal husbandry programs "in equality of conditions with men," protection for household workers in the cities, and the creation of an Indigenous Women's Department in SERNAM. Among the proposals submitted to then SERNAM Minister Adriana DelPiano by the Mapuche Women's Executive Secretariat in the Araucanía in 2000 were education completion programs, an "ethnocultural" educational focus that emphasizes equity between men and women, intercultural sexual education, family planning, and family violence programs, an intercultural mobile gynecological clinic, support for Mapuche women's leadership and participation, housing improvements, legal aid programs appropriate to the Mapuche worldview, and preferential access to land subsidies for Mapuche women heads of households (fieldnotes, November 3, 2000). In Santiago, proposals discussed in the Working Group with Urban Mapuche Women included creation of an "Indigenous Women's Center" with activities and programs for and by Mapuche women, creation of an Indigenous Women's Department staffed by Mapuche women within SERNAM, celebration of the International Day of the Indigenous Woman, spaces for indigenous women to display their crafts, and intercultural child care centers. Most of these proposals are gender-based but also specific to the concerns of Mapuche women. Because these were proposals conceptualized in terms of what SERNAM could actually do, many of them focus mostly on redistributive concerns. Nevertheless, like Mapuche demands more generally, they are related to recognition as well.

The second aspect of Mapuche women's discourse of difference is the argument that gender relations work differently among the Mapuche. This argument has three main facets—duality, complementarity, and transversality—all of which are rooted in the Mapuche worldview. Montecino (1995) explains that this worldview is based on a system of complementary opposing pairs: left-right, death-life, night-day, sickness-health, witch-machi, and so forth. One half of each pair makes no sense without the other, and, indeed, cannot exist without it. According to most western interpretations, women are associated with the negative pole in this system of opposing pairs. For the Mapuche, however, these representations have plasticity and capacity for reinterpretation, such that women can inhabit either pole (something that men cannot do) (ibid.).

Complementarity is reflected in the Mapuche deity Ngünechen, which is co-gendered and multigenerational. Ngünechen has four aspects: old woman, old man, young woman, and young man. Elisa Avendaño tells us that the men and the women always appear together, hand in hand. Bacigalupo (2003b) explains that machi represent complementarity in their practice, during which they cross genders and embody all four aspects of Ngünechen. In so doing, the machi "encompass all aspects of gender in fruitful complementarity, and . . . transcend gender, embody wholeness, and become divine."

The ideology of complementarity is also the basis for what were traditionally men's and women's roles in Mapuche communities: women responsible for the house, garden, small animal husbandry, and passing down culture, and men for larger-scale agriculture and the political sphere. The value placed on complementarity was revealed in the observations of some Mapuche women that the Chilean state's policies do not recognize the "transversal" or integrative character of Mapuche culture, and compartmentalize them (as women, youth, elderly, etc.). In their view, day-to-day activities and decision making in Mapuche culture are (in an ideal situation) much more integrative and oriented around equilibrium among all community members (young and old, male and female). They argued that complementary gender roles among the Mapuche do not necessarily signal inequalities between men and women.

Still, complementarity is by far the most diversely interpreted and contested aspect of Mapuche women's discourse, even among Mapuche women themselves. For some, it meant that all programs and policies coming out of a Chilean feminist perspective were suspect and inappropriate for Mapuche women. Interestingly, many of the women leaders in Santiago seemed to hold this view. These women were also less likely to organize exclusively as women or around women's issues per se. For instance, Margarita Cayupil, who was born and raised in Santiago and only recently became involved in the Mapuche movement, explained,

> To start, in our culture, the separation of work for just women doesn't exist. That doesn't exist. We have always said to SERNAM that we see women's work as a complement with men and the family, so having an

activity for just women unlinks or debilitates the nuclear family. . . . So the work that we do, we want to do it together with the family, taking into account the man as husband, and the children, not as a separated entity.

The Mapuche woman is complemented with her family, and the needs of the women are always going to be based on the family. One of the things is one always looks at the children, and one says, "I'm poor, I don't have resources, my child wants education," and one of women's needs could be more scholarships for the children to study. A need for health, too, but always the need of the woman . . . is intersected by all that is the nuclear family as a whole. So they are always going to be based on that.

Cayupil seemed to conceptualize complementarity in a way that went beyond the idea that women perform certain roles and men, others. Indeed, rather than focusing on specific and separate roles, she viewed complementarity in terms of another aspect of Mapuche worldview: the idea that decisions and activities are engaged in by the family as a whole. Some Mapuche cite this principle as a justification for demanding that the state institute policies and programs that incorporate the entire family. Cayupil herself argued that policies that focus exclusively on women, children, the aged, etc. represent an implicit threat to the survival of the Mapuche way of life (fieldnotes, August 9, 2001).

While it is certainly not only Mapuche women in Santiago who share Cayupil's views, these women were often much more insistent on a rigid conceptualization of complementarity and women's roles than were women in the Araucanía. This could be due in part to the closer relationship of some Mapuche women leaders in the Araucanía to some sectors of the Chilean women's movement. Conversely, that Mapuche women in the Araucanía have more access to "Mapuche" cultural resources, in the sense that there is a higher concentration of Mapuche in the region and it is ancestral Mapuche territory, may allow them to have a more flexible understanding of what it is to be Mapuche. Women who are trying to "be Mapuche" in Santiago (where they are much more of a minority) are more constantly at risk of being absorbed into the mass of Chilean women, and so are more rigorous in upholding complementarity as a standard by which they differentiate themselves. In addition, more of the women interviewed in the Araucanía had longer histories of participating in the movement, often in high profile positions, which may have led them to be less hesitant to confront biases and inequalities in the movement.[3]

Indeed, many of the women from the Araucanía were not so absolute in their interpretations of complementarity. They agreed that it was an important basis for gender relations among the Mapuche, but maintained that insofar as SERNAM's programs can be developed and delivered in a way that takes into consideration Mapuche worldview, they are important resources for Mapuche women. For example, Ana Llao argued in favor of taking advantage of available resources for women, and engaging in relevant national debates.

> The indigenous issue is not a vertical issue, but a horizontal one (that) crosses all issues, be it the women's issue, the economic issue. In other words, everything that has to do with the state, these are things that exist and I believe that we the Mapuche have to participate in this. We have to be always present in all those activities. And well, if it's necessary to talk about women, we have to talk about women. If it's necessary to talk about youth, we also talk about youth, and if it's necessary to talk about the aged . . .

Yet while she acknowledged the possibility that there is such a thing as the "subject of women," Llao was emphatic that ethno-cultural difference means that not all women can be treated the same. "It's not about arriving and applying policies for women without considering the particular cultural aspect."

For still others, complementarity was a resource to be used in fighting sexism in their daily lives. These women often suggested that sexism, or machismo, is a western phenomenon. When I asked her how the Coordinadora de Mujeres Mapuches came to talk about gender, Elisa Avendaño explained,

> For us the issue always was constitutional recognition of the Mapuche people. For us, women's work cannot be separated from men's work, because we (are) part of a people that self-differentiates from the wider society. When we differentiate (ourselves), we are trying to say that (in) our identity, our customs, (and those of) our brothers, machismo didn't exist. If we do an investigation into the past, machismo didn't exist. Machismo came into existence when (western) religion arrived and formal education arrived. That was when they told us, women's work over here, and men's work over there. And also in education, they told us, boys play with this kind of things and women do this other thing . . . and I think part of the Church always was preparing (a woman) to be a good mother, to be a good housewife, and not to be a good professional or a good leader or a good I don't know what, a woman who could do diverse things within the work world, within the social world, except that she was prepared to do certain things, *y eso se fue haciendo cultura*, over time this became culture within all society, be it Mapuche or Chilean.

Mapuche women who shared this perspective suggested that a return to a Mapuche past based on complementarity is a better alternative than SERNAM's approach to gender relations, which they interpreted as disparaging Mapuche traditions as well as Mapuche men, who have been their partners in resisting the oppression of the Chilean state and discrimination within Chilean society. Many also associated feminism with a desire for women to "surpass" men, which would mean a loss of the "balance" they perceived as an essential part of Mapuche worldview.

Many feminists are skeptical about these claims. They associate complementarity with a Parsonian functionalism that they have struggled to do away with. Furthermore, they do not believe what Mapuche women are saying, and suggest that complementarity as a basis for gender relations among Mapuche men and women is associated with the subordination of women. Zambrano (1987) has addressed this issue in her work. She argues that in the traditional Mapuche system, sex role segregation was not as rigid as in Ibero-American culture and men's roles were not valued above women's. However, she notes, Mapuche women have not achieved equal representation in decision-making positions, especially in national and regional organizations. Such organizations are more likely to have a political focus, whereas the local organizations led by women often tend to focus on material or cultural concerns. Interestingly, though, Mapuche women are more likely than their non-Mapuche counterparts to participate in all types of organizations (cultural and political organizations, community development groups, unions) and are also more likely than non-Mapuche women to achieve positions of authority in those organizations (SERNAM 1997). This type of leadership is evidenced by several of the women in this study, including Isolde Reuque and Elisa Avendaño, both of whom were vice presidents of Ad Mapu and Ana Llao, who was president of that organization. It is also evidenced by the Quintreman sisters who led the struggle against Ralco, and by Patricia Troncoso and Mireya Figueroa, two of the women who have been detained for their alleged participation in the Coordinadora Arauko Malleko.

Nevertheless, some Mapuche women themselves suggested that the ideal of complementary roles poses limitations for women. Isolde Reuque, for example, said that it may justify a lack of leadership opportunities for women outside of their communities, and that women who do achieve leadership roles in national-level organizations are often undervalued, not taken seriously, and left to assume menial tasks like secretarial work and serving tea. (Non-indigenous women who have participated in unions and political parties in the wider Chilean society have made similar complaints.)

Moreover, Mapuche women's discourse of complementarity (and of difference more generally) sometimes seemed like a form of "strategic essentialism." (Using Gayatri Spivak's term, I refer to the idea that they might have strategically presented themselves as different, with little to nothing in common with other women, in order to advance recognition of the Mapuche as a distinct people.) But whether or not what Mapuche women are saying is "true" and whether it is a form of "strategic essentialism" is beyond the scope of this chapter. As in any culture, there are instances of gender equality and gender inequality among the Mapuche. The important point here is that complementarity is a central aspect of how they distinguish themselves from Chilean women, and, more importantly, *of how they understand themselves.* To the extent that it is influenced by pressures from the Mapuche movement and the women's movement, their presentation of self in terms of difference may be partially a "strategic move." But reducing it to a response to those pressures would entail not taking Mapuche women on their word, a step that—ethically and methodologically—I am not prepared to take.

Outright rejection of the complementarity aspect of Mapuche women's discourse also ignores the "heterogeneity of their identifications" (Nelson 1999, 166–167) and reveals colonialist attitudes on the part of feminists. Nelson (ibid., 364) reflects on her own hesitations about analyzing gender politics among the Maya,

> I was trained as a feminist anthropologist to seek out these irritations and excitements, to aggressively listen for the way different voices sometimes break through, because they are a site of articulation where I can connect in transnational solidarity. I love it when the *mujer* speaks as a woman, saying what I want to hear. . . . But with the slight twist of gender in the first term, we are right back to Gayatri Spivak's original calculation of white women saving brown women from brown (and whiter) men and women.

I share Nelson's concerns, and while I think it is important to discuss gender issues among the Mapuche, I insist that Mapuche women's claims have to be taken seriously if advancement toward representing their interests is to be made. Bacigalupo (2003a) reminds us that first-world/colonialist feminist perspectives are often only marginally relevant to native women's experiences, and cautions that our constructions of gender and patriarchy are not universal. Following hooks

(1990), Mohanty (1991), and Spivak (1985), she criticizes first-world constructions as colonialist and ethnocentric and argues that "we need to attend to theories that start from the 'Margin' and see how they analyze and position themselves with regard to the 'Center'—and in turn look at how the presence of the Other creates the 'Center.'" Native women, she argues, must be given the opportunity to participate in theorizing about gender.

In fact, some Mapuche women have made interesting uses of complementarity to advance women's status. These women said that discrimination against women exists within Mapuche organizations and society, as it does in any society, and has resulted in problems for women such as an unfair burden in the household, fewer opportunities to take leadership positions, and domestic violence. Like Elisa Avendaño, they often attributed these problems to the influence that western patriarchal structure has had on the Mapuche. In this vein, Carolina Manque maintains that the infiltration of "machismo" among the Mapuche represents "the loss of values and the weakening of our roots and worldview" (1995, 17).

Rosa Rapiman, then director of the Casa de la Mujer Mapuche, explained that her organization works with men as well as women, partially because of the barriers men construct to prevent their wives from participating in activities outside of their homes and immediate communities,[4] and partially in order to reconstruct ancestral values based on equilibrium between women and men. She claimed that through a collaborative investigative process, men and women have gained in knowledge about traditional Mapuche views and the ways gender practices have changed through contact with western traditions. I asked Rapiman if feminism had a place in this kind of work.

> Well, feminism is a western concept, but I also think it means to work for women's rights. That is, in this case, not to think about surpassing the man, but just to work so that we are not inferior. So within this, I think that . . . for us and also the women we work with, we've worked so that the women value themselves, so they think that really, if they are married, they are partners, and that they shouldn't be the men's waitresses, but a partner. That is, to live in the equilibrium that is part of our worldview.

In Rapiman's discourse, complementarity and equilibrium were associated with equality between women and men. Again, it is important to note that not all Mapuche women share this perspective, and indeed, the Casa de la Mujer Mapuche was originally created by CEDEM, a Chilean feminist non-governmental organization. Nevertheless, some

Mapuche women have taken steps to work toward greater equality between women and men, from within their own cultural perspective. They simultaneously affirm their difference with Chilean women and work toward changing Mapuche women's status vis-à-vis Mapuche men.

The way Mapuche women frame demands for inclusion in spaces usually dominated by Mapuche men also reflects the ideals of equilibrium and complementarity. For instance, when Beatriz Painequeo was the urban indigenous representative to CONADI's council, she lobbied for greater inclusion of women: "I tried to put the issue of gender on the table—I couldn't make it happen—so that for once and for all, CONADI would also deal with it, because even though there are women who participate as leaders in different organizations, for me it is not enough, and it is not because I am a woman. I think we women are more consequential and insistent in what we do. When we propose something, we follow through on it until it is achieved." She clarified, though, that her intention was not to "feminize" CONADI: "That is like an extreme that doesn't benefit us. Within our culture, our people, there hasn't been that distancing or marginalization of men and women or a conflict between men and women. On the contrary, (the idea) is to work complementarily. But I think it is necessary to encourage women's participation, because it is not sufficiently equilibrated today." In sum, interpretations of complementarity are diverse, ranging from the idea that having different roles does not necessarily signal women's subordination, to the idea that complementarity implies an equal place for women in leadership and decision making. In any case, this is an important part of Mapuche women's gender discourse, both in terms of articulating difference vis-à-vis other women, and in terms of working toward change vis-à-vis Mapuche men.

The final aspect of Mapuche women's discourse of difference involves the assertion that Mapuche women experience forms of discrimination that are specific to being Mapuche *and* women. The women emphasized that the discrimination they suffer is different from that suffered by other women. They spoke of double, and often, triple discrimination: as women, as indigenous, and as the poor. And they insisted that many times, non-Mapuche women are the agents of that discrimination. There are numerous examples from my research. Several women claimed that Mapuche women are often not hired for jobs in which they would be attending the public (such as store clerks or bank tellers), because their physical features do not cohere with Chilean beauty standards, which value European physical characteristics. In addition, Mapuche women often receive substandard treatment in municipal offices and other public services. One anonymous leader from Cerro Navia said that she was often treated with suspicion, as if she were trying to get away with something rather than claiming the services that she rightfully deserved as a resident of her municipality. She also complained of being attended only after "whiter" women (interview, July 26, 2000; fieldnotes, December 13, 2000).

Finally, middle- and upper-class women employ Mapuche women as servants, exploiting their labor and sometimes resorting to ethnic slurs like "mapuchita," or "dirty Indian" to address them. When I asked her what she thought of feminism, Carolina Manque said it was a "legitimate current," but that "there has also been a certain discrimination, or a certain lack of preoccupation of many feminist movements as regards indigenous women." She told the story of her mother, who had been a servant in the Santiago home of a feminist who works in a women's non-governmental organization. "She was a feminist, but she treated my mother as 'shitty Indian.' She said that to her! And well, she would always say, 'you don't have rights, you have no rights.' . . . I said, 'This woman . . . is a feminist!?'" While surely all feminists do not share this woman's views, Manque's story vividly demonstrates that fighting against one form of injustice does not necessarily lead someone to develop a conscious position against all forms of injustice. That Mapuche women experience discrimination differently, and that they are often discriminated against by other women, indicates that all women's substantive experience of citizenship is not the same—they are not treated as "equals" of other women. This, along with the cultural differences and people-oriented goals summarized above, also implies that all women do not share the same interests.

By the first two aspects of their gender discourse—that their cause is that of the Mapuche as a whole and that gender roles work differently for them—Mapuche women argued that they are not the same as other women. By the third aspect—that they experience discrimination specific to being Mapuche women—they demonstrated that they are not treated as their "equals."

Contesting Assertions of Difference among Mapuche Women

The three aspects of Mapuche women's discourse emerged in some form in all of the interviews. However, individual women emphasized different aspects, and interpreted them in different ways. Many of the women mentioned that one of their most common debates with other Mapuche centered on the accusation that talking about women's issues would only create divisions within the movement as a whole. As almost all of the women I interviewed had some degree of interaction with SERNAM, none of them expressed the opinion that talking about women's issues was totally inappropriate. But the contested character of gender discourse among Mapuche women did emerge, as strongly evidenced by the above discussion of complementarity. In this section, I discuss three additional examples of how the "discourse of difference" is contested among Mapuche women themselves. All three examples demonstrate the importance of avoiding reifying or essentializing what it means to be a Mapuche woman.

The first example highlights differences between "rural" and "urban" Mapuche women. At a presentation of my preliminary results in Santiago in 2001, a young Mapuche woman who is part of the National Association of Rural and Indigenous Women, objected to my use of the expression "urban Mapuche" to define Mapuche who live in the city because, she said, "We are rural; we are not urban." A Mapuche social worker who was then working for ANAMURI likewise argued that the term was inappropriate because the urban/rural distinction had been imposed upon the Mapuche by force from the outside. She suggested that it was more appropriate to talk about "Mapuche in urban areas." These women's statements reflect the centrality of land, territory, and a specific way of life to many people's conceptualization of what it means to be Mapuche. Many feel that in the absence of a territorial basis for Mapuche identity, claims for recognition, autonomy, and self-determination will be weakened.

Nevertheless, their comments led to a rebuttal from Juana Huenufil, who said that as a Mapuche woman who was born and raised in Santiago, she had to disagree: urban Mapuche, in fact, do exist. She went on to say (implicitly critiquing the scholarly style in which the two women had commented on my presentation) that while it was fine for there to be Mapuche academics, it was important to consider the experience of the people at the grassroots, and that, in her experience as the leader of a small organization in La Pintana, urban Mapuche faced several concerns that were unique to living in the city. While in other ways her discourse had much in common with that of the other women, Huenufil's identity as a Mapuche woman was conditioned by her experiences as a Santiago resident and as a grassroots leader without university education. As Yuval-Davis (1997) cautions, it is necessary to avoid assuming that social groups are internally homogenous. Identity is not fixed, but rather, is shifting and context-driven. Moreover,

it is constantly produced, maintained, and reproduced through interactions with others (Nelson 1999). Thus, being "Mapuche" can mean
different things for different women in different contexts.

The second example involves the multiple meanings associated
with visión de pueblo, and centers on a *tragun* (in Mapudungun, a meeting with large attendance at which important issues are discussed) that
I was invited to attend in Santiago (fieldnotes, August 13, 2000). This
particular tragun brought together members of eleven organizations
from across Santiago in order to discuss the role of traditional Mapuche
authorities in urban Mapuche organizations. It was hosted by one of
the organizations, though a local non-governmental organization organized the event.

The tragun was an all-day event, and the afternoon was dedicated
to small group discussions on various themes, including the participation of women in Mapuche organizations. This discussion was attended
by about thirty women and one man, and was guided by a woman
leader of a Santiago organization. When one of the non-governmental
organization employees who had coordinated the event—a young
Mapuche social worker—stopped by to listen to the group's progress,
the conversation had turned to the influence of machismo within urban Mapuche organizations. The social worker looked alarmed, and cautioned the women that "machismo is a word that comes from feminism,"
adding, "in that sense, be careful girls, be careful because we don't have
anything to do (with feminism)." She then referred to Elisa Avendaño's
statement about autonomy: "Somebody said that we are not going to
achieve autonomy as women, we are going to achieve it as a people."
The social worker concluded that the point was not to talk about machismo, but "how we can make (men) legitimize us . . . in that we, the
women, are there already, administrating, organizing, demanding, making proposals." In this way, the social worker used Avendaño's statement to justify toning down women's claims that gender inequality was
a problem within their organizations, or at least to get them to express
it in less "feminist" language.

All of this was perplexing to me because I had also attended the
planning meeting for this event, where this social worker insisted that
the exclusion of women from positions of influence within Mapuche
organizations in Santiago had to be dealt with at the tragun. In several
personal conversations, as well, she had alleged that inequality was
prevalent within the organizations. However, she often qualified her
statements by reminding me that she was only Mapuche on her father's
side, and had grown up in Santiago—she felt this made her opinions

less authentically "Mapuche." Her cautions to the women thus appear to have been an effort to avoid contaminating what was intended to be a "Mapuche" discussion with what she considered to be western feminist thought. Ironically, several of the women went on to interpret Avendaño's statement in a way that the social worker hadn't intended. They said that yes, they are a people, and that this means equality between men and women. They added that if it is true that they are a people, and working together for the people, then it is necessary for men to open up more opportunities for women's participation. Thus, even what it means to be a people working together for autonomy was interpreted and framed in different ways by different women. For some, such as the social worker who was uncomfortable with the turn of the conversation, it was a way to tone down discussion of women's issues. For others, it was a way to call for greater participation and access to decision making for women.

The final example returns to the question of gender difference among the Mapuche. A few of the Mapuche women I interviewed (all of them from Santiago) suggested that because gender roles and norms in Mapuche culture were different than in dominant Chilean culture, issues like abandonment, domestic violence and divorce were not problems faced by Mapuche women. Margarita Calfio was a young Mapuche woman raised and educated in Santiago who, with her husband, made a political decision to move to Temuco because it is located in ancestral Mapuche territory. She worked as director of social planning at CONADI. While she agreed that it was possible that gender roles work differently for the Mapuche, Calfio expressed concern about what she considered to be a dangerous tendency to hide problems among the Mapuche.

> The other day I was talking with a Mapuche woman and we were talking about the issue of violence (against women), which worries me a lot. So I said to her, "But what can we do? We have to express this to the pertinent organisms," that we have to generate programs, what do I know. So she said to me, "No, we can't say that." "But why not?" "Because if we say that, the little help that we have is going to disappear." That is, it's like selling, to say, "Not in our Mapuche society, living in the countryside. In the community we have, like, harmonious relations, with reciprocity," all of the elements that they tell you about, that maybe in the genesis (was) like that, but today it's not that way, you see. And moreover, there is a conscious attempt to hide it, you know? And that is, like, dangerous. Very dangerous. For that reason I tell you that yes, there could be elements that differentiate (the Mapuche concept of gender from the Western one), but we haven't

bothered to analyze it and reflect deeply on it, more than just a discourse.

Calfio's comments suggest the negative impact that hegemonic gender discourses can have, within Mapuche culture as well as dominant Chilean society. She suggested that this Mapuche woman was reluctant to admit that violence is a problem in her community because she feared that the "support" they receive—presumably from a non-governmental organization or state agency—would be taken away if the Mapuche were shown to be less than idyllic. As noted above, Mapuche women also face opposing pressures from women's organizations and SERNAM to admit that machismo exists among the Mapuche. If they say it exists, they are presented—by SERNAM/the women's movement as well as by Mapuche men—as part of something that is against Mapuche men, and ultimately, against the cause they hold dear. It is as if indigenous peoples are not allowed to be complete, with their own problems and contradictions: if indigenous women admit problems, they are constructed internally and externally as somehow "less" indigenous (the women's movement says, "You're one of us!" and indigenous men say, "You're betraying our cause").[5] Calfio draws attention to the possibility that in the absence of autonomous spaces for the expression and development of Mapuche culture, women's issues are essentialized from the outside, and what it means to be Mapuche is also sometimes essentialized from within.

Mapuche women's gender identities (like those of all women) are heterogeneous and change depending on the context. As members of a subjugated people within Chile, their identities as Mapuche are often most salient. In other instances, they emphasize their roles as women within Mapuche society, or the specific experiences of being Mapuche women within Chilean society. Mapuche women's gender discourse indicates, however, that for them, being woman is always contextualized by being Mapuche. Indeed, even as they make gender-related demands, their focus is on the way that being Mapuche makes their experiences and concerns as women different from those of non-indigenous women. Mapuche women present themselves, and more importantly, understand themselves, as different from other women. Their presentation of self in terms of difference is influenced by pressures from the inside (the Mapuche movement) and the outside (the women's movement and SERNAM), but cannot be reduced to a product of those pressures. And as shall be seen in the following section, just as the Mapuche people's right to be a different and autonomous people is not recognized by the

Chilean state, Mapuche women's difference as women is seldom recognized or taken seriously within SERNAM's discourses and practices around women's rights.

THE CONTESTED REPRESENTATION OF MAPUCHE WOMEN

Beginning in October 2000, the Santiago non-governmental organization Cedesco ran a Saturday Leadership School for Women and Men Mapuche Leaders, which was funded by SERNAM's Civil Society Fund. As the pivotal event of the thirteen-session school, Carmen Melillan, coordinator of the project, organized a meeting between Mapuche women leaders and officials from several Municipal Women's Offices and SERNAM's Santiago office. Invitations were sent out a couple of weeks in advance. In their classes, the leaders had studied and critiqued the Indigenous Law, the Equal Opportunities Plan, and laws and programs established to benefit women. They held a special meeting a couple of days before the event in order to prepare a list of grievances, demands, and proposals to present to the officials. At this meeting, a woman who worked with another non-governmental organization and collaborated in the school suggested to the women that they present the list in Mapudungun. Juana Kolihuinka, the mild-mannered leader of Ko Kiyen, a local-level Mapuche women's organization in La Pintana, was elected to present the list. The day before the event, Cedesco employees called to confirm the attendance of the invited officials, but were told that no one from SERNAM would be able to make it. In the end, one SERNAM official attended the event. When she introduced herself, she said she could only stay for a few minutes, but that the issue was very important to her, and she wanted to at least stop by to greet the women. Before she had a chance to leave, Kolihuinka read the list of demands and grievances. The femocrat was understandably flustered, and at one point leaned over to Melillan, saying that someone was going to have to translate for her. When she concluded reading the list, Kolihuinka said, "I know that you didn't understand me, but it's not my fault that you don't understand me. . . . Probably it's all of your fault (for not making the effort to learn)." The official responded by saying that in order to work together, SERNAM and Mapuche women have to be able to understand each other. Kolihuinka countered that this was precisely the point (fieldnotes, December 16, 2000).

For the SERNAM official, at that moment, language was the principal obstacle to understanding. But for Mapuche women leaders, many of whom do not even speak Mapudungun, "not understanding" has to do with much more: the historical cause of their people, cultural differences, and experiences of ethnic and racial discrimination. Mapuche women are not the same as other women, is what Kolihuinka and the others present were saying. By reading the demands in Mapudungun, Kolihuinka emphasized Mapuche women's difference, and called for a response that would cease to allow non-indigenous women to be seen as the norm, thus moving the lived experience and worldviews of Mapuche and other indigenous women from the margins to the center. What has happened with all the demands and proposals made by Mapuche women based on this discourse of difference? In this section of the chapter I discuss four efforts of Mapuche women to have their interests represented by SERNAM. The first one illustrates the near complete absence of indigenous issues in SERNAM's early discourse. The following three highlight the additive approach to ethnicity that prevailed in SERNAM's later discourse. I go on to suggest two explanations for why these interactions have, from the standpoint of Mapuche women, been unsuccessful.

The Mesa Rural: Proposals without a Plan

In accordance with the mandate of the Indigenous Law, SERNAM established formal agreements (convenios) with CONADI at the national level and in the Araucanía in the mid-1990s.[6] Until the creation of the second Equal Opportunities Plan, however, efforts to represent indigenous women's interests within SERNAM were scarce, and rarely went beyond the inclusion of images of Mapuche women on SERNAM posters and pamphlets. Indeed, rural and indigenous women were not even mentioned in the first Equal Opportunities Plan. In response to this, groups representing these women petitioned SERNAM to form a committee in 1995—called the Mesa Rural—to create an "Equal Opportunities Plan for Rural Women." The Servicio Nacional de la Mujer agreed, but the resulting document (1997) was published not as a plan, but as "Proposals for Equal Opportunity Policies for Rural Women." And unlike the Equal Opportunities Plan, these proposals were not adopted as part of the presidential platform. Additionally, the specific issues faced by urban indigenous women (more than half the indigenous women in the country) were not addressed in either document. Furthermore, the Mesa Rural was effectively disbanded after the proposals were written, and was only reestablished in 2000.

Nevertheless, as a result of rural and indigenous women's complaints after their exclusion from the first plan, some changes took place, and SERNAM made some efforts to respond to Mapuche women's demands. Since 1999 in the Metropolitan Region as well as in the Araucanía, for instance, Mapuche organizations have had access to small grants for projects related to equal opportunities for women through an indigenous component in the Fondo de Sociedad Civil (Civil Society Fund), which was designed by SERNAM and is composed of funds from SERNAM, CONADI, PRODEMU, and FOSIS.[7] The Servicio Nacional de la Mujer also opened up to dialogue in some cases, and some Mapuche women expressed hope that this new "openness" would result in policies and programs more appropriate for Mapuche women. As the following cases demonstrate, however, SERNAM adopted an additive approach to "ethnicity," viewing it as one more impediment, rather than as a principal source of identity—as well as a means of distribution of power and domination in Chilean society—that creates differences in the perspectives of women and in their access to resources and decision making.

From Plan One to Plan Two: The Additive Non-Solution

In response to the criticisms of rural and indigenous women as well as pobladoras, SERNAM invited groups of women representing diverse sectors of society to participate in evaluating the first Equal Opportunities Plan prior to the creation of the second. Mapuche women in Santiago as well as in the Araucanía participated in these evaluations, and particularly in the Araucanía, contributed very specific proposals to the process. But as Erika López, former director of SERNAM in the Araucanía, pointed out, the second plan is made up of general objectives and lines of action, and as a result, few of these proposals actually appear in the plan. The women were left to protest that their time and efforts had been wasted.

According to various accounts, the Santiago evaluation process was particularly tense. It was a two-month, multistage process in which groups of women representing different sectors of society generated evaluations and proposals. They were brought together at the end to approve a final document that would be sent to the national level. The Mapuche women who participated protested that many had not even known the plan existed before they were invited to evaluate it. According to Margarita Cayupil, leader of Trawun Mapu in Santiago, the women also felt SERNAM was coming at them with pre-generated proposals for approval. In response, they decided they would submit proposals, but without the facilitation of SERNAM. Despite this, according to an anonymous SERNAM official, a couple of the Mapuche women

interrupted the final event, saying they were not represented in the proposals. She complained that the Mapuche women were organizationally immature, and commented, "Include them or don't include them,
they'll attack me all the same" (fieldnotes, March 27, 2000). Clearly,
both parties involved in this process displayed frustration and misgivings. The SERNAM official seemed to have expected that Mapuche
women would have been happy with being "included," but several
Mapuche women suggested that being stuck in the "same sack" as other
women is not the kind of inclusion they were looking for.

This interaction between Mapuche women and SERNAM officials
in Santiago hints at a central problem in the way SERNAM deals with
indigenous women today. Having shifted away from completely ignoring them, SERNAM now views them additively. According to Patricia
Hill Collins (1991, 222), additive approaches to oppression involve
"starting with gender and then adding in other variables such as age,
sexual orientation, race, social class, and religion." Such an approach
was clearly influential in the creation of the second Equal Opportunities Plan. Plan 2 is somewhat more promising than the first plan;
ethnicity or indigenous women are mentioned in fifteen of 147 total
lines of action (fourteen of thirty-one total objectives). Nevertheless,
indigenous women are presented almost exclusively in terms of being
an *especially* "marginal" or "vulnerable" group. Lines of Action that stem
from an additive approach include: "broadening and improving
women's access to legal services, especially women in disadvantageous
social, economic, ethnic and cultural, and geographic situations," and
"facilitating the opportunities for women, including the ethnic groups,
to participate in decision making related to the environment, which
influence their quality of life." Being indigenous is merely conceptualized as an additional barrier that makes access to resources and services
even more difficult for some women.

The alternative to the additive approach advocateᵤ by Collins
(1991, 222) "sees these distinctive systems of oppression as being part
of one overarching structure of domination." This entails "assuming
that each system needs the other in order to function," and brings attention to the ways that women's interests differ depending on their
place in this matrix of domination. Were SERNAM to enact policies
based on this conceptualization, several changes would take place.
Mapuche women would be involved with determining how gender interests and priorities are defined from the start. Moreover, SERNAM
would create lines of action that started from the Mapuche women's
perspective, rather than adding them into already existing plans.

Whether inclusion in SERNAM's written discourse would give Mapuche women more of an anchor from which to make claims on SERNAM remained to be seen when my research ended. But since SERNAM continued to ignore (or not understand) the centrality of indigenous identity to Mapuche women's gender identities, and to overlook the historical use of ethnic differences to maintain social divisions and hierarchies that result in inequalities among women, it seemed likely that Mapuche women would continue to be marginalized within SERNAM's vision of women's rights and interests.

Working Group with Urban Mapuche Women: The Problem with Diversity

In Santiago, Mapuche women from the Commission of Urban Indigenous Peoples (a network created in response to President Lagos's creation of Working Group for Indigenous Peoples) requested that the national office of SERNAM create a Working Group with Urban Mapuche Women. SERNAM agreed, and four meetings were held, starting on May 24, 2000.

Internal SERNAM documents on the Working Group demonstrate an inconsistent understanding of the importance of improving their representation of Mapuche women. In a document entitled *Minuta: Mujeres indígenas urbanas,* SERNAM acknowledges that it has a mandate to "eradicate all forms of discrimination." It also notes the state's recognition that "true democracy is only possible to the extent that each group and person feels part and represented by the diverse public policies that the state incorporates into its management." The document sets short-, medium-, and long-term challenges for SERNAM's work with Mapuche women, which include: "Incorporating them as a group of beneficiaries in the corresponding regions; visualizing them within the management and services that the programs offer to the community at the regional level." This second challenge seems to be getting at what is necessary: that SERNAM consistently consider the priorities and perspectives of Mapuche women. Nevertheless, the document then mentions a presidential mandate that all sectors of the government "design a programmatic agenda that integrates the wisdom and knowledge unique to the ancestral cultures." The mandate is presented as a positive step for SERNAM and other state agencies, but by focusing on integration and implying that indigenous peoples are the *past* of what is now Chile, it indicates the limits of "true democracy," as presently conceived and de-emphasizes the rights that recognizing indigenous peoples' status might entail.

The most visible result of this Working Group over the course of my fieldwork was the celebration of the International Day of the Indigenous Woman in Santiago on September 5, 2000. This was considered an important achievement by many of the women who participated. At the event, Adriana DelPiano spoke candidly of the difficulties SERNAM faces in confronting the issues of Mapuche women, and admitted that trying to understand where their concerns overlap with those of other women and in what ways they are different is a major challenge for SERNAM. Yet her speech revealed many of the problems with official state discourse vis-à-vis indigenous peoples. She repeated several times that the dialogues occurring between the Mapuche movement and the state were a question of how Chile could incorporate the "indigenous richness" that exists within the country. In the end, this was another example of folklorizing rhetoric. Rather than framing Mapuche women's demands in terms of recognition, DelPiano framed them in terms of diversity. Mapuche women's status as subjects with rights that may sometimes conflict with those of other women was downplayed.

Many Mapuche women would agree with DelPiano that recognizing diversity is a real need in Chile. Social work professor Hilda Llanquinao, for example, talked about her desire for non-indigenous Chileans to realize "that the other, even though they don't speak your language . . . even though they don't dress the same, they have feelings, they're a person." The problem is that official Chilean discourse focuses intently on diversity as a reason for creating reforms while de-emphasizing historical demands and Mapuche status as a people. Isolde Reuque talked about this problem in the context of the first three or four years after the national level SERNAM-CONADI convenio was signed.

> I think they took some time to learn about the people that were within (the country), what their specificity was, what was distinct, how they look, ah? Or to realize that yes, indigenous people existed. Before, they took it like "all the same," "we're all Chileans," but the indigenous part comes out later, and it comes out as a beautiful thing, something new that they are discovering. And "how exciting" and "how beautiful" with the new things they discover . . . (but it's) a vision of exotic things and not of an indigenous reality.

Reuque herself linked diversity to more fundamental recognition-based claims, and maintained that recognizing diversity involves acknowledging "the specificity of a pueblo with values, with its own internal debates," but also ideally it would in the long run entail self-managed economy, territory, autonomy, and respect for intellectual property.

At the celebration, DelPiano also said that Chile would be a differ-ent country if it acknowledged its mestizo identity as do many other Latin American countries. Acknowledging mestizaje, she suggested, makes us recognize a shared identity. The issue of mestizaje is *just as important* as that of indigenous peoples, and she would like to see CONADI address it. DelPiano accurately identified a problem: the wide-spread belief among Chileans that theirs is a racially homogenous so-ciety of European origin, and an almost universal denial of mestizaje among Chilean individuals (Aylwin 1998). But as noted in chapters 1 and 5, mestizaje discourses have been used in many countries through-out Latin America to deny the right to difference asserted by indigenous peoples. Mallon (1996, 171–172) identifies two strands of mestizaje dis-course. The first is "a liberating force that breaks open colonial and neo-colonial categories of ethnicity and race" and "rejects the need to belong as defined by those in power." The other is "an official discourse of na-tion formation, a new claim to authenticity that denies colonial forms of racial/ethnic hierarchy and oppression" by constructing and incor-porating indigenous peoples as "citizens." Mallon goes on to say that "as a discourse of social control, official mestizaje is constructed im-plicitly against a peripheral, marginalized, dehumanized Indian 'Other' who is often 'disappeared' in the process."

Official appeals to a shared mestizo identity such as DelPiano's im-plicitly (if not intentionally) undermine claims for status as a people. If everyone—Mapuche and Chilean alike—is mestizo, there is no need for the Mapuche to have differentiated cultural rights. The association of official mestizaje discourses with the forced disappearance of indig-enous cultures was a source of conflict at this event. Distrust of mestizaje, integration, and diversity discourses became especially clear when DelPiano suggested that indigenous women be incorporated as a cen-tral theme at the next International Women's Day celebration on the following 8th of March. Several Mapuche men and women objected that indigenous women need their own day because they are different and have often been discriminated against by non-indigenous women. One woman pointed out that maintaining the International Day of the In-digenous Woman and International Women's Day separate was impor-tant because many Mapuche beliefs and traditions have been subsumed and distorted by contact with non-Mapuches over time, as was the case with We Tripantu (Mapuche New Year, celebrated near the southern hemisphere's winter solstice in late June), which like many similar in-digenous celebrations throughout the region, was subsumed and reframed as the Roman Catholic holy day of Saint John. The woman explained that the Mapuche had to struggle to recover their traditional We Tripantu practices, and to legitimate it as a valid celebration. Thus, what seemed like appreciation of diversity to DelPiano was interpreted by several Mapuche individuals who heard her speech as an attempt to incorporate them and in effect, to make them disappear.

Clearly, Mapuche women's activism has led SERNAM to consider diversity. But diversity alone is not sufficient to address Mapuche women's claims for cultural rights. Ultimately, focusing on diversity complements SERNAM's additive approach. Whereas recognizing Mapuche women as members of a different people would entail significant structural changes in the ways priorities are established and decisions are made, a discourse of diversity permits SERNAM to continue conceiving of them as members of a greater whole ("women"), who simply need to be integrated.

Mapuche Women's Executive Secretariat: Selling Programs to the Mapuche

In practice, the additive approach is also evident in the extension of already-existing programs toward Mapuche women, instead of the development of new programs or policies that start from their perspective. An example of this occurred when proposals were submitted by the Mapuche Women's Executive Secretariat to DelPiano in a formal ceremony held in the Araucanía in November 2000.

The Servicio Nacional de la Mujer's regional office in the Araucanía displayed increasing willingness to work with Mapuche women. For instance, a regional document acknowledged the "lack of equality policies for Mapuche women that are based on real needs and expectations" (Matte 1999), and in my interviews with Erika López, then director of the regional office, she recognized that measures to address the needs of Mapuche women in the region were long overdue. She added, though, that regional offices are severely limited in the extent to which they can make their programs cater to regional needs. Programmatic as well as budgetary decisions are made at the national level, characteristic of the still highly centralized Chilean state.

Despite these limitations, under López's supervision SERNAM-IX took some steps toward addressing Mapuche women's demands. In 2000, Karin Treulen, a Mapuche advisor, was hired. She was responsible for organizing the "Mapuche Women's Executive Secretariat," a group of academics, non-governmental organization workers, government bureaucrats, and members of Mapuche women's organizations. The objective of the Secretariat was to create a list of proposals that would be integrated into the regional development plan as well as to form the basis for a Regional Equal Opportunities Plan for Mapuche Women. The proposal-developing process was very participative, integrating the four groups involved.

DelPiano's immediate response at the ceremony during which she was presented with the proposals was disappointing. Her major policy announcement was the creation of two intra-family violence centers for the Araucanía, one of which would be easily accessible to Mapuche women. The point is not that these centers were unwanted or unnecessary, but that rather than giving serious consideration to the proposals submitted by Mapuche women, DelPiano merely announced that Mapuche women would be assured access to the centers whose creation had been decided in a different context. Servicio Nacional de la Mujer officials often explained that it is difficult to incorporate women's proposals because annual budgets are determined approximately one year in advance. This argument holds little water, however, when it is used year after year and no changes are put into effect. Moreover, Mapuche women sometimes interpreted the extension of already-existing programs to them as an attempt to impose discourses and priorities that do not reflect reality or their own priorities. Once again, Mapuche women were simply "added-in" to SERNAM's pre-established understanding of what equal opportunities for women means.

Still, in the Araucanía, SERNAM began to respond to Mapuche women's demands by initiating this process, and this should not be overlooked. The willingness of López and Treulen to try to address Mapuche priorities—which was virtually non-existent in the Metropolitan Region and was inconsistent at the national level—demonstrates that the state is not a monolithic actor. Mapuche women are more likely to have their demands addressed when sympathetic actors exist within the state, although this is limited by centralized decision making and budgetary constraints.

In 2001 SERNAM backed up their verbal commitment to Mapuche women in the Araucanía by signing a national-level agreement with CONADI that designated 50 million pesos for agricultural development, intercultural health care and intra-family violence prevention, and leadership training, among other initiatives ("SERNAM y CONADI" 2001). While this effort was a significant gesture toward change in the relationship between SERNAM and Mapuche women, 50 million pesos, or less than 10 dollars per intended beneficiary, indicates both the severely limited budgets of SERNAM and CONADI, and the lack of priority conferred to Mapuche women by the state in general. In January 2002, however (after my fieldwork ended), a Mapuche woman, Rosa Rapiman of the Casa de la Mujer Mapuche, was designated regional director of SERNAM. Whether she would be able to implement programs and policies from a perspective more in line with Mapuche women's priorities remained to be seen, though her tenure ended in May 2003, before she could conceivably put substantial changes into effect.

When taken together, these four cases show that while SERNAM had recently begun to recognize the need to address Mapuche women's priorities, its main strategy was an additive approach that failed to acknowledge Mapuche women's assertions of cultural difference. Issues such as the ways some women are implicated in the discrimination suffered by others, possible cultural differences in gender relations, and the need for intercultural programs, were still not on SERNAM's agenda.

THE ROOTS OF THE PROBLEM: POWER DIFFERENCES AND STATE CONTEXT

Why has achieving the representation of Mapuche women's interests in SERNAM been so difficult? I suggest that there are two reasons. First, Mapuche women do not have access to the limited power made available to women within the Chilean state. And second, insofar as they conflict with state socioeconomic and ideological goals, many of the specific demands of Mapuche women, like those of the Mapuche movement more generally, remain unaddressed.

The scenarios presented above demonstrate that all women do not share equally in determining SERNAM's agenda for the woman citizen. The problem is not just that women don't have access to power structures and decision making, it is that even among women, access is differentiated. The Servicio Nacional de la Mujer's discourse of women's citizenship is based on a universalistic conceptualization of equality, in which being indigenous is not considered to be a central part of some women's identity or a characteristic that influences how power is distributed in Chile. The social locations (educated, non-poor, non-indigenous) of the women who work at SERNAM have given them access to more powerful positions. Mapuche women, on the other hand, do not have access to influence how central concepts like "women," "women's interests," and "equality" are defined. Much as Zinn and Dill (2000) suggest is the case for women of color in the United States, women and their interests are defined by SERNAM in such a way as to normalize and centralize the experience of women with higher education, who are not poor, or indigenous. In the process, the experiences of Mapuche women are marginalized and constructed as "outside" the experiences of "the Chilean woman citizen." Of course, many Mapuche women in this study also constructed themselves as "other than" the Chilean woman citizen, seeking to have their priorities addressed on this basis. This proved difficult because SERNAM's model tended to reduce Mapuche women's assertions of difference to something that could be added on to what SERNAM assumed were the core experiences of all women.

My interviews and conversations with women who work in SERNAM reflected institutional and personal ambivalence about dealing with the concerns of indigenous women. Many mentioned that the "willingness" to incorporate the priorities of Mapuche women existed. But this willingness did not easily translate into action. Apart from the limits imposed by being a state institution, there was a lot of fear and hesitation involved. And in some cases, the "willingness" that people told me about was hard to detect. For example, in one of my attempts to find out what had happened to the Working Group with Urban Mapuche Women, which had been started by the National Office of SERNAM, it was explained to me that the responsibility had been transferred to the Metropolitan Region Office. I commented that this was perplexing, because I had recently been told by someone at the regional office that no program for Mapuche women existed. The answer I received was, "What can I tell you? No one wants to touch the issue" (fieldnotes, November 13, 2000).

Some women in SERNAM were reflective about the lack of efforts to adequately represent Mapuche women. Valeria Ambrosio, head of programs in the National Office of SERNAM and former director of SERNAM-RM gave her perspective on why SERNAM hasn't tried to address Mapuche women's demands and said,

> The truth is that the institution as such, never had the resources and never has made a major effort for indigenous women, because it was supposed that CONADI was the institution that had to make that effort, and what we have to do is incorporate a gendered perspective within (CONADI). But the work with CONADI has not been easy. . . . The indigenous women are not interested either, because for them the recovery-oriented racial struggle becomes much more important than the gender struggle, you understand. Lastly, the issue of poverty becomes much more relevant. So it is not easy. On the other hand they have a very militant attitude (*una actitud muy reivindicativa*) with a lot of permanent battle against the state or against whomever, so this doesn't make dialogue easy. But apart from this, lastly, there is a historical experience that one can understand, and this is part of their story. As an institution, we should open up to the issue of the

indigenous woman. And I hope that with this new administration we have the opportunity to do so. At least there is the intention, the willingness.

Ambrosio's reflections reveal the obstacles perceived by women in SERNAM when it comes to "opening up" to Mapuche women. In her view, lack of resources, lack of clarity in their relationship with CONADI, Mapuche women's apparent lack of interest, the ways that poverty compounds their problems, and Mapuche militancy all combine to make reaching out to Mapuche women a challenge that SERNAM has generally avoided confronting. At the same time, her statements reflect the dominant position that in order to be served, Mapuche women must fit themselves into the gender priorities predetermined by non-indigenous femocrats.

Ambrosio's reference to CONADI as the responsible agency points to another difficulty. Often in conversations with women at SERNAM, I got the impression that they saw their duty toward indigenous women in terms of assuring that CONADI incorporated a gender perspective, but not in terms of SERNAM itself assuming the responsibility to assure that the policies it advocated were free of bias against indigenous women. As noted above, SERNAM and CONADI have signed agreements to work together in pursuance of policies to benefit indigenous women. Very little has come out of these agreements, however, other than a short series of workshops for Mapuche women in the Araucanía. Moreover, according to several CONADI employees, CONADI had no specific policies directed at women, and little reflection had been made as to what role CONADI should take vis-à-vis women (fieldnotes, April 17, 2000 and December 6, 2000). A former CONADI employee in Santiago further explained that sensibility about gender at CONADI did not go any further than saying, "It would be good to know more about this," just as in SERNAM, sensibility about indigenous issues does not go far beyond a general interest or willingness (fieldnotes, August 9, 2001).[8] Others in CONADI expressed ambivalence about whether it was appropriate to deal with gender at all; they questioned whether the concept could be reconciled with Mapuche values like complementarity and transversality. This situation is further complicated by the fact that like SERNAM, CONADI does not have the power to fund or implement its own programs in other than pilot form. As a result of institutional limitations as well as a lack of serious reflection about Mapuche women on the part of both agencies, Mapuche women found little support in either.

The construction of Mapuche women as "outside" SERNAM's sphere of responsibility contributed to the additive approach to addressing Mapuche women's demands. It cohered, as well, with SERNAM's redistributive focus to equality. The Servicio Nacional de la Mujer tried to fit Mapuche women into a discourse of equality that did not recognize their priorities or identities. Some women in SERNAM appeared to have struggled with this issue, but of course saw it from a western perspective of what it means to work in favor of women's interests. Erika López, for instance, explained that she felt establishing adequate programs or policies for Mapuche women was complicated, because although Mapuche women issued demands, they often questioned the very concept of gender on which SERNAM's work is supposedly based: "They criticize that western concepts are incorporated and are imposed upon an indigenous culture. . . . That is, (they say), 'The issue of gender, this has been an issue of the greater society that has interrupted and many times has come to divide us.' So with that argument, how do you define a public policy for Mapuche women?" López recognized that to a great extent, Mapuche women were coming from a different perspective on how gender roles operate, and she talked about the difficulties that might be encountered, were an attempt made to implement policies from the perspective of two worldviews that sometimes contradict one another. She expressed ambivalence about undertaking such a measure, questioning whether it was possible to create programs from Mapuche women's perspective of difference that would fit within SERNAM's mission of promoting a gender perspective in state programs and policies. She also questioned whether it was appropriate to deliver policies from a (western) gender perspective to Mapuche women who didn't necessarily share that perspective. Altogether, her reflections point to the difficulty of recognizing "difference" within social policies, particularly in the context of a highly centralized state.

Some femocrats suggested that talking about power differences among women takes attention away from the struggles of women more generally. (Some feminists in the United States make this argument about postmodernism.) In her comments after a presentation of my work in Temuco, López said that she considered my paper to be an accurate portrayal of the current situation, and agreed that SERNAM had not adequately represented Mapuche women's concerns. She added, though, that she felt it was necessary to recognize that the state also has not met its commitments to women in general, and the fact that SERNAM does not have the power to fund or implement its own programs and has to turn to other ministries for financial backing and to carry out programs puts major limits on what SERNAM can do. López concluded that women in general are not viewed by the state as subjects of rights (fieldnotes, August 1, 2001). López's comments make sense from the perspective of a middle-class, non-indigenous woman. But they also elide Mapuche women's assertion that they do not feel (and to some extent, do not consider themselves) part of the wider group of women to which López referred.

Even if SERNAM more fully opened itself up to representing Mapuche women's priorities, it is hard to say what the corresponding programs and policies would look like. Mapuche women who worked in the state had a unique perspective on this issue. They acknowledged that SERNAM and the state's responses have been inadequate, but they found it difficult to come up with the answers from a policy perspective. An anonymous woman who worked at CONADI explained that the differences between Mapuche women and women in SERNAM are partially due to differing priorities. She said, "Today indigenous peoples are concerned with other issues, and not the role of men or women within indigenous worldviews." But when asked what she thought of how SERNAM has dealt with indigenous issues, she commented,

> I am not particularly convinced. I think the issue of equal opportunities has to do with the recognition of differences between distinct peoples, first of all. Recognition and the acceptance of the differences between different peoples. There has to be acceptance. And also the differences between men and women from different peoples and between men and women of the same people, too. . . . The truth is I am not satisfied with [their] work. . . . How they have dealt with the problems or indigenous issues really [treats them like] folklore, and is very reduced to the issue of poverty. It doesn't satisfy me, let's say, but nor do I have an alternative. I don't have the answer to this, I don't know how to deal with it.

A more adequate approach might entail centering the indigenous/non-indigenous dynamic as one of the principal matrices of power and domination in society in SERNAM's policy, programs, and discourse, much as feminist movements have insisted on centering gender. But still, what would policies specific to Mapuche women—that do not reduce their issues to poverty and vulnerability—actually look like? *Which* problems faced by non-Mapuche women are not faced by Mapuche women, or are confronted in a different way? And what effects do the cultural differences that make "being a woman" different for Mapuche women actually have in the daily experiences? Margarita Calfio, the young Mapuche director of social planning at CONADI, expressed concern about how to go beyond simply saying, "We are not represented and our worldview is different," to actually operationalizing those differences. When I asked her what she thought of the criticism that SERNAM tries to impose a western concept of gender that does not fit with Mapuche worldview, she said,

> I think that could be true, but give me the elements that make me differentiate western policy from the gender policy that Mapuche women should have. I have asked that hundreds of times, because there are women who say, "But this can't be! They don't consider us, they don't consider our worldview." And then I say, "What do you do differently? Give me concrete elements. Okay, the worldview, but that is a concept that doesn't say much to me, it is very broad. It's your vision of the world . . . . but tell me what it is that differentiates the issue of gender for the Mapuche or indigenous people from what it is not." And I think that we haven't been capable of elaborating something solid, theoretical, to say, "Yes, this is what we want, the contents of (the programs and policies)." . . . I don't think that has happened yet, there is not a reflexive process, and that is needed.

At this point, Calfio went on to make her comments, cited above, about how a lack of reflection on the issues faced by Mapuche women can sometimes result in dangerous situations, such as the denial of domestic violence. The problem is thus how to create an environment in which the unique views of Mapuche women are respected enough so that they can engage in the reflexive process Calfio described without feeling subsumed by SERNAM and the western conceptualization of gender.

Beyond power differences among women, there is a second reason that SERNAM has been so unsuccessful in representing Mapuche women's priorities. This is related to the broader economic and ideological goals of the state. Insofar as they conflict with these goals, many of the specific demands of Mapuche women, like those of the Mapuche movement more generally, remain unaddressed. The Servicio Nacional de la Mujer's discourse and actions can only be understood in the context of the larger state. As in the rest of the state, when Mapuche women's demands were incorporated into SERNAM's agenda, it was not historical injustice or cultural difference that SERNAM recognized. Rather, as noted above, policies directed at indigenous women were linked to poverty alleviation and "vulnerability," and at integrating them into a wider group of women by appreciating their "diversity." So DelPiano's focus on diversity and SERNAM's additive approach make sense, not just because Mapuche women's demands represent a challenge to how they perceive women's rights and interests, but because Mapuche demands more generally are perceived as a similar threat to the integrity of the Chilean nation.

But just saying that SERNAM, like the rest of the state, does not recognize Mapuche women's difference does not capture the whole problem. At the presentation of my work in Temuco, Isolde Reuque commented that researchers have a tendency to want to put everything into neat categories, but what Mapuche women want is participation as a people as a whole, and not to be compartmentalized into different social segments. Arguably, several of the Mapuche women I interviewed would suggest otherwise, that dealing with indigenous women's issues *should* be a priority of SERNAM. The tension between seeking recognition as a people and dealing with their specificities as women is present in the discourse of almost all of the women I interviewed, including Reuque. Yet her point is important: if the state does not recognize the Mapuche as a people, it does not really matter what SERNAM is doing for women.

The Mapuche have a distinct way of looking at things, Reuque went on to say, and there is so much talk about equality, but the respect for difference that is necessary before equality can become a reality still does not exist (fieldnotes, August 1, 2001). This claim to difference cannot be encapsulated in appeals to diversity or equality, and it cannot be assuaged by redistributive programs. Rather, it is linked to a demand for recognition of Mapuche status as a people which is inherently opposed to state interests, and to Chilean citizenship as it is presently conceived.

CONCLUSION: CITIZENSHIP, DIFFERENCE, AND MAPUCHE WOMEN'S ACTIVISM

Mapuche women's claims, based on visión de pueblo, draw attention to the differences and inequalities that exist among women. They present a challenge to SERNAM's portrayal of the interests of Chilean women citizens, which is based fundamentally on the principle of equality between women and men. The shortcomings of SERNAM in this regard match the reticence of the wider state to deal with claims based on cultural difference and historical injustice.

That is, in their interactions with SERNAM, Mapuche women face many of the same difficulties faced by the Mapuche people as a whole in interactions with other state agencies. Mapuche women's demands are based in difference, which is ultimately related to the idea that the

Mapuche are a distinct people. Many of their demands nonetheless focus on redistributive issues, such as access to work, land, health care, and education, and these are the demands more likely to be taken up by SERNAM, as they can be easily "added in" to the demands of other women. The relationship of these demands to the historical claim for recognition of Mapuche status as a people is downplayed by SERNAM, which prefers to frame them in terms of diversity. In this sense, and unsurprisingly, the relationship of Mapuche women to SERNAM parallels the relationship of the people as a whole to the Chilean state. More problematically, as noted in chapter 5, when projects are funded, the leaders involved often do not explicate the link to cultural recognition, as they are pleased to get any resources at all, and indeed, have very real needs related to redistribution. The end result, however, often seems to be cooptation of Mapuche demands rather than recognition of cultural difference.

Some Mapuche women question altogether the point of formally issuing demands to the state or participating in meetings to develop proposals in coordination with the state. They argue that the solution to the Mapuche conflict does not lie in public policy; Mapuche women's claims are one part of broader reivindicaciones over a historical conflict that is unlikely to be resolved by increasing funds for multicultural education or intercultural health programs. The construction of a strong movement that focuses on historical demands is thus more important than negotiating with the state. Carolina Manque, for example, argued that in the context of an oppressive and colonialist state, establishing a strong movement of Mapuche women that empowers them while struggling for justice for the people as a whole, is a more important goal (email correspondence with author).

In the first part of this chapter, I showed that even though they emphasized that their demands are coterminous with those of the movement as a whole, Mapuche women sometimes make gender-based demands, which are rooted in a discourse of difference. I then discussed how Mapuche women's and SERNAM's gender discourses and practices have come into conflict with one another, resulting in the exclusion of Mapuche women's priorities from SERNAM's discourse and programs. Power differences among women and an additive approach to indigenous women's concerns are central factors in explaining why Mapuche women have had little success in gaining representation in SERNAM. As part of the state, SERNAM necessarily follows state strategy vis-à-vis the Mapuche: it avoids conceiving Mapuche women's demands as claims for cultural rights, relying instead on an additive approach and a loose treatment of diversity. Mapuche women are excluded from the state women's policy machinery, but that policy machinery is by and large obliged to stay within parameters set by statewide priorities—which have specific impacts on indigenous peoples, but also, on women.

Addressing indigenous people, not only in terms of a loosely conceived "diversity" or an additional "vulnerable" sector, but also as participants in a historical relationship that has resulted in the depredation of their societies, cultures, and nations, as well as modern-day discrimination and the devaluation of their cultures, would mean radically changing the way SERNAM and the state (and indeed, the nation itself) is organized. It would entail recognition of differentiated cultural rights as part of the citizenship regime, which is currently based on individual rights. The unique challenge that Mapuche women pose to state-driven gender discourse indicates possibilities for the growth of a critical politics around cultural difference and historical injustices, which could pressure for greater recognition of cultural rights. It also contributes to the development of a greater understanding of the intersections and disjunctures between indigenous peoples' rights and women's rights. The possibilities for guaranteeing cultural rights as a part of Chilean citizenship, and how the case of Mapuche women compares to that of the pobladoras, will be further addressed in the final chapter.

7

WHY DIFFERENCE MATTERS

At the beginning of this book, I asked whether it is possible to accommodate differences among women within laws, policies, and agencies that are designed to help women achieve equality with men. I examined this question by looking at the cases of Mapuche women and pobladoras in relation to SERNAM and the rest of the women's policy machinery in Chile. In this chapter, I draw the two cases together and discuss their implications for the representation of differences among women in official discourse and practices around women's rights. My goal is to enhance our understanding of how actors who differ by gender, class, and *pueblo* are articulated into re-established democracies. My conclusions fall along three interrelated lines. First, the cases demonstrate that "women's interests" are not univocal. Official policies and discourse often treat them that way, however, eliding differences among women. Second, power differences among women combine with the larger context of goals related to national development and identity to limit the possibility that pobladora and Mapuche women's demands for rights based in difference will be addressed. And finally, movements that focus on redistribution and recognition have divergent implications for the expansion of citizenship.

THERE'S NO SUCH THING AS "WOMEN'S INTERESTS"

In their interactions with the state women's policy machinery, pobladoras and Mapuche women understand and present themselves, their priorities, and their activism in terms of their differences with other women. Pobladoras assert that their interests and priorities are not always the same as those of middle-class women. Mapuche women maintain that their indigenous heritage and continuing struggles as a people mean that their priorities are not the same as those of other women. Neither group sees itself represented in the state. Based on these assertions of difference, they make specific demands and proposals to the state women's policy machinery.

While both pobladora and Mapuche women's claims are rooted in a sense of difference, how they frame their claims is distinct. The central issue for pobladoras is more closely linked to redistribution than to recognition, while the opposite is true for Mapuche women. The pobladoras ultimately desire to make the source of their difference with other women—socioeconomic inequality—disappear. That is, pobladoras want to be integrated with other, more economically secure, women. While they desire to be recognized and invited to participate on the basis of their specific skills and contributions as pobladoras, they see this participation as their main route to inclusion. Conversely, although Mapuche women's claims are sometimes similar to those of pobladoras, most of them are linked to recognition. Mapuche women express a desire for their difference to be acknowledged and respected, not made to disappear. Their demands involve the recognition of cultural difference, not some essential "womanhood" they share with others. In terms of policy, this might entail the creation of parallel structures or the establishment of policies that, from the beginning, are rooted in the Mapuche worldview.

Fraser (1997) and other scholars, such as Yuval-Davis (1997), argue that emphasizing recognition and identity politics has worked to the detriment of many contemporary social movements by reifying group differentiations and lending itself to multiculturalism as a policy response. Fraser instead supports a movement strategy that focuses on deconstructing and destabilizing group differentiation while simultaneously focusing on socialist remedies for structural inequalities. This strategy seems to cohere with pobladoras' objectives. However, Mapuche women, and the Mapuche people as a whole, challenge Fraser's idea of blurring the boundaries of identity politics in a way that other groups do not. The struggles of indigenous peoples focus not just on rectifying cultural and socioeconomic injustices within a given system, but on gaining autonomy from that system. As Young (1997) puts it, in this case, recognition is the end in itself as well as a means to economic justice. The recognition of cultural difference and rights ultimately entails the radical reorganization of how power and resources are distributed in Chile.

It is indeed important to avoid reifying what it means to be Mapuche (and the women who participated in this study demonstrate significant variation in what this identification means to them) as well as to recognize the occasions in which Mapuche demands overlap with those of other social groups. Nevertheless, indigenous peoples do not fit easily within social movement strategies that focus on destabilizing group differentiations. Nor would their objectives be met were this to take place. In fact, policies that blurred differentiations through assimilation, integration, and mestizaje have been used in the past to further exploit and marginalize indigenous people.

Pobladoras are also much more likely than Mapuche women to organize around "women's issues." Gender plays a predominant role in how pobladoras describe their identities as well as how they justify their activism and their demands. Pobladoras' greater focus on gender reflects their greater contact with middle-class feminists, and the fact that they were more integrated into the women's movement during the dictatorship than were Mapuche women. Consequently, many middle-class feminists who participated in the movement and are now part of the state possess sensitivity to class-based difference. Their sensitivity to class issues, however, stands in stark contrast to their ignorance about cultural difference and rights. Except for CEDEM/PEMCI, few women's movement actors reached out to Mapuche women during the dictatorship.

Mapuche women themselves are often reluctant to identify their claims as "women's issues." Responding in part to pressures from the outside (women's movement actors) and the inside (Mapuche movement actors), they are insistent that even when they make specific claims as women, their central objective is to achieve recognition of the rights of the people as a whole. Expressing the ways that their gender identities differ from those of non-indigenous women is thus central to Mapuche women's public gender discourse and how they frame their claims for rights. Their stance toward SERNAM is often much more oppositional than that of pobladoras also because femocrats are so reluctant to believe what Mapuche women are saying, and to realize that their demands are categorically distinct from demands made solely on the basis of class inequalities.

The distinct priority that Mapuche women and pobladoras give to "women's issues" per se coheres with how they frame demands. Pobladoras seek socioeconomic redistribution. They also seek redistribution of decision-making power in the state women's policy machinery, and they do so because they perceive their gender-related goals as at least similar to those of middle-class women. Mapuche women, in contrast, focus more on cultural recognition, and their claims vis-à-vis the women's policy machinery (for indigenous women's departments, and so on) are related to creating space for recognizing difference *and for being Mapuche* within it, or sometimes, alongside it. In both cases, however, the women's claims challenge the notion of "women's interests" promoted from within the state. Class and ethno-cultural differences and inequalities structure women's identities and interests in distinct ways.

REPRESENTING DIFFERENCES AMONG WOMEN IN THE STATE

Mapuche women's and pobladoras' claims for rights on the basis of difference are in effect demands for the expansion of women's citizenship in Chile. What happens to these claims when they are issued to the state? On a general level, the two cases display some similarities. My findings indicate that, as they assert to be the case, many of the priorities of Mapuche women and pobladoras are excluded from the work of the state women's policy machinery. In both cases, this appears to be due to two main factors. First, Mapuche women and pobladoras do not have access to the limited power made available to women within the Chilean state. Decisions about how "women," "women's issues," and "equality" are defined are made by middle-class, non-indigenous, formally educated women. Despite their history of cross-class activism, such women often do not acknowledge the ways that their class positions afford them power and benefits denied to pobladoras. They often fail to recognize the power differences between themselves and indigenous women as well. Moreover, because women's citizenship itself remains contested and only limited space and resources are allotted to women, the women with power within the state women's policy machinery are reluctant to dedicate those resources to Mapuche women's and pobladoras' concerns or to incorporate their participation in a meaningful way. In the end, Chile's gendered citizenship regime is experienced differently by women on the basis of class and indigenous status.

The second reason that the priorities of the two groups are seldom addressed goes beyond the women's policy machinery. Insofar as they conflict with hegemonic socioeconomic and ideological goals, many of the claims of pobladora and Mapuche women (and of poor and Mapuche people more generally) remain unaddressed. The Servicio

Nacional de la Mujer and the Municipal Women's Offices are part of the state, and as such, are unlikely to contradict dominant interests and strategies in resolving the claims of poor and indigenous people. This places significant limitations on what pobladoras and Mapuche women are likely to achieve.

During the dictatorship pobladores objected to the lack of respect for human rights under the military regime, and their collective identity—lo popular—emphasized their desire for an end to economic marginalization and a deep desire to be part of Chilean society. They sought democracy, but also redistribution—which would ultimately result in their integration into the benefits of modernity. Now that democracy has returned, the poor and working-class activists that remain—particularly the pobladoras—continue to demand inclusion and redistribution. However, the state's approach to social policy (involving self-help, targeting, preparing individuals for the market, and competitions for scarce funds) has proven ineffective in combating inequality. And since social policy has been reframed to focus on responsibilities and opportunities, it is difficult to make claims that associate social policy with citizenship rights. Participation is a policy focus, but it is implemented in terms of self-help programs, rather than in the inclusive terms emphasized by pobladoras. Social spending has increased, but sectoral targeting is privileged above the recognition of social rights.

The Mapuche have a distinct relationship to national development goals. Chilean national development in many cases threatens Mapuche existence. Moreover, a unitary Chilean national identity is used to justify national development initiatives as beneficial to all and to delegitimate Mapuche claims that they are a people with an inherent right to self-determination. Hegemonic goals in the global economy delimit what kinds of demands will be taken up by the state and also in what ideological framework that will happen. The state carefully frames Mapuche claims and selectively responds to certain demands. Historical reivindicaciones become socioeconomic problems, and diversity is appreciated, but cultural rights are not recognized. This effectively assuages some movement actors and thereby helps to contain the Mapuche movement.

Both cases demonstrate the importance of looking at the state-citizen relationship from above and below. Certainly, Mapuche women's and pobladoras' claims for the expansion of rights are impelled from below. What they are able to achieve, however, has everything to do with expectations being handed down from above, both in terms of

SERNAM's expectations for how women should perceive their gender interests, and the state's expectations for how rights will be conceptualized in the democratic-neoliberal era. The claims that are incorporated into the state are likely to be those that most cohere with hegemonic material and cultural objectives.

OPPOSING IMPLICATIONS FOR EXPANDING CITIZENSHIP

The two cases have divergent implications for the expansion of citizenship. By this I mean three things. First, the content of demands, the context in which they are made, and the actors involved all play important roles in determining which citizenship claims are taken up by the state (i.e., *how* citizenship is likely to be expanded and for whom). Second, Mapuche and pobladora demands for the expansion of citizenship actually pose very different challenges to the citizenship regime. The pobladora case points to the need to take universal social rights more seriously and to consider the links between representation and participation, whereas, in order for Mapuche claims to be addressed, differentiated cultural rights would have to be recognized. Finally, citizenship is a limited grounds for making progress around the expansion of rights for the poor and indigenous peoples alike. While fraught with contradictions, a human rights paradigm may be more relevant to the struggles of both groups.

How the state responds to demands depends on not just what those demands are—whether they are based in recognition or redistribution—but on who makes them and in what context. Specifically, in the current context, it appears that Mapuche demands for redistribution are more likely to be positively received than are their demands for recognition. Taken alone, this might suggest that redistribution claims are easier to get through than recognition claims. But paradoxically, pobladora demands related to redistribution receive little attention. Moreover, both the women's movement and the Mapuche movement were successful in achieving demands based in recognition at the transition to democracy. And perhaps most importantly, upon closer inspection it is apparent that the reception of Mapuche demands is actually not so simply delineated on the basis of recognition and redistribution; the redistribution demands that can be reframed as socioeconomic problems and the recognition demands that can be reduced to "diversity" are both taken up by the government. The recognition demands that would result in more substantial redistribution of power and resources, however, are flatly rejected. What the findings suggest, then, is that the types of goals that motivate people to form movements *as well as* the ideological and economic context in which those goals are pursued are important to whether movements are successful in advancing their claims.

But why do Mapuche demands garner more of a response than do those of pobladoras? While it is made up of a multitude of actors who frequently disagree with one another about goals and strategies, the Mapuche movement is growing in visibility if not in internal cohesiveness. Perhaps partially as a result of the opportunities opened up by the Concertación's commitment to decentralization and local level participation, the Mapuche have managed to pose issues that challenge Chilean national identity and development goals. In order to maintain national and international legitimacy, state actors have had to respond to Mapuche claims. They have done so, as well, because elite/state losses would be much greater were claims for autonomous territory and self-government to become more generalized. The corresponding strategy, as noted above, has involved framing Mapuche demands in terms that foster integration, emphasize redistributive issues like agricultural development and land buybacks, and reduce recognition to a loose conception of diversity. Unsurprisingly, this strategy is reproduced in SERNAM's representation of Mapuche women's priorities.

The pobladora movement, on the other hand, appears to have fallen into disarray and ineffectiveness since the end of the dictatorship. There is substantial sympathy for the pobladoras' cause within the women's policy machinery, particularly when compared to Mapuche women. Yet pobladoras haven't been able to present a compelling cause that draws public attention or the activism of large numbers of poor and working-class women and men. Perhaps this is because many pobladora claims have been at least discursively taken up by the state. Concertación leaders have made inequality, poverty, and participation priorities of the democratic regime. Dispute over the *quality* of the Concertación's commitment to these issues seldom garners significant public attention in the current context, in which the big goal, democracy, has been accomplished. The focus on citizen responsibilities under neoliberalism likewise invalidates such claims, particularly because the type of integration the pobladoras are asking for implies a degree of socialism that is simply not an option in the neoliberal-democratic world order. That the remaining pobladora activists link their demands for redistribution to participation creates an additional barrier: not only are their redistribution demands not addressed to the extent that pobladoras wish but femocrats also refuse to recognize their ability to make specific contributions through direct participation.

In a sense, then, Mapuche claims for the expansion or redefinition of rights seem to be taken more seriously than those of pobladoras. To the extent that pobladoras' claims during the dictatorship were taken up by the Concertación, their movement was successful. But organizing to make demands for the expansion of social rights or to challenge the Concertación's commitment to redistribution has not resonated with a broad enough social base to garner a significant response in the current context and femocrats are reluctant to involve pobladoras in decision making. The Mapuche, in contrast, have built a more compelling movement in the neoliberal-democratic era. However, to the extent that their claims for recognition are consistently de-emphasized or delegitimated by state actors in favor of an integrative, redistributive approach, their goals have yet to be met. In both cases, the way in which claims are taken up by the state creates a difficult situation, in which negotiating with the state often results in the appropriation of leaders and some movement objectives while more substantial goals are left by the wayside.

What would addressing the claims of Mapuche women and pobladoras mean for citizenship in Chile? My comments pertain to the women's policy machinery and to the state more generally. For pobladoras, the problem today is that socioeconomic rights that guarantee a minimum standard of living for all citizens were curtailed during the dictatorship and have never gained status as completely legitimate claims under the Concertación—at least not in the social democratic sense that was part of lo popular. Despite the Concertación's discursive commitment to citizenship rights and participation, the ways that policies are carried out (and the hegemonic national development goals behind them) do not meet pobladoras' expectations for democracy. For citizenship to be expanded in such a way as to represent pobladoras' priorities, universal socioeconomic rights that go beyond "opportunities" would have to be installed as part of the citizenship regime, and pobladoras would have to be personally involved in the process.

While greater access to social rights might address some of their demands, the universal individual rights paradigm is problematic for the Mapuche, men and women alike. More appropriate to their claims would be what Iris Young (1990) calls differentiated citizenship. Young argues that the universal individual rights of citizenship do not protect all people equally, that "equality" written from a certain cultural (and racial and gendered) perspective often results in the delegitimation and exclusion of other perspectives and lifestyles. Justice necessitates guaranteeing rights specific to particular groups of people. The lack of representation of Mapuche claims will not be resolved unless differentiated cultural (and often collective) rights are recognized as part of citizenship. Moreover, because many of their demands are related to autonomy and self-determination, it is possible that even guaranteeing differentiated cultural rights is not an adequate solution, and that the ultimate answer to Mapuche claims lies outside of the citizenship relationship.

Is it possible to represent claims for rights based in difference in the state? Or are conflicts over women's citizenship inevitable? Overall, as a state strategy to represent women's interests, and ultimately, to integrate women more fully as subjects of citizenship rights, SERNAM does a poor job of incorporating claims of difference. Yet the cases of Mapuche women and pobladoras demonstrate that answering this question entails going beyond women's citizenship to look at the citizenship regime as a whole. Power differences among women as well as hegemonic goals in the context of the (neoliberal) global political economy place limits on the chances that Mapuche women's and pobladoras' priorities and interests are represented. To guarantee that all women, and all citizens, are treated as full subjects of rights would entail taking two distinct but not necessarily contradictory steps to reform SERNAM and Chilean citizenship as a whole. These are to guarantee cultural rights and to establish a higher common standard of socioeconomic rights among all citizens. These steps are unlikely to be taken in the current context, however, in which improving Chile's position in the global economy is privileged above women's rights, indigenous rights, and socioeconomic equality.

Human rights accords may prove essential to struggles for the expansion of rights in the context of the global neoliberal-democratic order. In Chile, this is especially true as it seems increasingly possible that the next president will be from the political right. Pobladora, indigenous, and feminist activists are likely to find such an administration very unsympathetic to their demands.

Unlike citizenship rights, which represent a balance between the struggles of citizens from below and elite/state efforts to control and articulate the interests of social actors from above, a human rights paradigm views rights as fundamental to the existence of human beings, standards that no person should have to live without. Sjoberg et al.

(2001, 33) define human rights as consisting of "the social claims of individuals (or groups) upon organized power relationships as a means of enhancing human dignity." Human rights claims thus represent potential constraints on organized power—elite and state power, but multinational and transnational corporate power as well.

This assertion cannot be made without some qualifications, however. Beginning with the Universal Declaration of Human Rights in 1948, human rights have been conceptualized in terms of protecting the individual from state violence and have focused in particular on civil and political rights. Like the concept of citizenship, this conceptualization of human rights has spurred critiques from feminists and indigenous peoples alike. Both groups assert that the universalization of human rights has served to elide significant differences within humankind. Feminists have noted that the distinction between the public and private spheres is reflected and reproduced in the dominant human rights discourse. Whereas men may tend to face violations of civil and political rights in the public sphere, violations of women's human rights are more likely to occur in the private sphere, often at the hands of their male family members (Bunch 1990; Charlesworth 1995). The dominant conceptualization of human rights has thus left women unprotected in the sphere in which they are most vulnerable.

Indigenous peoples frequently critique the human rights paradigm for its bias toward individual rights. Until recently, few human rights documents have recognized the centrality of cultural and collective rights to indigenous peoples' continued existence. Even more importantly, the United Nations system (made up, of course, of member states that ultimately work with their own interests in mind) fails to recognize the sovereign rights of indigenous peoples to self-determination and self-government, and is careful to qualify the meaning of the word "peoples" when it is used in official documents. Thus, international human rights accords have frequently failed to provide the guarantees indigenous peoples need to advance their claims.

Despite these limitations, both women and indigenous peoples have often found more success framing their appeals in terms of human rights rather than citizenship. Feminists' struggle to redefine "women's rights as human rights" (Bunch 1990) has led to significant international attention to the multitude of ways that violence impinges upon women's rights on a daily basis, usually in the private sphere. Feminists have also mobilized around the "second generation" of human rights, which comprises social and economic rights.[1] These rights are often most immediately relevant to the lives of women, though as

Naples (2002) and Desai (2002) note, they are frequently the most difficult to enforce. Moreover, focusing on these rights may imply that civil and political concerns are somehow irrelevant to women (Bunch 1990). Still, social and economic rights have formed the basis for local feminist mobilizations as well as transnational solidarities (Desai 2002). In addition, they are central to pobladoras', and to a lesser extent, Mapuche women's, claims.

Indigenous peoples have also made advances in the international human rights realm. A Working Group on Indigenous Populations, established under the United Nations High Commissioner for Human Rights in 1982, submitted a draft declaration on the rights of indigenous peoples in 1993, which has since been working its way up to the General Assembly for consideration. The United Nations also declared 1995–2004 the International Decade of the World's Indigenous People. While these are largely symbolic gestures, some real advances have taken place as well. Though significant limitations and restrictions are imposed in almost all cases, in recent years nations such as Bolivia, Nicaragua, Ecuador, and Colombia have taken legal and/or constitutional measures to recognize indigenous rights to identity, participation, territory, and/or self-government. One of the most exciting advances at the regional level was the 2001 Awas Tingni case in which the Inter-American Human Rights Court found the Nicaraguan government in violation of indigenous territorial rights after it granted a forestry company a concession on indigenous lands. Nevertheless, fifteen months after the case was closed, Nicaragua had yet to fully comply with the decision, indicating the difficulties of enforcing international law (ILRC 2003).

The implementation of human rights accords is of central importance in guaranteeing social and economic rights, which are often subordinate in national constitutions. In addition, as Stavenhagen (1996) points out, human rights standards provide a defense against those who might argue that economic and social rights are not rights at all, but rather, policy objectives. They are also central to reframing the struggle of indigenous peoples against the state. Insofar as the goal of the modern state is to have a monopoly of legitimate power, it is predictable that states would be reluctant to admit claims for cultural rights—particularly insofar as these imply self-government and autonomous territory. Nevertheless, the existence of standards for indigenous rights at the international level may mean that recognizing them is necessary in order to maintain legitimacy with the international community.

While recognizing socioeconomic, cultural, and collective rights begins to address the priorities expressed by pobladora and Mapuche women, it does not directly address how these concerns relate to others that are more explicitly linked to gender, or how class and indigenous movements sometimes subordinate women's rights to those of the "common good," as if women were not a part of it (just as SERNAM tends to subordinate class and indigenous concerns to those of "women"). Continued efforts will have to be made by feminist scholars and activists in order to show the links between socioeconomic, cultural/collective, and women's rights without subsuming one within the other.

Many changes need to take place before human rights are enforced. Movements need to be attentive in formulating their demands in the language of rights rather than as ameliorative requests (Roxborough 1997). In addition, while the human rights paradigm conceptualizes rights in terms that supercede the powers of nation states, it is still representatives of nation states who create the actual human rights accords. Thus, how human rights are operationalized and implemented continues to be limited by elite interests at the national and international levels. Moreover, the mere existence of standards does little to guarantee that nation states will adhere to them, though recent events, including the detention of Pinochet in London from October 1998 until March 2000, suggest that some are taking them seriously. Ultimately, human rights accords will be indispensable in defending the rights of people—and of peoples—against the rights of "organized power."

CONCLUSION

Why should anyone care about whether or not pobladora and Mapuche women's priorities are represented in Chile's National Women's Service? Conflicts within women's movements are clearly not limited to Chile. If women's movements are to be relevant to defending women's rights in the twenty-first century, we are going to have to find ways to take seriously claims for rights that are based in differences among women. Moreover, despite the increasing support of the international community for indigenous rights, conflicts between indigenous peoples and nation states continue to escalate throughout the world. Citizenship rights and difference are in some ways antithetical to one another, and the expansion of rights in the context of neoliberalism is unlikely. Yet confronting this dilemma is central to defending the rights of women and men worldwide.

The cases examined in this book therefore have important implications for mobilizing around rights—women's rights as well as those of other groups—more generally. Femocrats' failure to adequately represent the priorities of Mapuche women and pobladoras suggests that the creation of women's policy machineries within states is not enough to assure that all women's priorities are addressed. This is true because of limitations inherent in promoting women's rights from within the state, but it is also true because women in greater positions of power tend to promote issues important to them. Is it possible to build alliances among groups of women in ways that do not elide differences among them? This is a key question facing women's movements worldwide, and numerous theorists and practitioners have worked to find the answer. One promising possibility may be found in what Collins (1991) refers to as the advancement of a humanist vision based on coalition politics, Sandoval (2000) calls the Methodology of the Oppressed, and Yuval-Davis (1997) titles transversal (as opposed to universal) politics.

Each of these perspectives relies on the concept of standpoint. The theorists contend that there is no one truth and all forms of knowledge are situated and partial. Moreover, throughout history, dominant groups have subordinated oppressed groups' ways of knowing because the dominant have an interest in claiming that they speak an absolute, unbiased truth. (Foucault called the knowledge of oppressed groups "subjugated knowledge.") But when all knowledge is recognized as partial, possibilities for dialogue and understanding emerge. When this occurs, these authors contend, coalition politics are possible. As Collins explains (1991, 236): "Each group speaks from its own standpoint and shares its own partial, situated knowledge. But because each group perceives its own truth as partial, its knowledge is unfinished. Each group becomes better able to consider other groups' standpoints without relinquishing the uniqueness of its own standpoint or suppressing other groups' partial perspectives." Successful coalitions are likely to be formed around issues rather than identity, involving mobilization, as Yuval-Davis puts it, "not in terms of who we are, but what we want to achieve" (1997, 126). Coalition politics also avoids the reification of identities, such that power differences within social groups are openly acknowledged: class, race, gender, and so forth are interlocking aspects in the matrix of oppression. In such a system, as Yuval-Davis (ibid., 129) puts it, "dialogue, rather than fixity of location, becomes the basis of empowered knowledge."

While these coalitions may begin by centering subjugated experiences and knowledge and decentering the dominant perspective, Collins suggests, citing Elsa Barkely Brown (1989), that eventually these dialogues will come to the point where, rather than decentering any one standpoint, the center is constantly "pivoted." This idea is reminiscent of Elisa Avendaño's comments in chapter 1. She spoke of recognizing and respecting the struggle of non-Mapuche feminists, and acknowledged that they could be advocates on behalf of Mapuche women. At the same time, she asked for the recognition that only Mapuche women are able to feel what it means to be Mapuche based on a lifetime of unique experiences. That is, she asked that Mapuche women's standpoint be respected as a valid, if partial, form of knowledge. Many pobladoras asked the same when they spoke of their desire to have their ability to make unique contributions recognized.

This perspective says more about the capacity of different groups within civil society to engage in activism around common goals than it does about the relationship of those groups to the state. Nevertheless, it does indicate a potential way for groups like Mapuche women, pobladoras, and middle-class feminists to work for change together on some issues, while allowing for diverse viewpoints and struggles in which not everyone in a given coalition participates. In this situation, dominant women might feel less compelled to verify whether subordinated groups' assertions of difference are valid or not, and the extent to which women from subordinated groups feel their class, race, or ethnic identities threatened by aligning themselves with feminists might also be lessened. This form of working toward social and political change is unlikely to work in all cases. Indeed, as Yuval-Davis points out, it is not always possible to reconcile the positions of different individuals and groups. Nevertheless, coalition politics offers perhaps the most hope for future alliances among diverse groups of women.

Appendix: Research Sites, Sample, and Design

In chapter 1, I discussed several issues related to the design of this project and ethical issues that arose over the course of carrying it out. In this appendix, I provide supplementary information about design issues, the research sites, and the sample. I completed the fieldwork for this project in Chile in summer 1999 and between February 2000 and January 2001. I made a follow-up trip to Chile in summer 2001 in order to share results with research subjects and other interested individuals in the form of formal presentations and personal conversations. Some additional data was collected at that time.

Reliability and validity are the central standards by which social scientists judge the merit of research. In qualitative research, reliability refers to "auditability." The data presented in this book is reliable in the sense that I am able to explain to others what I did and why I did it. This appendix and the reflections on methodology and ethics in chapter 1 represent an effort to make my activities transparent to others. In addition, my fieldnotes compose an auditable record of my activities related to this project. Validity is the question of whether the interviews ascertained what I intended them to ascertain. Two issues are at stake—did I ask the right questions and did I have access to respondents' true feelings and impressions. I addressed the first through careful consideration of the topics addressed in the interviews and by paying attention to the types of questions asked by others who have done similar research. To a certain extent, my methodological approach obligates me to believe my respondents, but as noted in chapter 1, I took steps to build trust with my respondents before interviewing them and observing their activities.

RESEARCH SITES

From the high Andes and the Atacama Desert in the north, to the Mediterranean-like wine growing regions of the central valley, mountainous lake-dotted landscape of the near south, and spectacular glaciers of Patagonia, Chile is an environmentally diverse and aesthetically stunning country. A skinny country, it stretches along almost 2,700 miles of the South American Pacific coast but on average is only slightly more than 110 miles wide. The Andes mountain range runs the length of most of the country, which is bordered by Peru to the north and Bolivia and Argentina to the east. Approximately 4.4 percent of the population is indigenous according to the 2000 CASEN national survey of households, though the 1992 Census put this figure at around 10 percent (MIDEPLAN 2002; see chapter 5, note 1 for a discussion of the issues surrounding these estimates). The Mapuche are the vast majority of the indigenous population, followed by the Aymara and Rapa Nui. Aside from the Spanish, who arrived in South America over 500 years ago, Chile experienced significant German, English, and Italian immigration. Today, the country is divided into thirteen administrative regions. I focused my investigation on two of these: the Metropolitan Region, which is the most populous, and Region IX, which has the highest relative Mapuche population.

According to the 1992 Census, the Metropolitan Region is home to 5.2 million persons (39.4 percent of the total Chilean population). I focused my interviews in the capital city of Santiago. Although Santiago is just one of six provinces in the region, over 93 percent of the region's population resides there. A significant proportion of Chile's Mapuche population—between 20 and 50 percent, depending on the estimate—lives there as well. Because it is the capital city and the country's major metropolis, Santiago was also a site of concentrated resistance against the dictatorship. The province of Santiago is administratively divided into thirty-two comunas, or municipalities. Santiago is a modern city, and almost all of its residents have access to electricity, indoor plumbing, and so on. Nevertheless, it is an extremely unequal city, in which residents of some municipalities have standards of living similar to the wealthiest residents of the United States, and others are direly poor.

I focused my interviews and fieldwork in two working-class/poor municipalities: Cerro Navia and La Pintana. While the poverty rate for Santiago as a whole is 14.2 percent, in Cerro Navia, it is 23.9 percent and in La Pintana, 31.1 percent (MIDEPLAN 2001).[1] A Human Development Index, created specifically for Chile by the United Nation's Development Program and the Chilean government, paints a somewhat different picture.[2] Out of a total of 333 Chilean municipalities, La Pintana ranked 120th and Cerro Navia 135th in level of human development. The relatively medium rankings indicate that residents of these two municipalities have access to services and income that they would not likely have in other, particularly rural, parts of the country. However, the results also show that twelve of the twenty-five municipalities with the highest levels of human development—including the top six—are in Santiago. This inequality is visible, of course, as residents of Cerro Navia and La Pintana are more likely to lack basic services and paved roads (though this is increasingly uncommon anywhere in Santiago), have access to only lower quality schools and health care, and live in self-constructed or publicly subsidized housing. These municipalities are also associated with violence and delinquency. I chose Cerro Navia and La Pintana for two reasons. First, both of them have high Mapuche populations compared with other comunas in the region.[3] And second, both were largely created through *tomas de terreno,* have experienced rapid population growth over the past four decades, and have histories of significant pobladora activism. In addition to the Cerro Navia and La Pintana focus, though, in cases of particular interest, I conducted interviews with women from other municipalities.

Region IX is also called the Araucanía, a title that derives from *araucano,* the name assigned to the Mapuche by early Spanish settlers. In relative terms, the region continues to be home to more Mapuche people than any other region; over 25 percent of the population is Mapuche according to the 2000 CASEN survey and the 1992 Census. This represents nearly 33 percent of the country's total indigenous population. In some of the region's comunas, such as Saavedra, Galvarino, and Nueva Imperial, the Mapuche are the majority. Given that the Mapuche warded off the Spanish and later the Chileans until the late 1800s, the region was integrated into the Chilean nation much later than other parts of the country. While Temuco is the seat of commerce and regional government, the region has a high rural population (almost 39 percent), and agriculture, forestry and fishing composes 27 percent of the region's gross internal product (Matte Casanova 1999).[4] This percentage is shrinking, though forestry's contribution is on the rise.

In 2000, a greater proportion of the population was poor in the Araucanía than in any other region of the country: 32.7 percent, compared to 20.6 percent for the nation as a whole (MIDEPLAN 2001). The region's municipalities with high rural Mapuche populations are among the poorest in Chile. The Araucanía's municipalities also have some of the lowest levels of human development in the country. Out of thirty municipalities, twenty-four ranked low or very low in human development. Children in some rural Mapuche areas have to make significant daily commutes in order to attend school; this problem becomes more complex as they grow older and have to go farther to find the nearest middle or high school. It is common for students to board during the week in nearby towns in order to attend classes. Many drop out altogether. Health care is another significant problem. Access is low, ethnic discrimination common, and infant mortality rates in Mapuche communities are high. Dirt floors and lack of plumbing are commonplace; some areas only received access to electricity as late as the 1990s (unusual in Chile). And as noted in chapter 5, land is scarce and, often, deteriorated.

SAMPLE DETAILS AND BIOGRAPHICAL SKETCHES OF MAIN INTERVIEWEES

I conducted approximately sixty formal, open-ended, semi-structured interviews, divided among Mapuche women and pobladora activists, members of other poor women's organizations, such as Centros de Madres and Capillas, government employees, non-governmental organization workers, and participants in SERNAM's jefas de hogar program. The vast majority of these were audiotaped. The formal interviews were supplemented by informal conversations, informational interviews, and participant observations. The sample has both strengths and weaknesses. Its main strength, I think, is that it has allowed me to contrast the gender discourses of three very distinct groups of women, and to see where they intersect and where they contradict one another. A central limitation, on the other hand, is that while they are the leaders of organizations and make claims to representativeness, the Mapuche and pobladora women interviewed do not necessarily represent the universe of Mapuche and pobladora women—even those who participate in organizations.

My access to the women I interviewed and spent time with, particularly women in the state and the pobladoras, was facilitated by my affiliation with FLACSO-Chile where Teresa Valdés, a well-known and respected Chilean sociologist and women's movement activist, served as my advisor. Ana María Ordenes of the non-governmental organization Solidaridad y Organización Local (SOL, Solidarity and Local-level Organization) also facilitated my access to pobladora activists associated with REMOS, and Lilian Medina and Alicia Monsálvez of the Women's Office in Cerro Navia helped me establish contacts with a number of women in that comuna. My access to Mapuche women was aided by contacts made during my preliminary trip to Chile in summer 1999. In particular, Julio Tereucan of the Indigenous Studies Institute at the Universidad de la Frontera in Temuco and Carmen Melillan from Cedesco, a non-governmental organization in Santiago that works with Mapuche organizations, facilitated my entry.

Mapuche Women Leaders

The purpose of my interviews with Mapuche women leaders was to find out what their priorities were, how they felt those priorities were represented in the state, and what gender had to do with those priorities. The interviews focused on the respondent's personal activism history; her organization's activities, interactions with state agencies, and demands on the state; and her views on the relevance of gender to her activism. Participants were necessarily women who had had some degree of contact with SERNAM; as a result, leaders of organizations that have chosen an explicit strategy of non-interaction with the state are not represented in this sample. In addition, since I focused exclusively on the Metropolitan Region and the Araucanía, women leaders in Regions VIII and X, which also have significant Mapuche populations, were not included.

In Santiago, I conducted ten interviews with leaders of local-level, sociocultural Mapuche associations. About half of these women were born in Santiago; the other half had migrated from Mapuche communities in the south. They were diverse in terms of their personal activism histories as well as the degree of contact they had had with the state and other organizations. Political work was seldom their sole or even principal activity; most also focused on cultural recuperation or creating spaces (physical and psychosocial) for being Mapuche in the city. Their organizations were small, with between ten and forty members, and most had both women and men as members. Women, however, almost always formed the majority and tended to be the most active participants. Most participants were poor or working class. This is the predominant type of Mapuche organization in Santiago.

Several of these women were involved in the Urban Indigenous

Commission, which represented the urban Mapuche in the Working Group with Indigenous Peoples set up by President Lagos shortly after he took office in 2000. These women also demanded the creation of what came to be known as SERNAM's Working Group with Urban Mapuche Women. Others had participated in leadership training and other projects sponsored by the non-governmental organization Cedesco. I also conducted participant observations with several of these organizations—attending workshops, meetings, ceremonies, and interactions with government representatives. Their biographies are as follows:

At the time of our interview, María Hueichaqueo was president of Taiñ Adkimn, which means Our Knowledge in Mapudungun. The organization was founded in the early 1990s and runs culture and language workshops for children, as well as traditional Mapuche crafts workshops for adults. Hueichaqueo also participated in the Urban Indigenous Commission, the Working Group with SERNAM, and ran for, but lost, the position of Urban Advisor to CONADI. She was also involved with numerous Cedesco activities. She was in her early thirties, born in Santiago, and married with three children. Interviewed in La Pintana, July 26, 2000.

Juana Kolihuinka was president of Ko Kiyen, or Water of the Moon. In her forties at the time of our interview, she immigrated to Santiago when she was fifteen years old, and worked for some time as a domestic servant. She formed Ko Kiyen in the late 1990s with the purpose of salvaging Mapuche culture in the city. The organization was initially formed as a women's organization, but in response to some criticism, now includes men as well. She had strong ties to Cedesco. She was married with two daughters. Interviewed in La Pintana, August 23, 2000.

Born in Santiago, Juana Huenufil has been an activist around Mapuche issues since she consciously assumed her Mapuche identity at the age of sixteen. In her forties at the time of our interview, she was married to José Painequeo, director of the Indigenous Affairs Office in the municipality of La Pintana. Her organization, Inchiñ Mapu, was formed in the early 1990s, and focuses on cultural issues. Having participated in the Urban Indigenous Commission and SERNAM's working group, Huenufil was active in establishing a political presence for the Mapuche as well. Interviewed in La Pintana, October 11, 2000.

One anonymous leader was interviewed in Cerro Navia. Born in Santiago, she was in her late thirties, and participated in a number of other organizations before founding her current one in conjunction with a number of other Mapuche women in early 2000. She had close ties with Cedesco. She was married and had several children. Interviewed in Cerro Navia, July 26, 2000.

María Huichalao, president and founder of the Mapuche Council of Cerro Navia, immigrated to Santiago at the age of eighteen to work as a domestic servant. Her organization was active in the ministry of health's Intercultural Health Program, and collected money in support of the struggle against Ralco. She was fifty years old at the time of our interview, married with children. Interviewed in Cerro Navia, October 23, 2000.

Over seventy years old when we met, María Pinda, founder of Katriwala, had a long history of activism. She began as a human rights activist when her son was detained during the dictatorship, and eventually shifted her attention to the Mapuche cause. She was active in the movement to create CONADI and the Indigenous Law, had participated in a variety of international indigenous forums, went to New York for Beijing +5, and was active in the Coordinadora de Mujeres Mapuches. She was separated from her husband. One of her daughters is Amelia Gaete, former director of the Indigenous People's Office in the municipality of Cerro Navia. Interviewed in Cerro Navia, November 3, 2000.

Beatriz Painequeo was cofounder of Folilche Aflaiai (People of the Eternal Root), one of the only Mapuche organizations in existence in Santiago during the dictatorship. She, too, was active in the movement to create CONADI, and was the urban advisor to CONADI from its inception until 2000. She was active, as well, in the Urban Indigenous Commission. Interviewed in Ñuñoa, November 28, 2000.

With her brother, Margarita Cayupil founded Trawun Mapu in the comuna of La Granja in 1996. The organization focused on cultural recuperation, as well as countering discrimination in the city. She was active in the Urban Indigenous Commission and had had some interaction with Cedesco. She was separated and had one daughter. Interviewed in La Granja, September 11, 2000.

Nelly Hueichan was the leader of Trepein pu Lamñen, an organization in Peñalolen that focused on social support and transmitting Mapuche culture to children. The organization started as only women, but gradually came to include children and men (usually the family members of the participants). Hueichan was also the head of the Indigenous People's Office in the municipality. Interviewed in Peñalolen with other members of the organization, October 14, 2000.

While not explicitly a leader of a Mapuche women's organization, Silvia Carfil was an active participant in one. She was also a child care worker at a community center run by the Lutheran Church in San Ramón. There she served as an advisor to Trafwin, a group of non-Mapuche women that focused on informing themselves and the public about Mapuche culture and the political situation. Trafwin, incidentally, is also a member of REMOS (see pobladora organizations in the following section). Interviewed in San Ramón, November 8, 2000.

In addition to these interviews, I benefited from conversations with other organizations in Cerro Navia, Renca, and Pudahuel, as well as numerous Mapuche leaders from throughout the region at events sponsored by various institutions.

In the Araucanía, I interviewed seven recognized leaders in the Mapuche movement, most of who started as leaders from rural communities. All of them lived in Temuco at the time of our interviews, and many worked in institutions that served Mapuche communities. Many of them were associated with the Coordinadora de Mujeres Mapuches, a network of Mapuche women established in order to have a political and social presence, which was virtually inactive by 2000. Most of these women participated actively in the creation of the Indigenous Law as well as in the Beijing World Women's Conference process. Many were among the most visible participants in the historical (and continuing) Mapuche struggle. They had a history of interactions with the state:

Hilda Llanquinao, professor of social work at the Universidad de la Frontera, was active in various Mapuche organizations before the dictatorship, including the Unión Araucana and the Federación Araucana el Toqui. She was married, and probably in her early sixties. Interviewed in Temuco, May 23, 2000.

Carolina Manque was a social worker and cofounder of Aukiñko Domo, a non-governmental organization that works exclusively with Mapuche women. She was active in the Coordinadora de Mujeres Mapuches as well as SERNAM's Mesa Rural, and attended the World Women's Conference in Beijing. She was in her early thirties, was separated at the time and had one child. Interviewed in Temuco, May 26, 2000.

Elisa Avendaño was active in the Centros Culturales Mapuches (the most important organization during the dictatorship, which later became Ad Mapu—see chapter 5) from their inception. During the dictatorship, she came to be vice president of Ad Mapu. She was later active in the Coordinadora de Mujeres Mapuches and the Mesa Rural. At the time of our interview, she was a singer-songwriter in Mapudungun and had a small culture/music organization. She was around forty years old and had one son. Interviewed in Padre las Casas (Region IX), August 2, 2000.

Isolde Reuque was a cofounder of the Centros Culturales Mapuches, and a vice president of Ad Mapu during the dictatorship. She later founded an association of rural Mapuche women, called Kellukleayñ pu Zomo, or Helping Among Women. She participated in the Coordinadora de Mujeres Mapuches and the Mesa Rural, went to Beijing, and at the time of our interview, was serving as a special advisor on indigenous issues to President Lagos. She was married and had one daughter. Interviewed in Temuco, August 3, 2000.

One anonymous college graduate was interviewed. Earlier, she had been active in the Communist Youth and at the time of interview, was vice president of a national rural and indigenous women's organization. She was married and in her early thirties. Interviewed in Santiago, September 26, 2000.

Rosa Rapiman was director of the Casa de la Mujer Mapuche, a nongovernmental organization that provided training and assistance in selling traditional craftwork, in addition to recovering traditional designs. The Casa also focused on Mapuche women's rights and organizational support. She participated in the Coordinadora de Mujeres Mapuches and the Mesa Rural. She was in her thirties, married, had one child and was expecting her second. Shortly after my fieldwork ended, she was named director of SERNAM in the Region. Interviewed in Temuco, July 6, 1999 and October 27, 2000.

Ana Llao is the only woman to have achieved the presidency of Ad Mapu, which she held when the Mapuche organizations signed the Nueva Imperial Agreement with then soon-to-be president Aylwin. She was active in the Coordinadora de Mujeres Mapuches and the Mesa Rural, and attended the Beijing Conference. She was in her forties, separated, and had one child. Interviewed in Temuco, October 27, 2000.

I also benefited from several conversations with a second anonymous woman who resides in Temuco.

Most of my interactions with Mapuche women leaders in rural Mapuche communities consisted of informal conversations at workshops hosted by local-level organizations, non-governmental organizations, or state agencies, including ones held by Corporación Unión Araucana in Curarrehue, Puren and Nueva Imperial and an assembly-style meeting held by the regional office of SERNAM, at which Mapuche women's demands were presented to Minister DelPiano. Most rural Mapuche women's organizations in the region focus on small-scale economic activities, such as craftwork, greenhouse production of flowers and vegetables, egg farming, or "ethno-tourism." I had the opportunity to visit a few such organizations, including an ethno-tourism organization in Padre las Casas, various groups associated with PRODEMU (Program for Women's Development), and groups working with non-governmental organizations. Almost all of the rural women leaders I spoke with were very poor and had little formal education. I conducted formal interviews with representatives from two associations in rural Mapuche communities:

One anonymous woman headed a small association that was struggling to prevent the construction of a dump near its community. This woman also participated in SERNAM's Women Heads of Households Program in the municipality of Temuco. Interviewed in Temuco, May 24, 2000.

Juanita Curío, Flor Caniumilla, and Ruth Tureo formed the directive of Wanglen ("Star" in Mapudungun). This was a women's agricultural group that had recently split off from a group run by men, which they felt did not represent their needs. They also focused on cultural-political issues and women's rights. Wanglen was made up of about forty small collectives from rural areas of the municipality of Villarrica. Interviewed in Temuco, December 6, 2000.

Pobladora Leaders

Pobladora organizations, also known as women's social organizations, are made up of poor and working-class women. As discussed in chapter 2, most of these organizations were created during the dictatorship and formed part of a women's movement whose main goal was bringing about the return to democracy. Many of the pobladora organizations, however, also focused on practical needs, such as how to keep food on the table, and women's issues, such as self-esteem, sexuality, and domestic violence. Almost all of these organizations are on the left end of the political spectrum, and in a nation that remains closely divided in terms of support or opposition to Pinochet, they do not represent the totality of poor and working-class urban women. They do, however, represent the main social organizations that have remained visible and active in their communities since the return to democracy. Most of these activists were young mothers when they began their activism; at the time of my fieldwork, most were between forty and sixty years old, and several were grandmothers.

I conducted a total of eleven interviews with leaders of pobladora organizations. These interviews focused on the same general issues and had the same purpose as the interviews with Mapuche women. Again, I tried to focus on the municipalities of La Pintana and Cerro Navia, though I also included the poor and working-class comuna of Renca because it was an example of a municipality in which women's organizations had a close working relationship with the municipal government and significant local resources were being invested in women's programs. I also conducted participant observations with several of these organizations—attending workshops, meetings, and interactions with government representatives.[5]

The majority of the pobladoras I interviewed were associated with REMOS. The Red de Mujeres de Organizaciones Sociales was one of the main post-dictatorship networks of pobladora organizations, and emphasized making demands of the state and exercising control ciudadano on state programs. It brought together over forty organizations, and had received technical support from the non-governmental organization SOL. Each member organization was small, consisting of between five and twenty women, but often serving many more through sexual education, violence prevention, personal development, and other services:

One anonymous leader was interviewed in La Granja. Her organization was founded in 1991 with the assistance of a Maryknoll volunteer, though its members had been active throughout the dictatorship, mainly in organizations associated with the Church. Its main activities involved conducting workshops and other activities to improve women's awareness of issues related to personal development and sexuality. She was in her mid-fifties, married, and had three children. Interviewed in La Granja, April 12, 2000.

Lucía Benvenuto was president of the Casa de la Mujer Laura Rodríguez in La Pintana, which had its roots in the early years of the dictatorship and the creation of *comedores infantiles* (community kitchens to feed children) under the shelter of the Church. The women who participated in the comedores eventually formed anti-dictatorship "workshops" that focused on human rights work and solidarity campaigns. Once democracy was reestablished, the Casa focused on personal development, using handicraft workshops as a way to get women interested in participating. Benvenuto was director of REMOS when I interviewed her. She was in her late forties, married, and had three sons. She also worked for pay sporadically, taking in laundry or ironing. Interviewed in La Pintana, April 13, 2000.

In her mid-forties at the time of our interview, María Molina was coordinator of the Coordinadora Luisa Toledo in La Pintana. During the dictatorship the Coordinadora was part of the Coordinadora San Ricardo, which focused on human rights and women's issues. Since the return to democracy, it has provided training in child abuse prevention, sexuality, drug addiction, personal development, and other areas. Molina initially became active at the initiative of a Spanish volunteer who came to her door in 1978 and invited her to create an organization with other women. When I interviewed her, she was also a representative on the Partido por la Democracia's municipal council. She was married and had three daughters. Interviewed in La Pintana, April 25, 2000.

An anonymous woman in her early twenties was a participant in a Renca organization that focused on a variety of issues, including personal development, education, and child care. She was single and had one child. Interviewed in Renca, June 29, 2000.

Aída Moreno was founder and president of the Casa de la Mujer Huamachuco in Renca, which was established shortly after the end of the dictatorship with support from private donors associated with the Catholic Church. Its activities were diverse, including personal development, job training, education, psychological services, community libraries, child care, and so on. It survived in part on funds derived from World Vision, an international non-governmental organization whose services the Casa also administers. The now separated wife of a leftist radical, Moreno did not become an activist until after the dictatorship started and her home was raided by military police. Invited to participate early on in a Church-sponsored group, she became an outspoken critic of the dictatorship, and was also active in the Movimiento de Mujeres Pobladoras (MOMUPO), a popular feminist network. She had five adult children. Interviewed in Renca, July 3, 2000.

Hilda Muñoz was president of Mikempai (Women of Peace, in Diaguita), an organization in Renca that focused on domestic violence prevention. She was a catechism teacher in the 1960s, and during the 1970s was trained as a "health volunteer," also under the Catholic Church. She was active in numerous health-oriented organizations throughout the dictatorship, had contact with various feminist organizations, and eventually came to focus on domestic violence. She was treasurer of REMOS and an officer in the Women's Network of Renca when I interviewed her. She was in her sixties, married, and had three children. Interviewed in Renca, October 17, 2000.

Ana Pichulmán was president of REMOS at the time of our interview. She was a Mapuche woman and a communist, but had chosen to focus her struggle on women's issues. She was active in human rights groups during the dictatorship, when her husband was imprisoned and her daughter detained. In the late 1980s, she also founded an organization dealing with women's rights. Interviewed in Santiago, October 18, 2000.

Mercedes Montoya was secretary of REMOS and headed the Women's Program at Servicio Paz y Justicia (SERPAJ, Peace and Justice Service), a human rights non-governmental organization that was active throughout the dictatorship. Interviewed in La Florida, July 9, 2000.

At the time of my fieldwork, no pobladora organizations in Cerro Navia were members of REMOS. Women I interviewed found this strange, noting that Cerro Navia had been a central area of resistance against the dictatorship. Some hypothesized that the high level of poverty in the municipality led many women who previously participated in organizations to seek employment outside of the home, leaving them with less time for participation in organizations. Whatever the case, I interviewed three pobladora organizations in Cerro Navia, all of which had similar orientations and engaged in similar activities to the REMOS groups:

The Organización de Mujeres Educadoras de Pudahuel (OMEP) started as a group of young pregnant women brought together by Quaker volunteers in the mid-1980s. They were trained to teach others about women's health issues, including pregnancy, AIDS, violence, and sexuality. They used theatre as an educational tool. Four members were interviewed in Cerro Navia, April 12, 2000.

Mujeres Creando Futuro was the only pobladora organization in this sample that was not organized (or at least composed of women who were) during the dictatorship. Its members came together in a 1996 personal development workshop organized by a non-governmental organization, which was held as part of a free gasfitters course offered by the municipality in conjunction with the water utility. Its participants ranged in age from around twenty-eight to over sixty. Three members were interviewed in Cerro Navia, April 28, 2000.

Most of the women who formed Rayen Mahuida originally lived in the municipality of Maipú, but were *erradicadas*[6] to Cerro Navia (which was then part of Pudahuel) in 1979. In Maipú, they were supported by the Catholic Church and two missionaries (one Chilean, one Belgian), who also eventually transferred their work to Cerro Navia. Once they were in Cerro Navia, the women organized around their most immediate need: feeding their children. Eventually, they established community kitchens, bulk buying initiatives, women's workshops, and arpillera workshops, among other activities. At the time of our interview, they had constructed and ran a child care center, and organized activities for teens and women. They had limited prior contact with REMOS. Interviewed in Cerro Navia, May 5, 2000.

Other Urban Women's Organizations

As explained in chapter 2, the term "pobladora organizations" generally refers to those created in resistance to the dictatorship, associated with the political left, and having some linkages to the women's movement. In order to acquire some perspective on the similarities and differences between these organizations and other forms of activism among women in similar socioeconomic conditions, I conducted two interviews each with Centros de Madres and Capillas, or Catholic Church-based "solidarity" groups, and one interview with a women's group in Temuco.

Discussed in some detail in chapter 2, Centros de Madres are typically organizations of more conservative women who supported the Pinochet regime. Today, their activities center on arts and crafts and providing members with a social outlet. They are usually made up of twenty to thirty women, most of whom are over fifty years old. Both of the Centros de Madres I interviewed were located in Cerro Navia. In both cases, the interviews took place during the Centro's weekly meeting, in the form of a group discussion. Both Centros chose to appear anonymously. Interviewed in Cerro Navia on May 9, 2000 and May 16, 2000.

Capillas, or Grupos Solidarios, are social outreach groups operating within individual Catholic parishes. During the dictatorship, many of them worked in radical resistance to the dictatorship. For instance, one of the groups I interviewed provided emergency medical care to citizens who were hurt in conflicts with military police. (The possibility of being turned in to the authorities was great if injured individuals went to a public hospital.) At the time of our interview, however, their activities tended to focus on delivering services to particularly needy families within their churches. Capillas tend to be very small groups, usually made up of less than ten members, most of whom are over fifty years of age. Both of my Capilla interviews took place in Cerro Navia. The women interviewed were Claudia Fuentes of the Grupo Solidario Pequeño Simón (July 21, 2000), and three women from the Grupo Solidario Capilla San Francisco Xavier (July 22, 2000).

There are few women's organizations in Temuco, and I was unable to locate any associated with anti-dictatorship resistance. I did, however, interview women from the Grupo de Gimnasia Recreativa y Deportiva de la Rueda (La Rueda Women's Sports and Recreation Group), an organization sponsored by a local mental health clinic that links mental health training to physical fitness classes. Interviewed in Temuco, August 3, 2000.

Government

I conducted interviews with government employees that interacted with Mapuche and pobladora women at the local, regional, and national levels. The purpose of these interviews was to understand the services the agencies offered, particularly as they pertained to Mapuche and/ or pobladora women, their interactions with organizations, and the respondents' personal motivations for doing the work that they did. Many of those interviewed had been active in some form of resistance during the dictatorship.

I conducted the following interviews with SERNAM employees at the national and regional levels:

A social worker by training, Valeria Ambrosio had worked at SERNAM since its inception. She was a former regional director of the Metropolitan Region's Office, and at the time of our interview, was national director of programs. She spent some of the dictatorship years in exile in England, but returned to work in the areas of teen pregnancy and women's mental health. She was a member of the PPD and had grown daughters. Interviewed in Santiago, May 19, 2000.

Natacha Molina spent some years in exile in Costa Rica and Mexico, where she was introduced to feminism. She participated in the feminist movement when she returned to Chile in 1984 and was active in creating the first democratic government's platform around women's issues and designing the proposal for the creation of SERNAM. Though technically no longer a femocrat at the time of our interview, for four years (1996–2000) she was deputy director of SERNAM. Prior to and after that, she worked at the Instituto de la Mujer, a non-governmental organization that she cofounded in 1987, which conducted academic studies about women and also provided empowerment and educational workshops for women. Interviewed in Santiago, August 13, 2001.

Trained as a teacher, Erika López was regional director of SERNAM in the Araucanía from 1994 until 2002. At the time of our interview, she was in her thirties, and had been a member of the Christian Democrat Party since 1985. She was married and had two children. Interviewed in Temuco, October 26, 2000.

Cecilia Fernández was head of the family violence program at SERNAM in the Araucanía. She was a social worker by training, and had worked in the Ministry of Education, where she developed training programs about family violence for teachers, before coming to SERNAM. She was married and around thirty years old. Interviewed in Temuco, May 24, 2000.

An anonymous mestiza femocrat was interviewed at SERNAM in the Araucanía. She was single and in her late twenties. Interviewed in Temuco, August 1, 2000.

One anonymous woman was interviewed at SERNAM in the Metropolitan Region. She was in her fifties and had a history of activism within the women's movement. Interviewed in Santiago, March 27, 2000.

Informational interviews were also conducted with several other SERNAM femocrats at the national and regional levels.

I interviewed two Mapuche women who work at the National Corporation for Indigenous Development (CONADI):

Margarita Calfio was head of Social Management at CONADI's national office in Temuco. Born and raised in Santiago, she was active in a Mapuche student organization there before moving to Temuco explicitly in order to reside in ancestral Mapuche territory. She was also active in a Mapuche organization called Liwen. She was married and in her early thirties. Interviewed in Temuco, December 5, 2000.

I interviewed a young, anonymous social worker who headed a division of CONADI's Santiago Office. Though she was of Mapuche descent, she did not participate in Mapuche (or other) organizations prior to working in CONADI. Interviewed in Santiago, November 30, 2000.

I also benefited from informational interviews with several other CONADI employees in Santiago and Temuco.

I conducted some interviews, mainly informational, with employees of PRODEMU, the Program for Women's Development which is the successor of CEMA-Chile, and is directed by the first lady. The Program for Women's Development initially focused on arts and crafts activities for women, but at the time of my fieldwork, its objectives were being shifted to be more in line with those of SERNAM. These informational interviews were conducted in both Santiago and Temuco. In addition, I benefited from numerous conversations with an anonymous Mapuche woman fieldworker at PRODEMU in the Araucanía. I also conducted an in-depth interview with Caty Orellana, provincial director of PRODEMU in Santiago. During the dictatorship, she was a young pobladora. She very actively resisted the military regime, and cofounded Las Domitilas, a popular feminist collective named after a Bolivian miner's wife and activist Domitila Barrios de Chungara. She was in the process of completing a degree in public administration. Interviewed in Santiago, September 20, 2000.

I also interviewed municipal employees because, despite Chile's high level of centralization, the municipal level is where women's major day-to-day interactions with the government take place. In addition, I wanted to see if there were more possibilities for participation in decision making or greater representation of Mapuche and pobladora priorities at this level. Many of those interviewed were Municipal Women's Office employees:

Olivia González was territorial coordinator of the Women's Office in La Pintana. She participated during the dictatorship in programs supported by the Catholic Church's Vicaría Sur and communal kitchens, and by making, and eventually teaching others how to make and export, arpilleras. Originally hired for her skills as an arpillerista, she had worked in the municipal office for eight years, and had a short-wave radio show for the discussion of women's issues. Interviewed in La Pintana, May 18, 2000.

Alicia Monsálvez worked in the Women's Office in Cerro Navia. At the time I interviewed her, she was also president of the Socialist Party there. During the dictatorship, she was active in human rights groups. She had worked for the municipality for six years. In the beginning, she worked in the Community Organizations Department, but was later transferred to the Women's Office. She was about forty years old, married, and had three children. Interviewed in Cerro Navia, July 19, 2000.

Lilian Medina became director of the Women's Office in Cerro Navia in 1997. Like many of the women in the Municipal Women's Offices, she took the position not out of a commitment to women's rights, but because she needed a job. Nevertheless, she made a sustained effort to explicitly link the Office's activities to women's rights and has a long history of human rights activism. She was forty-one years old, and had recently chosen to become a single mother. Interviewed in Cerro Navia, July 27, 2000.

Social worker Jessica Orrego directed the Women's Program in Renca from 1997 until early 2001. She built the program into one of the municipality's strongest and best-funded departments, and helped establish the Red de Mujeres de Renca, a network of forty women's social organizations. Before coming to the municipality, she worked with women's economic development projects in rural areas through a non-governmental organization and in a program for pregnant teens. However, she said it was not until she began to work in the Women's Program and had contact with SERNAM that she consciously integrated a gender perspective into her activities. She had her first child shortly after our interview. Interviewed in Renca, October 30, 2000.

Elena Rivera was in charge of training programs in the Women's Office in Pudahuel, where she had worked for six years at the time of our interview. She had been active in Church-based organizations for most of her life, and said her own experience as a separated woman raising two children on her own, who began her university training after getting her job at the municipality, taught her that women have the capacity to learn and achieve even when their economic means and social support are limited. Interviewed in Pudahuel, April 13, 2000.

I also benefited from conversations with a femocrat at the Women's Office in El Bosque.

I also conducted informational interviews with three Heads of Municipal Indigenous Affairs Offices in the Metropolitan Region and had conversations or informational interviews with several other government employees at the regional and municipal levels in the Araucanía.

Non-governmental Organizations

I conducted in-depth interviews with individuals who worked with non-governmental organizations that support Mapuche women or pobladoras in order to get their impressions about the organizations and their activities and demands, as well as the state's representation of them. These included Carmen Melillan, a Mapuche social worker who directed a program at Cedesco that provided support for Mapuche organizations in Santiago (Santiago, June 30, 2000); Angélica Willson from CEDEM, a feminist academic non-governmental organization with close ties to Mapuche women's organizations in Temuco (Santiago, October 30, 2000); and Mercedes Montoya and Marisol Leiva from the women's program at the human rights non-governmental organization SERPAJ (La Florida, July 9, 2000). Additional conversations and informal interviews were granted by numerous other women's and Mapuche non-governmental organization workers in Santiago and Temuco, as well as by several scholars in both cities.

Rural Leaders

I interviewed Francisca Rodríguez, longtime communist agricultural union leader, proponent of women's rights, and cofounder of ANAMURI, which is the major Chilean organization uniting indigenous and non-indigenous women, for her perspectives on how these two groups of women can unite their struggles and bring their demands to the state. Interviewed in Santiago, June 21, 1999 and September 11, 2000.

Participants in the Women Heads of Households Program

I interviewed seven participants in SERNAM's jefas de hogar program in order to understand the perspectives of beneficiaries of SERNAM's programs, and how these differ from or cohere with those of Mapuche and pobladora leaders. Six of these interviews were conducted in Temuco, one in Cerro Navia. I also participated in several municipal level activities for these women in Cerro Navia. Few of them were organized outside of the program. They were generally under thirty-five, since there is an age limit on participation. Although they were supposed to be single mothers, in Temuco women who were married were still allowed to participate.

Notes

1 WOMEN'S RIGHTS AND REPRESENTING DIFFERENCE

1. "State women's policy machineries" is a United Nations term for the range of policies, programs, ministries, etc. designed to represent women's interests in the state. In Chile, it includes SERNAM, the Municipal Women's Offices, and other peripheral agencies, such as the Programa de Desarrollo de la Mujer, PRODEMU (directed by the First Lady).
2. By "expansion" I mean broadening the kind of rights that are guaranteed as part of full citizenship as well as deepening the content of rights, such that the substantive experience of them more closely matches the expectations of citizens.
3. *Criollo* refers to people of Spanish descent born in the Americas.
4. Kymlicka gives additional consideration to cultural diversity as justification for group-differentiated rights.
5. It is important to note that indigenous peoples generally distinguish themselves from ethnic groups by noting that they are not a subset of immigrants to a given place, but a nation or people possessing rights to a territory that was invaded and appropriated from them.
6. Unless otherwise noted, all translations from Spanish to English (from interviews and other primary and secondary sources) are my own.

2 WOMEN'S ACTIVISM AND THE CHILEAN STATE

1. Four Latin American countries granted women the vote before World War II, four during the war, and twelve after it. Chilean women were granted the vote in 1949, after decades of activism (Miller 1991).
2. By no means is appealing to women's civic duty as mothers a strategy unique to Pinochet. Evans (1989) documents the emergence of the ideology of "Republican Motherhood" during the United States Revolutionary War. The ideology mobilized women around the notion that it was their patriotic duty to raise future citizens dedicated to the good of the nation. Republican Motherhood resurfaced during the struggle for woman suffrage, when proponents and opponents alike used the concept to justify their positions. As well, Teddy Roosevelt appealed to a similar responsibility when he spoke of (white) women's duty to have more children in order to avoid "race suicide."
3. Other important women's organizations and networks associated with political parties, such

as Mujeres de Chile (MUDECHI, Women of Chile), which was formed by communist women, did not have a feminist orientation.

4. Baldez (2001) draws an interesting parallel between the political strategies of Poder Feminino and Mujeres por la Vida along these lines. Both groups used non-partisanship to assert women's ability to rise above the bickering and maneuvering among male-dominated political parties, and called for unity among the parties in order to achieve their goals. Both also appealed to essentialist notions of women's moral superiority, and were successful in bringing about greater political unity among men.

5. Under national and international pressure for a return to democratic rule, and confident the Chilean people wanted him to remain as their leader, Pinochet agreed to this plebiscite. Had the "Sí" vote won, Pinochet would have stayed on as dictator and president of Chile for eight more years.

6. Though, as Teresa Valdés notes in her comments on Guzmán (n.d.), "national machineries" focusing on women's issues have a longer history in Chile. The first Juridical Women's Office was established in 1949, and various presidents have established offices aiming to promote women's integration since that time. However, SERNAM is the first agency established by law rather than presidential decree.

7. Figure reported is from the 2000 CASEN national household survey, reported by MIDEPLAN minister Krauss and SERNAM director DelPiano in 2001. Though there are significant problems with comparability of data collection methods over time and with underestimation (particularly until 1976 when census data was replaced with more specific labor surveys), women's labor force participation has been steadily increasing over time, from around 21.9 percent in 1960, to 22.3 percent in 1970, 27.6 percent in 1976, 30 percent in 1980, and 31 percent in 1990 (Valdés and Gomariz 1992).

---

3   NATIONAL DEVELOPMENT, SOCIAL POLICY, AND THE POOR

1. It should be noted that just because such a common identity existed, it does not mean that all pobladores unconditionally shared in the ideals reflected by lo popular. In fact, Pinochet had plenty of supporters among the poor and working classes.

2. Unfortunately, the drop in pobladora participation has not been documented in quantitative terms. Also, the drop in popular sector participation more generally is not to say that there are not any organizations in the poblaciones today. Territorial organizations like juntas de vecinos (community councils), youth groups, sports clubs, elderly clubs, etc. abound in many neighborhoods. These organizations, however, do not generally make demands for the expansion of citizenship rights, as do many pobladora organizations, particularly those belonging to REMOS.

3. This had the potential to be a democratizing measure, but, for a number of reasons, was not. First, of course, the dictatorship and lack of elections precluded democratic rule at the municipal level. Second, decentralization only occurred in terms of carrying out policies. Municipalities could not make policy or design decisions. Finally, municipal wealth was (and continues to be) so disparate that poorer municipalities could not provide services equal in quality to those of richer municipalities.

4. She also maintains that the Concertación's focus on overcoming poverty is different in comparison to that of the military regime because it privileges social investment over handouts, responds to diverse situations of poverty with more flexible and participative programs, and tries to sensitize those who implement policies to generate opportunities for social and economic integration.

5. According to Meller (1999), in 1996, the richest 20 percent of Chileans received approximately 57 percent of total income; the poorest 20 percent received only 4.5 percent. These figures (along with the inequality figures noted in the text) have remained relatively stable since 1987. The Gini Index is a common measure of income inequality, with 0.0 representing a completely equal income distribution and 1.0 a completely unequal distribution. Chile's Gini Index is 0.57, which compares to 0.38 for the United States and 0.25–0.30 for most European countries. (Meller cites data from the Inter-American Development Bank 1999. The United States Census Bureau [2000] reports the United States' Gini coefficient to be around 0.44.) Income is highly concentrated in Chile. Meller notes that if the Gini coefficient is calculated without the richest 10 percent, the coefficient goes down to 0.27, on par with northern European countries. In comparison, calculating the Gini coefficient without the top 10 percent for the United States (based on the initial 0.38 figure) gives a result of 0.34. Even for other Latin

American countries with high levels of inequality, the figure does not change nearly as substantially.

6. Paley (2001) similarly uses the concept of "marketing democracy" to emphasize the influence of free market ideology on the content of contemporary democracy (and also to highlight the extent to which this brand of democracy has been marketed to Chilean citizens).

7. At least one Lagos administrative initiative that got underway after my fieldwork had ended—the health sector reform—did refer to rights rather than opportunities. Its slogan was: "Because Health is a Right, Chile Wants Reform."

8. In a 1998 study, I similarly found that Bolivian non-governmental organizations had difficulty balancing their need for funding from international aid agencies with their role as advocates for the poor and critics of structural adjustment.

9. De La Maza points out that an additional factor that limits poblador organizations' capacity to make citizenship demands is that they are no longer linked to networks that engage in political mobilizations.

10. Moreover, state agencies whose work focuses on a specific subgroup of society, including FOSIS (the poor), SERNAM (women), and CONADI (Indians), generally are not permitted to carry out their own programs in other than pilot form. They determine desired outcomes as well as technical and administrative guidelines, and depending on the specific program, call non-governmental organizations, other private entities, or municipalities to compete for the job by submitting proposals and potential budgets. Insofar as they are designed with the intent of generating and supporting participation in civil society, the creation of concursos for funding social project proposals is distinct from the subcontracting of non-governmental organizations and other private entities as executors of programs, consultants, or project/policy evaluators.

11. The Servicio Nacional de la Mujer (unlike many other state agencies) responded to pobladoras' demand that an "affirmative action" mechanism in benefit of pobladora organizations be inserted into its own competitive fund (known as the Civil Society Fund).

---

4   PARTICIPATION AND THE REPRESENTATION OF POBLADORAS IN THE STATE

1. I thank Susan Franceschet for her cogent reflections on the relationship between representation and participation.

2. In this sense, my argument differs somewhat from that of Baldez (1999, 2002), who suggests that there is some intentionality on the part of the Concertación (and the Christian Democrats in particular) to undermine SERNAM's linkages with women's organizations.

3. Although my conversations with them focused on interactions with the women's policy machinery, pobladoras' critiques of state participation discourses encompassed other state agencies, as well. Some of these critiques are found in this chapter, and others in chapter 3.

4. The Servicio Nacional de la Mujer also encouraged the evaluation of services and attention received in the CIDEMs (Women's Rights Information Centers located in SERNAM's regional offices) through the use of comment cards.

5. The REMOS leaders' concerns about their ability to assume a representative role seemed to have become more acute some time after they became completely autonomous from SOL (the non-governmental organization that helped create REMOS) in late 2000–early 2001. While gaining their autonomy was an important step for the network, it also meant losing important financial and technical support from SOL. By 2003, this situation had led several organizations to return to SOL, which was creating a new network of popular women's organizations.

6. In addition, much of the remainder of international funding is now channeled through FOSIS, a state agency. Some pobladoras observe that a significant amount of funding ends up getting eaten up in the state bureaucracy, further reducing the funds available to social organizations. Moreover, funds administered through FOSIS tend to fit within the neoliberal social policy paradigm described in chapter 3. Finally, many larger non-governmental organizations have become dependent on the state, working as subcontractors in program implementation and carrying out state-sponsored studies. As a result, many are reluctant to issue serious criticisms of the state.

7. Susan Franceschet's insights were crucial in formulating this argument.

8. Ibid.

5   STATE GOALS, NATIONAL IDENTITY, AND THE MAPUCHE

1. The 2000 CASEN national socioeconomic survey of households found that 666,319 persons belonged to one of Chile's indigenous peoples, representing a total of 4.4 percent of the general population, and that over 85 percent of the indigenous in Chile are Mapuche (MIDEPLAN 2002). The CASEN figures are substantially lower than those derived from the 1992 Chilean census, in which approximately 10 percent of Chileans self-identified as Mapuche, Aymara, or Rapa Nui; over 90 percent of these identified as Mapuche. The discrepancy is widely attributed to the phrasing of the question. The CASEN asked individuals if they *belonged to* one of the eight indigenous peoples legally recognized in Chile, while the census asked individuals if, as Chileans, they *considered themselves part of* one of the three most populous indigenous peoples. Some have posited that heightened consciousness of indigenous roots at that time, as 1992 was the quincentennial of Columbus's invasion of America, may have contributed to the higher estimate, as well (Valdés 1999). The discrepancy in the estimates is especially marked for the Metropolitan Region. The 1992 Census found that around 50 percent of the indigenous population resided there, representing about 10 percent of the regional population; the 2000 CASEN puts those figures at 23.7 percent and 2.6 percent, respectively. The CASEN figures thus may exclude individuals who feel that their migration—or their parents' migration—means that they no longer "belong" to a given community, despite the fact that they still self-identify as indigenous. In the 2002 Census, the question was phrased similarly to the CASEN, and preliminary results are on par with that survey ("Censo ayuda" 2003). (A 1996 CASEN survey also found similar results.) There are various political and social reasons to favor one result over the other. See Bañados and Fredes (2003) and Valdés (1999) for additional debate on this issue.
2. The Mapuche Cultural Centers were created with the support of the Catholic Church in 1978. They incorporated a large number of communities in Regions VIII, IX, and X, and as such were illegal under a dictatorship rule that limited the range of cultural centers to a single municipality. The centers were therefore reorganized as a trade organization (*gremio*), the Asociación Gremial de Pequeños Agricultores y Artesanos Ad Mapu (Ad Mapu Association of Small Scale Farmers and Artisans). Until 1983 (when a leftist coalition won internal elections and more moderate sectors left the organization) Ad Mapu was the most broad-based Mapuche organization of all time, representing as many as 1,500 communities (Mallon 1999; Reuque Paillalef 2002).
3. Some organizations, most importantly the Consejo de Todas las Tierras, did not sign this pact.
4. According to the Indigenous Law, Mapuche who choose to establish legal standing as an organization can do so as either a community or an association. The distinction between the two is not important for the purposes of this book.
5. In 1966, the Universal Declaration of Human Rights was codified into two covenants, one of which is the Covenant on Civil and Political Rights.
6. My sources on Ralco include Aylwin (1998, 1999) and Nordbo (2000).
7. According to Van Cott's (2000) survey of eighteen Latin American nations, ten had ratified the International Labor Organization's Convention 169 by 1998.
8. Interestingly, extreme rightist organizations are beginning to use the concept of mestizaje to diminish Mapuche claims for autonomy and self-government. Their idea seems to be that if all Chileans are mestizo and therefore have claims to Mapuche ancestry, then no Mapuche has the right to claim special rights (see, for example, Fundación Chile Unido 1999).
9. Fenelon (1997, 277) notes that throughout their relations with the United States the Lakota have been similarly categorized as "hostiles," "aliens," or "friendly Indians with potential for becoming good citizens." It is also important to note that the Chilean right generally demonstrates even less support for Mapuche demands and criticizes the Concertación for its indigenous land policy and its (in rightists' opinion) failure to uphold the rule of law.

6   VISIÓN DE PUEBLO AND THE REPRESENTATION OF MAPUCHE WOMEN IN THE STATE

1. It is not my assertion that the women I interviewed are representative of all Mapuche women who participate in the movement. As noted in the introduction, the Mapuche women I interviewed had engaged the concept of "women's issues" at some level, and most had had some

contact with SERNAM, PRODEMU, or Municipal Women's Offices. Moreover, because my sample is limited to women in the Araucanía and Santiago, I could not capture any differences that may exist between these women and those in Regions VIII and X, where there are also significant Mapuche populations.

2. This working group was solicited of SERNAM by Mapuche women from the Commission of Urban Indigenous Peoples in 2000. It will be discussed in greater detail later in the chapter.

3. Moreover, while most of the Santiago leaders in this study had migrated to the city or were the children of migrants, they differed in some ways from the majority of Mapuche living in Santiago. In her study of Mapuche women who migrated to Santiago (mostly to work as domestics), Rebolledo (1995, n.d.) noted that many developed a greater sense of autonomy from the strictures of cultural norms and were compelled to reconsider and adjust their self-perceptions as well as their identities vis-à-vis non-Mapuches, and urban and rural Mapuche. This adjustment surely occurred among the Santiago leaders in this sample, but its outcome seems to have been different from what Rebolledo observed of the domestics in her study, who found a degree of freedom in their separation from their families and communities. While the leaders I interviewed frequently did redefine "being Mapuche" in ways specific to life in Santiago, by choosing to organize around being Mapuche and reaffirming their identity as such, they differed from the majority of Mapuche in the city.

4. Many pobladoras said that they also had to overcome this problem in order to participate in organizations.

5. Calfio suggested that something similar takes place with discourses that present indigenous people as "protectors of the environment." She argued that this discourse often does not reflect contemporary reality, but that funding agencies are giving them money to be protectors of the environment, and so, in order to have access to needed funds, they have to pretend and ignore possible environmental problems caused by their modern behaviors.

6. ARTICLE 39(c) of the law establishes that CONADI must "encourage the participation and the integral development of the indigenous woman, in coordination with the National Women's Service."

7. The Fund existed prior to 1999, but in that year, CONADI was invited to collaborate and a percentage of the resources was reserved for indigenous women's projects. The Program for Women's Development (PRODEMU) is directed by the first lady. The Social Solidarity Fund (FOSIS) was established as a state agency by former president Aylwin, and most international aid for social programs is funneled through it.

8. The creation of an Indigenous Women's Program in CONADI's Santiago Office in 2001 might represent a change in this attitude.

7 WHY DIFFERENCE MATTERS

1. The inclusion of these rights as part of international agreements has traditionally been promoted by countries of the third world and the former Soviet Union while the United States and western Europe have focused on civil and political rights (Desai 2002).

APPENDIX

1. Poverty is an income-based measure in Chile. A household is poor when its monthly income per capita is less than two times the value of a basket of basic alimentary goods in urban areas, and 1.75 times that value in rural areas. In 2000, the poverty line in urban zones was set at 40,562 pesos (approximately 65 dollars) and 27,349 in rural areas (about 45 dollars). Income includes earnings of household residents as well as monetary state subsidies (MIDEPLAN 2001).

2. The index includes a measure of "potential years of life lost" (the difference between potential and actual life span); adult literacy, schooling coverage (all levels); school enrollment; schooling levels; per capita household income; and per capita household income corrected for poverty.

3. According to figures derived from the 1992 Census, the Mapuche represent 12.7 percent of the population in Cerro Navia and 14.6 percent in La Pintana, compared to about 10 percent for the Metropolitan Region as a whole. Because these figures are based on the 1992 Census, they may be higher than other estimates. (See the first endnote in chapter 5 for a discussion of discrepancies in available estimates of Chile's indigenous population.) No more recent figures were available at the time of publication. The most important point is that Cerro Navia and La

Pintana both have high Mapuche populations relative to other municipalities in the Metropolitan Region.

4. Agriculture, forestry, and fishing is followed by personal services, commerce, construction, and industrial manufacturing.

5. Renca's poverty rate is 25.7 percent. Its Human Development Index ranking is 114.

6. This is the term that refers to the process of forced relocation of entire poblaciones—which often started as illegal settlements—to other parts of the city. The process resulted in greater segregation, as poblaciones were relocated from wealthier areas to poorer ones.

Bibliography

"Acuerdo en senado sobre las etnias." 2002. *El Sur*. Concepción, Chile. July 5, 2002. Available: *http://www.soc.uu.se/mapuche/*.

Alvarez, Sonia. 1998. "Latin American Feminisms 'Go Global': Trends of the 1990s and Challenges for the New Millennium," 293–324 in *Cultures of Politics/Politics of Cultures: Re-visioning Latin American Social Movements*, edited by Sonia Alvarez, Arturo Escobar, and Evelina Dagnino. Boulder: Westview Press.

———. 1990. *Engendering Democracy in Brazil: Women's Movements in Transition Politics*. Princeton: Princeton University Press.

Alvarez, Sonia, Arturo Escobar, and Evelina Dagnino. 1998. "Introduction: The Cultural and the Political in Latin American Social Movements," 1–32 in *Cultures of Politics/Politics of Cultures: Re-visioning Latin American Social Movements*, edited by Sonia Alvarez, Arturo Escobar, and Evelina Dagnino. Boulder: Westview Press.

Anthias, Floya and Nira Yuval-Davis. 1989. "Introduction," 1–15 in *Woman-Nation-State*, edited by Nira Yuval-Davis and Floya Anthias. London: MacMillan.

Anzaldúa, Gloria. 1987. *Borderlands/La Frontera: The New Mestiza*. San Francisco: Spinsters/Aunt Lute.

Aylwin, José. 2001. "El acceso de los indígenas a la tierra en los ordenamientos jurídicos de América Latina: Un estudio de casos." Document prepared for CEPAL's Agricultural Development Unit and the CEPAL/GTZ project, "Mercado de tierras rurales."

———. 2000. "Los conflictos en el territorio mapuche: Antecedentes y perspectivas." *Revista Perspectivas*. 3(2). Universidad de Chile. Available: *http://www.xs4all.nl/~rehue/*.

———. 1999. "Indigenous Peoples' Rights in Chile and Canada. A Comparative Study." Master's of Law Thesis, University of British Columbia, Canada.

———. 1998. "Indigenous People's Rights in Chile: Progresses and Contradictions in a Context of Economic Globalization." Paper presented at the Canadian Association for Latin American and Caribbean Studies XXVIII Congress. March 19–21, 1998. Available: *http://www.xs4all.nl/~rehue*.

Bacigalupo, Ana Mariella. 2003a. "Rethinking Identity and Feminism: Contributions of Mapuche Women and Machi from Southern Chile." *Hypatia* 18(2): 32–57.

———. 2003b. "The Struggle for Machi Masculinities: Colonial Politics of Gender, Sexuality and Power in Chile." Forthcoming in *Ethnohistory*. 50(3).

———. n.d. "Gender Passages and Contested Sexualities: Ideology and Practice in Mapuche Shamanism." Unpublished Manuscript.

Baldez, Lisa. 2002. *Why Women Protest: Women's Movements in Chile*. Cambridge: Cambridge University Press.

———. 2001. "Nonpartisanship as a Political Strategy: Women Left, Right, and Center in Chile," 273–297 in *Radical Women in Latin America: Left and Right*, edited by Victoria González and Karen Kampwirth. University Park, PA: The Pennsylvania State University Press.

———. 1999. "La política partidista y los límites del feminismo de estado en Chile," 407–433 in *El modelo chileno: Democracia y desarrollo en los noventa*, edited by Paul Drake and Iván Jaksic. Santiago: Lom Ediciones.

Bañados, Francisco and Iván Fredes. 2003. "Mapuches de Santiago acusan al INE de cometer 'genocidio estadístico.'" *El Mercurio*. Santiago, Chile. March 29, 2003. Available: *http://www.soc.uu.se/mapuche*.

Barrios de Chungara, Domitila (with Moema Viezzer). 1978. *Let Me Speak! Testimony of Domitila, a Woman of the Bolivian Mines*. London: Stage 1.

Bell, Percival. 2001. "Es un error de diagnóstico creer en subversión mapuche." *El Sur*. Concepción, Chile. February 11, 2001. Available: *http://www.soc.uu.se/mapuche/*.

Benería, Lourdes. 1992. "The Mexican Debt Crisis: Restructuring the Economy and the Household," 83–104 in *Unequal Burden: Economic Crises, Persistent Poverty and Women's Work*, edited by L. Benería and S. Feldman. Boulder: Westview Press.

Bengoa, José. 1999. *Historia de un conflicto: El estado y los mapuches en el siglo XX*. Santiago de Chile: Planeta.

———. 1992. "Mujer, tradición y shamanismo: Relato de una machi mapuche." *Proposiciones* 21: 132–155.

———. 1985. *Historia del pueblo mapuche. Siglo XIX y XX*. Santiago de Chile: Ediciones Sur.

Blumer, Herbert. 1986 (1969). *Symbolic Interactionism: Perspective and Method*. Berkeley: University of California Press.

Bordo, Susan. 1993. *Unbearable Weight: Feminism, Western Culture, and the Body*. Berkeley: University of California Press.

Brown, Elsa Barkley. 1989. "African-American Women's Quilting: A Framework for Conceptualizing and Teaching African-American Women's History." *Signs* 14(4): 921–929.

Bunch, Charlotte. 1990. "Women's Rights as Human Rights: Toward a Re-Vision of Human Rights." *Human Rights Quarterly* 12: 486–498.

Butler, Judith. 1990. *Gender Trouble: Feminism and the Subversion of Identity*. New York: Routledge.

Caldeira, Teresa. 1990. "Women, Daily Life and Politics," 47–78 in *Women and Social Change in Latin America*, edited by Elizabeth Jelin. Geneva, Switzerland: UN Research Institute for Social Development.

Calfio, Margarita. 1997. "'La autonomía no la vamos a conseguir como mujeres, la vamos a conseguir como pueblo': Entrevista a Elisa Avendaño, dirigenta de la coordinadora de mujeres de instituciones y organizaciones sociales mapuche." *Liwen* 4: 104–112.

"Censo ayuda a mejorar políticas indígenas." 2003. *El Sur*. Concepción, Chile. April 19, 2003. Available: *http://www.soc.uu.se/mapuche/*.

Charlesworth, Hilary. 1995. "Human Rights as Men's Rights," 103–113 in *Women's Rights Human Rights: International Feminist Perspectives*, edited by J. Peters and A. Wolper. New York: Routledge.

Chuchryk, Patricia. 1994. "From Dictatorship to Democracy: The Women's Movement in Chile," 65–107 in *The Women's Movement in Latin America: Participation and Democracy*, edited by Jane Jaquette. Boulder: Westview Press.

Cleary, Eda. 1987. "El papel de las mujeres en la política de Chile: Acerca del proceso de emancipación de mujeres chilenas durante la dictadura militar de Pinochet." Unpublished Master's Thesis. Alemania Federal.

Collins, Patricia Hill. 1991. *Black Feminist Thought: Knowledge, Consciousness, and the Politics of Empowerment*. New York: Routledge, Chapman, and Hall.

Comisión Asesora en Temas de Desarrollo Indígena. 1999. *Informe*. Santiago: MIDEPLAN.

Comisión de Constitución, Legislación, Justicia y Reglamento. 2003. Informe de la Comisión de Constitución, Legislación, Justicia y Reglamento, recaído en el encargo que le hiciera el Senado respecto del conflicto mapuche en relación con el orden público y la seguridad ciudadana en determinadas regiones. Boletín No. S 680-12. Santiago: Senada de Chile. Availble: *http://www.lyd.cl*.

Congreso Nacional de Chile. 1993. *Ley 19253* (Indigenous Law). Available: *http://www.bcn.cl*.

———. 1991. *Ley 19023* (Law establishing SERNAM). Available: *http://www.bcn.cl*.

Cooley, Charles Horton. 1902. *Human Nature and the Social Order*. New York: Scribner's.

Coordinadora de Mujeres de Organizaciones e Instituciones Mapuches. 1995. *Memoria. Encuentro*

Nacional de Mujeres Indígenas. Temuco: Coordinadora de Mujeres de Organizaciones e Instituciones Mapuches.

"Critican soluciones a demandas mapuches." 1999. *El Mercurio.* Santiago de Chile. August 7, 1999. Available: *http://www.soc.uu.se/mapuche/.*

Curilem, María and Carmen Melillán. 1997. "Mujer Mapuche" *Actas seminario mapuche de Cerro Navia.* Available: *http://www.xs4all.nl/~rehue/.*

Das, Veena. 1995. *Critical Events: An Anthropological Perspective on Contemporary India.* Delhi: Oxford University Press.

De La Maza, Gonzalo. 1999. "Los movimientos sociales en la democratización de Chile," 377–405 in *El modelo chileno: Democracia y desarrollo en los noventa,* edited by Paul Drake and Iván Jaksic. Santiago: Lom Ediciones.

Desai, Manisha. 2002. "Transnational Solidarity: Women's Agency, Structural Adjustment, and Globalization," 15–33 in *Women's Activism and Globalization: Linking Local Struggles and Transnational Politics,* edited by Nancy A. Naples and Manisha Desai. New York: Routledge.

Díaz, Pía. 2001. "Se posterga clausura de la cumbre sobre racismo." *El Mercurio.* Santiago de Chile. September 8, 2001. Available: *http://www.soc.uu.se/mapuche/.*

Dietz, Mary G. 1989 (1987). "Context Is All: Feminism and Theories of Citizenship," 1–24 in *Learning about Women: Gender, Politics and Power,* edited by Jill K. Conway, Susan C. Bourque, and Joan W. Scott. Ann Arbor: University of Michigan Press.

ECLAC. 1999. *Participation and Leadership in Latin America and the Caribbean: Gender Indicators.* Santiago de Chile: ECLAC.

Eisenstein, Hester. 1991. *Gender Shock: Practicing Feminism on Two Continents.* Boston: Beacon Press.

Escobar, Arturo. 1992. "Culture, Economics, & Politics in Latin American Social Movements Theory & Research," 62–85 in *The Making of Social Movements in Latin America: Identity, Strategy, and Democracy,* edited by Arturo Escobar and Sonia Alvarez. Boulder: Westview Press.

Espinosa, Pilar. 2003. "Pehuenches piden hoy paralizar central Ralco." *El Mercurio.* Santiago de Chile. May 30, 2003. Available: *http://www.soc.uu.se/mapuche/.*

Espinoza, Vicente. 1993. "Pobladores y participación. Entre los pasajes y las anchas alamedas." *Proposiciones* 22: 21–53.

Esteva, G. 1997. "The Zapatistas and Current Political Struggle." Paper presented at the Second Encounter for Humanity and Against Neoliberalism. Spain, July 1997.

Evans, Sara M. 1989. *Born for Liberty.* New York: Free Press.

Fenelon, James V. 1997. "From Peripheral Domination to Internal Colonialism: Socio-Political Change of the Lakota on Standing Rock." *Journal of World-Systems Research* 3: 259–320.

Fernández, Roberta. 1994. "Abriendo Caminos in the Brotherland: Chicana Writers Respond to the Ideology of Literary Nationalism." *Frontiers* 14(2): 23–50.

Fitzsimmons, Tracy. 2000. *Beyond the Barricades: Women, Civil Society and Participation after Democratization in Latin America.* New York: Garland.

Flores, Gabriela, Cristina Llanquileo and Jeannette Paillan. 1995. "Conclusiones del Primer Congreso Mujeres Indígenas Urbanas Región Metropolitana." Conference Proceedings. August and September 1995, Región Metropolitana, Chile.

Franceschet, Susan. 2001a. "Women in Politics in Post-Transitional Democracies: The Chilean Case." *International Feminist Journal of Politics* 3(2): 207–236.

———. 2001b. "Gender and Citizenship: Democratization and Women's Politics in Chile." Unpublished Doctoral Dissertation. Carleton University (Canada).

Fraser, Nancy. 1997. *Justice Interruptus: Critical Reflections on the "Postsocialist" Condition.* New York: Routledge.

Fraser, Nancy and Linda Gordon. 1994. "Civil Citizenship against Social Citizenship? On the Ideology of Contract-Versus-Charity," 90–107 in *The Condition of Citizenship,* edited by Bart van Steenbergen. London: Sage.

Frei, Eduardo Jr. 1998. *Mensaje Presidencial: 21 de mayo de 1998.* Santiago: Ministerio Secretaría General de Gobierno.

Friedman, Elisabeth J. 1998. "Paradoxes of Gendered Political Opportunity in the Venezuelan Transition to Democracy." *Latin American Research Review* 33(3): 87–135.

Frohmann, Alicia and Teresa Valdés. 1993. "Democracy in the Country and in the Home, the Women's Movement in Chile." *FLASCO-Chile Serie Estudios Sociales No. 55.* Santiago: FLACSO.

Fundación Chile Unido. 1999. "Los mapuches y la identidad chilena." *Correinte de opinión* 13. May.

Gobierno de Chile (MIDEPLAN) and Programa de Desarrollo de las Naciones Unidas (UNDP). 2000.

"Desarrollo humano en las comunas de Chile." *Temas de desarrollo humano sustentable No. 5.* Santiago: MIDEPLAN/UNDP.

"Gobierno descarta autonomía para el territorio mapuche." 2001. *El Sur.* Concepción, Chile. February 2, 2001. Available: *http://www.soc.uu.se/mapuche/.*

"Gobierno reinstala en el Senado el concepto de pueblo originario." 2002. *Diario El Gong.* Temuco, Chile. July 7, 2002. Available: *http://www.diarioelgong.cl.*

Gould, Jeffrey L. 1998. *To Die in This Way: Nicaraguan Indians and the Myth of Mestizaje, 1880–1965.* Durham: Duke University Press.

Grupo Iniciativa Chile. 1997. *Las mujeres campesinas, indígenas y asalariadas agrícolas en la plataforma de acción de Beijing. Proyecto estrategias de acción política post-Beijing.* Santiago: Grupo Iniciativa.

———. 1994. *Mujeres: Ciudadanía, cultura y desarrollo en el Chile de los noventa. Hacia la IV conferencia mundial sobre la mujer y el foro no gubernamental. Beijing, 1995.* Santiago: Grupo Iniciativa.

Grupo de Salud Llareta. 2001. "Las diversas interpretaciones de la 'participación': Entre el ser actor y ser utilizado para el beneficio de otros." Paper presented at the 2001 Congress of the Latin American Studies Association. Washington, DC. September 6–8, 2001.

Guzmán, Virginia. n.d. "Gestión pública y equidad de género." Ciclo de debates del consejo académico, Santiago: SERNAM.

Hale, Charles R. 1996. "*Mestizaje,* Hybridity, and the Cultural Politics of Difference in Post-Revolutionary Central America." *Journal of Latin American Anthropology* 2(1): 34–61.

Hall, Stuart. 1996 (1986). "Gramsci's Relevance for the Study of Race and Ethnicity," 411–440 in *Stuart Hall: Critical Dialogues in Cultural Studies,* edited by David Morley and Kuan-Hsing Chen. New York: Routledge.

Haraway, Donna. 1988. "Situated Knowledges: The Science Question in Feminism and the Privilege of Partial Perspective." *Feminist Studies* 14(3): 575–599.

Hipsher, Patricia. 2001. "Right and Left-Wing Women in Post-Revolutionary El Salvador: Feminist Autonomy and Cross-Political Alliance Building for Gender Equality," 133–164 in *Radical Women in Latin America: Left and Right,* edited by Victoria González and Karen Kampwirth. University Park, PA: The Pennsylvania State University Press.

Hirshman, Albert O. 1970. *Exit, Voice, and Loyalty: Responses to Decline in Firms, Organizations, and States.* Cambridge, MA: Harvard University Press.

hooks, bell. 1990. *Yearning: Race, Gender, and Cultural Politics.* Boston: South End Press.

Huenchuán, Sandra. 1995. "Mujeres indígenas rurales en la Araucanía: Huellas demográficas y de sus condiciones de vida." Available: *http://www.xs4all.nl/~rehue/.*

Indian Law Resource Center (ILRC). 2003. "The Awas Tingni Case—Fifteen Months Later: The Challenges to the Implementation of the Decision of the Inter-American Court of Human Rights." Written in collaboration with International Human Rights Law Group. January 16, 2003. Available: *http://www.indianlaw.org.*

Inter-American Development Bank (IADB). 1999. *Facing Up to Inequality in Latin America.* Washington, DC: IADB.

International Labor Organization. 1989. *C169 Indigenous and Tribal Peoples Convention.* Available: *www.ilo.org.*

Jaquette, Jane S. 1994. "Women's Movements and the Challenge of Democratic Politics in Latin America." *Social Politics* 1(3): 335–340.

Jayawardena, Kumari. 1986. *Feminism and Nationalism in the Third World.* London: Zed Books.

Jelin, Elizabeth. 1996. "Women, Gender, and Human Rights," 177–224 in *Constructing Democracy: Human Rights, Citizenship, and Society in Latin America,* edited by Elizabeth Jelin and Eric Hershberg. Boulder: Westview Press.

———, ed. 1990. *Women and Social Change in Latin America.* Geneva: UN Research Institute for Social Development.

Jelin, Elizabeth and Eric Hershberg. 1996. "Convergence and Diversity: Reflections on Human Rights," 215–224 in *Constructing Democracy: Human Rights, Citizenship, and Society in Latin America,* edited by Elizabeth Jelin and Eric Hershberg. Boulder: Westview Press.

Krauss, Alejandra. 2001. "Pobreza e indigencia e impacto del gasto social en la calidad de vida 2000." Press conference of minister of planning and cooperation. Santiago, June 28, 2001.

Krauss, Alejandra and Adriana DelPiano. 2001. "Situación de la mujer en Chile 2000." Press conference. October, 2001.

Kymlicka, Will. 1995. *Multicultural Citizenship: A Liberal Theory of Minority Rights.* New York: Oxford University Press.

"La demanda de la mujer rural." 1986. Document from the Primer Encuentro de la Mujer Rural, held in Punta de Tralca, Chile in July 1986.

Lagos, Ricardo. 2001. *Mensaje presidencial: 21 de mayo del año 2001*. Santiago: Ministerio Secretaría General del Gobierno.

———. 2000. *Mensaje presidencial: 21 de mayo del año 2000*. Santiago: Ministerio Secretaría General del Gobierno.

———. 1999. *Programa de gobierno: Para crecer con igualdad*. Santiago de Chile: Concertación de Partidos por la Democracia.

Lavanchy, Javier. 1999. "Perspectivas para la comprensión del conflicto mapuche." Available: *http://www.xs4all.nl/~rehue/*.

Lister, Ruth. 1997. *Citizenship: Feminist Perspectives*. New York: NYU Press.

Mallon, Florencia. 1999. "Cuando la amnesia se impone con sangre, el abuso se hace costumbre: El pueblo mapuche y el estado chileno, 1881–1998," 435–464 in *El modelo chileno: Democracia y desarrollo en los noventa*, edited by Paul Drake and Iván Jaksic. Santiago: Lom Ediciones.

———. 1996. "Constructing *Mestizaje* in Latin America: Authenticity, Marginality, and Gender in the Claiming of Ethnic Identities." *Journal of Latin American Anthropology* 2(1): 170–181.

Mann, Michael. 1987. "Ruling Class Strategies and Citizenship." *Sociology*. 21(3): 339–354.

Marshall, T. H. 1992 (1950). *Citizenship and Social Class*. Concord, MA: Pluto Press.

Matear, Ann. 1995. "The Servicio Nacional de la Mujer (SERNAM): Women and the Process of Democratic Transition in Chile, 1990–1994," 93–117 in *Neo-liberalism with a Human Face: The Politics and Economics of the Chilean Model*, edited by David E. Hojman. Liverpool: University of Liverpool Institute of Latin American Studies.

Matte Casanova, Janette. 1999. *Balance regional de políticas de igualdad de oportunidades para las mujeres, 1994–1999*. Temuco: SERNAM IX Región.

McClintock, Anne. 1997. "'No Longer in a Future Heaven': Gender, Race, and Nationalism," 89–112 in *Dangerous Liaisons: Gender, Nation, and Postcolonial Perspectives*, edited by Anne McClintock, Aamir Mufti, and Ella Shohat. Minneapolis: University of Minnesota Press.

Mead, George H. 1934. *Mind, Self and Society: From the Standpoint of a Social Behaviorist*. Chicago: University of Chicago Press.

Meller, Patricio. 1999. "Pobreza y distribución del ingreso en Chile (década de los noventa)," 41–64 in *El modelo chileno: Democracia y desarrollo en los noventa*, edited by Paul Drake and Iván Jaksic. Santiago: Lom Ediciones.

Melucci, Alberto. 1984. "An End to Social Movements?" *Social Science Information* 23: 819–835.

Metoyer, Cynthia Chavez. 2000. *Women and the State in Post-Sandinista Nicaragua*. Boulder: Lynne Rienner.

MIDEPLAN. 2002. "Análisis de la VIII Encuesta de Caracterización Socioeconómica Nacional (CASEN 2000)." *Documento no. 14: Etnias y pobreza en Chile 2000*. Santiago: MIDEPLAN. Available: *http://www.mideplan.cl*.

———. 2001. *Pobreza e indigencia e impacto del gasto social en la calidad de vida. Informe ejecutivo*. Santiago: MIDEPLAN. Available: *http://www.mideplan.cl*.

———. 2000. "Ministra Krauss respondió a demandas de mujeres mapuches urbanas," Press release. Available: *http://www.mideplan.cl/prensa/prensa79.html*.

Miller, Francesca. 1991. *Latin American Women and the Search for Social Justice*. Hanover, NH: University Press of New England.

Mills, C. Wright. 1959. *The Sociological Imagination*. New York: Oxford University Press.

Mohanty, Chandra Talpade. 1991. "Under Western Eyes: Feminist Scholarship and Colonial Discourses," 51–80 in *Third World Women and the Politics of Feminism*, edited by Chandra Talpade Mohanty, Ann Russo, and Lourdes Torres. Bloomington: Indiana University Press.

Mohanty, Chandra Talpade, Ann Russo, and Lourdes Torres. 1991. *Third World Women and the Politics of Feminism*. Bloomington: Indiana University Press.

Molina, Natacha. 1986. *Lo femenino y lo democrático en el Chile de hoy*. Santiago de Chile: VECTOR.

Molyneux, Maxine. 2000. "Twentieth-Century State Formations in Latin America," 33–81 in *Hidden Histories of Gender and the State in Latin America*, edited by Elizabeth Dore and Maxine Molyneux. Durham: Duke University Press.

———. 1986. "Mobilization without Emancipation? Women's Interests, State, and Revolution," 280–302 in *Transition and Development Problems of Third World Socialism*, edited by Richard R. Fagen, Carmen Diana Deere, and Jose Luis Coraggio. New York: Monthly Review Press.

Montecino, Sonia. 1995. *Sol viejo, sol vieja: Lo femenino en las representaciones mapuche.* Santiago: SERNAM.

Moser, Caroline. 1996. *Confronting Crisis: A Comparative Study of Household Responses to Poverty and Vulnerability in Four Poor Urban Communities.* Washington, DC: The World Bank.

Muga, Ana. 2002. "Orígenes: 'Meter plata para neutralizar los conflictos.'" *El Siglo* 184. Available: *http://www.soc.uu.se/mapuche/.*

"Mujeres mapuches indignadas con intendenta." 2001. *El Diario Austral.* Temuco, Chile. January 20, 2001. Available: *http://www.soc.uu.se/mapuche/.*

Naples, Nancy A. 2002. "The Challenges and Possibilities of Transnational Feminist Praxis," 267–281 in *Women's Activism and Globalization: Linking Local Struggles and Transnational Politics,* edited by Nancy A. Naples and Manisha Desai. New York: Routledge.

Narayan, Uma. 1997. *Dislocating Cultures: Identities, Traditions, and Third World Feminism.* New York: Routledge.

Nelson, Diane M. 1999. *A Finger in the Wound: Body Politics in Quincentennial Guatemala.* Berkeley: University of California Press.

Nordbo, I. 2000. "The Destiny of the Bíobío River. Hydro Development at Any Cost." Available: *http://www.soc.uu.se/mapuche/.*

Oficina de la Mujer El Bosque. 1996. "Conclusiones: Cumbre de Mujeres de El Bosque Elena Caffarena." Conference proceedings. August 6, 1996. El Bosque, Santiago, Chile.

Orrego, Jéssica and Adela Martínez. 1999. "Informe final II Congreso de Mujeres de Renca." Conference proceedings. September 10, 1999. Renca, Santiago, Chile. Published in November 1999.

Oxhorn, Philip. 1995. *Organizing Civil Society: The Popular Sectors and the Struggle for Democracy in Chile.* University Park, PA: Penn State Press.

Paley, Julia. 2001. *Marketing Democracy: Power and Social Movements in Post-Dictatorship Chile.* Berkeley: University of California Press.

Petras, James and Fernando Ignacio Leiva with Henry Veltmeyer. 1994. *Democracy and Poverty in Chile: The Limits to Electoral Politics.* Boulder: Westview Press.

Portes, Alejandro. 1997. "Neoliberalism and the Sociology of Development: Emerging Trends and Unanticipated Facts." *Population and Development Review* 23(2): 229–260.

Power, Margaret. 2002. *Right-Wing Women in Chile: Feminine Power and the Struggle against Allende 1964–1973.* University Park, PA: The Pennsylvania State University Press.

———. 2000. "Class and Gender in the Anti-Allende Women's Movement: Chile, 1970–1973." *Social Politics* 7(3): 289–308.

Pratt, Mary Louise. 1996. "Overwriting Pinochet: Undoing the Culture of Fear in Chile." *Modern Language Quarterly* 57(2): 151–163.

Pringle, Rosemary and Sophie Watson. 1998. "'Women's Interests' and the Post-Structuralist State," 203–223 in *Feminism and Politics,* edited by Anne Phillips. New York: Oxford University Press.

Provoste, Patricia. 1997. "Los servicios públicos y los derechos de las mujeres: Hacia una modernización de la gestión pública," 43–64 in *Instituto de la Mujer: Veredas por cruzar 10 años.* Santiago: Instituto de la Mujer.

———. 1995. *La construcción de las mujeres en la política social.* Santiago: Instituto de la Mujer.

Raczynski, Dagmar. 2002. "Políticas sociales y de superación de la pobreza de Chile." Paper presented at Andrew W. Mellon Fellowship Program in Latin American Sociology 2002 Annual Workshop in conjunction with Center for Latin American Social Policy (CLASPO). University of Texas at Austin, February 28, 2002.

———. 1999. "Políticas sociales en los años noventa en Chile. Balance y desafíos," 125–154 in *El modelo chileno: Democracia y desarrollo en los noventa,* edited by Paul Drake and Iván Jaksic. Santiago: Lom Ediciones.

———. 1998. "Para combatir la pobreza en Chile. Esfuerzos del pasado y desafíos del presente," 191–231 in *Construyendo opciones. Propuestas económicas y sociales para el cambio de siglo,* edited by René Cortázar and Joaquín Vial. Santiago de Chile: CIEPLAN and Dolmen Ediciones.

———. 1995. "Focalización de programas sociales: Lecciones de la experiencia chilena," 217–255 in *Políticas económicas y sociales en el Chile democrático,* edited by Crisóstomo Pizarro, Dagmar Raczynski, and Joaquín Vial. Santiago de Chile: CIEPLAN/UNICEF.

Raczynski, Dagmar and Rossella Cominetti. 1994. "La política social en Chile: Panorama de sus reformas." *Serie reformas de política pública número 19.* Santiago de Chile: CEPAL.

Raczynski, Dagmar and Claudia Serrano, eds. 2001. *Decentralización: Nudos críticos.* Santiago de Chile: CIEPLAN/Asesorías para el Desarrollo.

Rebolledo, Loreto. 1995. "Factores de clase, género y etnia en la migración de mujeres mapuche,"

407–423 in *Mujeres: Relaciones de género en la agricultura*, edited by Ximena Valdés et al. Santiago: CEDEM.

———. n.d. "Los cambios de 'personalidad' en mujeres mapuche migrantes: Consideraciones en torno a la identidad." Unpublished Manuscript. Santiago: Universidad de Chile Programa Interdisciplinario de Estudios de Género.

Red de Mujeres de Organizaciones Sociales (REMOS). n.d. "Jornadas de reflexión y análisis del Plan de Igualdad de Oportunidades. Conclusiones y propuestas." Unpublished Conference Proceedings. Santiago.

Reilly, Charles. 1996. "Complementing States and Markets: The Inter-American Development Bank and Civil Society." Paper presented at the North-South Center Conference Multilateral Approaches to Peacemaking and Democratization in the Hemisphere. April 11–13, 1996.

Reuque Paillalef, Rosa Isolde. 2002. *When a Flower is Reborn: The Life and Times of a Mapuche Feminist* (edited, translated, and with an introduction by Florencia E. Mallon). Durham: Duke University Press.

Richards, Patricia. 1998. "Finding the Loma Santa: The Limits of NGOs as Promoters of Civil Society in Bolivia." M.A. Thesis, The University of Texas at Austin.

Roberts, Bryan. 1996a. "The Social Context of Citizenship in Latin America." *International Journal of Urban and Regional Research* 20(1): 38–65.

———. 1996b. "The Social Dimensions of Citizenship and Social Policy in Latin America." Paper presented at 50th Annual Meeting of ANPOCS. Caxambu, Brazil. October 22–26, 1996.

Rossel, Eduardo. 2000. "Duras críticas por rechazo a reforma sobre pueblos indígenas," *La Tercera*. Santiago de Chile. October 19, 2000. Available: *http://www.soc.uu.se/mapuche/*.

Roxborough, Ian. 1997. "Citizenship and Social Movements under Neoliberalism," 57–78 in *Politics, Social Change and Economic Restructuring in Latin America*, edited by W. Smith and R. Korzeniewicz. Miami: North-South Western Press.

Royal Commission on Aboriginal Peoples. 1996. *Final Report*. Ottawa, Ontario: Canada Communication Group.

Sandoval, Chela. 2000. *Methodology of the Oppressed*. Minneapolis: University of Minnesota Press.

Schild, Verónica. 2000. "Neo-liberalism's New Gendered Market Citizens: The 'Civilizing' Dimension of Social Programmes in Chile." *Citizenship Studies* 4(3): 275–305.

———. 1998. "New Subjects of Rights? Women's Movements and the Construction of Citizenship in the 'New Democracies,'" 93–117 in *Cultures of Politics/Politics of Cultures: Re-visioning Latin American Social Movements*, edited by Sonia Alvarez, Arturo Escobar, and Evelina Dagnino. Boulder: Westview Press.

———. 1995. "NGOs, Feminist Politics, and Neo-Liberal Latin American State Formations: Some Lessons from Chile." *Canadian Journal of Development Studies* 16(Special Issue): 123–147.

———. 1994. "Recasting 'Popular' Movements: Gender and Political Learning in Neighborhood Organizations in Chile." *Latin American Perspectives* 21(2): 59–80.

———. 1990. "The Hidden Politics of Neighbourhood Organizations: Women and Local Level Participation in the Poblaciones of Chile." *Canadian Journal of Latin American and Caribbean Studies* 15(30): 137–158.

Schneider, Cathy Lisa. 1995. *Shantytown Protest in Pinochet's Chile*. Philadelphia: Temple University Press.

Seidman, Gay W. 1999. "Gendered Citizenship: South Africa's Democratic Transition and the Construction of a Gendered State." *Gender & Society* 13(3): 287–307.

Senado de Chile. 2003. 42nd Ordinary Session. April 29, 2003. Transcript available: *http://www.senado.cl*.

———. 1999a. Special Session. June 16, 1999. Transcript available: *http://www.senado.cl*.

———. 1999b. Special Session. July 7, 1999. Transcript available: *http://www.senado.cl*.

SERNAM. 2001. "Ejes temáticos." Available: *http://www.sernam.gov.cl*.

———. 2000. *Plan de igualdad de oportunidades entre mujeres y hombres. Lineamientos generales, 2000–2010*. Santiago: SERNAM.

———. 1997. *Propuestas de políticas de igualdad de oportunidades para las mujeres rurales*. Santiago: SERNAM.

———. 1996. *Plan de igualdad de oportunidades para las mujeres: 1994–1999*. Santiago: SERNAM.

———. n.d. "Minuta. Mujeres indígenas urbanas." Unpublished document, Departamento de coordinación intersectorial, sector rural.

SERNAM-IX Región. 1999. *Plan regional de igualdad de oportunidades. Región de la Araucanía*. Santiago: SERNAM.

SERNAM-Región Metropolitana. 1999a. *Balance y proyecciones. Plan de igualdad de oportunidades, 2000–2010*. Santiago: SERNAM-RM.

——. 1999b. *Plan regional de igualdad de oportunidades. Región Metropolitana.* Santiago: SERNAM.
"SERNAM y CONADI apoyan a mujeres mapuches." 2001. *El Diario Austral.* Temuco, Chile. March 23, 2001. Available: *http://www.soc.uu.se/mapuche/.*
Sjoberg, Gideon, Elizabeth A. Gill, and Norma Williams. 2001. "A Sociology of Human Rights." *Social Problems* 48(1): 11–47.
Social Watch. 2001. "About Social Watch." Available: *http://www.socwatch.org.uy.*
"Spanish Energy Giant Thwarts Indigenous Land Agreement." 2003. *Santiago Times.* Santiago de Chile. February 28, 2003.
Spivak, Gayatri. 1994. "Can the Subaltern Speak?" 66–111 in *Colonial Discourse and Post-Colonial Theory: A Reader,* edited by P. Williams and C. Christman. New York: Columbia University Press.
——. 1985. "Three Women's Texts and a Critique of Imperialism." *Critical Inquiry* 12(1): 262–280.
Stavenhagen, Rodolfo. 1996. "Indigenous Rights: Some Conceptual Problems," 141–159 in *Constructing Democracy: Human Rights, Citizenship, and Society in Latin America,* edited by Elizabeth Jelin and Eric Hershberg. Boulder: Westview Press.
Stephen, Lynn. 2001. "Gender, Citizenship, and the Politics of Identity." *Latin American Perspectives* 28(6): 54–69.
Sternbach, Nancy Saporta, Marysa Navarro-Aranguren, Patricia Chuchryk, and Sonia E. Alvarez. 1992. "Feminisms in Latin America: From Bogotá to San Bernardo." *Signs* 17(2): 393–435.
"Suprema dio luz verde para Ralco." 2002. *El Sur.* Concepción, Chile. January 29, 2002. Available: *http://www.soc.uu.se/mapuche/.*
Toledo, Victor. 1998. "Derechos y territorios: Bases para las políticas públicas y ciudadanía del pueblo mapuche." Unpublished Manuscript. Temuco.
——. 1997. "Todas las aguas. El subsuelo, las riberas, las tierras. Notas acerca de la (des) protección de los derechos indígenas sobre sus recursos naturales y contribución a una política pública de defensa." *Liwen* 4: 36–79.
Turner, B. 1990. "Outline of a Theory of Citizenship." *Sociology* 24(2): 189–217.
"Última década: Distribución del ingreso no mejora." 2001. *El Mercurio.* Santiago, Chile, July 14, 2001.
United States Census Bureau. 2000. "Income 1999." Available: *http://www.census.gov/hhes/income/income99/99tablef.html.*
Valdés, Marcos. 2001. "Políticas públicas, planificación, y pueblos indígenas en Chile." Available: *http://www.mapuche.cl.*
——. 2000. "Analisis de coyuntura." Available: *http://www.mapuche.cl.*
——. 1999. "Instrumentos de cuantificación de población indígena: El Censo de Población y Vivienda 1992 y Encuesta de Caracterización Socioeconómica Nacional CASEN 1996." Available: *http://www.soc.uu.se/mapuche/.*
——. 1996. "Notas sobre la población mapuche de la Región Metropolitana: Un avance de investigación." *Pentukun* 5: 41–66.
——. n.d. "Entre la integración y la autonomía: La mirada intelectual del conflicto mapuche." Available: *http://www.mapuche.cl.*
Valdés, Teresa. n.d. "Comentarios de Teresa Valdés" (regarding "Gestión pública y equidad de género" by Virginia Guzmán). Ciclo de debates del consejo académico. Santiago: SERNAM.
Valdés, Teresa and Enrique Gomariz, eds. 1992. *Mujeres latinoamericanas en cifras. Chile.* Madrid: Instituto de la Mujer/Ministerio de Asuntos Sociales de España. Santiago de Chile: FLACSO-Chile.
Valdés, Teresa and Marisa Weinstein. 1993. *Mujeres que sueñan. Las organizaciones de pobladoras en Chile: 1973–1990.* Santiago: FLACSO-Chile.
——. 1988. "Mujer, acción y debate II: Se hace camino al andar." *Material de discusión #111.* Santiago: FLACSO-Chile.
Valdés, Teresa, Marisa Weinstein, Isabel Toledo, and Lily Letelier. 1989. "Centros de madres 1973–1989. ¿Sólo disciplinamiento?" *Documento de trabajo #416.* Santiago: FLACSO-Chile.
Valenzuela, María Elena. 1998. "Women and the Democratization Process in Chile," 47–74 in *Women and Democracy: Latin America and Central and Eastern Europe,* edited by Jane Jaquette and Sharon Wolchik. Baltimore: The Johns Hopkins University Press.
——. 1987. *La mujer en el Chile militar: Todas íbamos a ser reinas.* Santiago: Ediciones Chile y America (CESOC).
Van Cott, Donna Lee. 2000. *The Friendly Liquidation of the Past.* Pittsburgh: University of Pittsburgh Press.

Vecchione, Judith, exec. prod. 1993. *In Women's Hands.* Video produced by WGBH Boston. South Burlington, VT: Annenberg/CPB Collection.

Wade, Peter. 1997. *Race and Ethnicity in Latin America.* Chicago: Pluto Press.

Walby, Sylvia. 1996. "Woman and Nation." 235–254 in *Mapping the Nation*, edited by Gopal Balakrishnan. London: Verso.

————. 1994. "Is Citizenship Gendered?" *Sociology* 28(2): 379–395.

Waylen, Georgina. 1996a. "Democratization, Feminism, and the State in Chile: The Establishment of SERNAM," 103–117 in *Women and the State: International Perspectives*, edited by S. Rai and G. Leivesley. London: Taylor and Francis.

————. 1996b. *Gender in Third World Politics.* Buckingham: Open University Press.

Weinstein, Marisa. 1997. "Políticas de equidad de género y participación de las mujeres." Santiago: FLACSO-Chile (Nueva serie Flacso).

Westwood, Sallie and Sarah Radcliffe. 1993. "Gender, Racism and the Politics of Identities in Latin America," 1–29 in *Viva: Women and Popular Protest in Latin America*, edited by Sarah Radcliffe and Sallie Westwood. New York: Routledge.

Young, Iris Marion. 1997. "Unruly Categories: A Critique of Nancy Fraser's Dual Systems Theory." *New Left Review* 222: 147–160.

————. 1990. *Justice and the Politics of Difference.* Princeton: Princeton University Press.

Yuval-Davis, Nira. 1997. *Gender & Nation.* London: Sage.

————. 1993. "Gender and Nation." *Ethnic and Racial Studies* 16(4): 621–632.

Zambrano, Mireya. 1987. "Mujer Mapuche: Organización y participación." *Serie agricultura y sociedad* 5: 85–104.

Zinn, Maxine Baca and Bonnie Thornton Dill. 2000 (1997). "Theorizing Difference from Multiracial Feminism," 23–29 in *Gender Through the Prism of Difference*, Second Edition, edited by M. Baca Zinn, P. Hondangneu-Sotelo, and M. Messner. Boston: Allyn and Bacon.

Index

About the Author

PATRICIA RICHARDS is assistant professor of sociology and women's studies at the University of Georgia. She received her Ph.D. in sociology at the University of Texas at Austin in 2002, where she was a Mellon fellow in Latin American sociology and received a university-wide Outstanding Dissertation Award for 2002–2003.